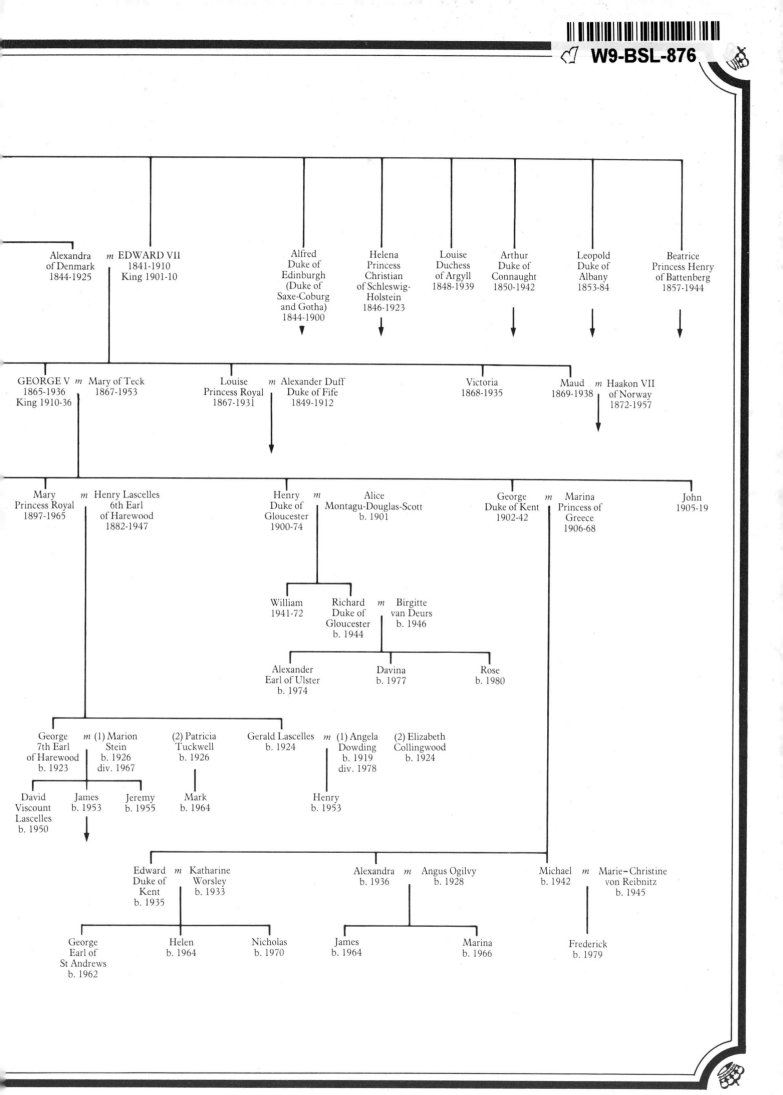

Alexandra
of Denmark
1844-1925

m EDWARD VII
1841-1910
King 1901-10

Alfred
Duke of
Edinburgh
(Duke of
Saxe-Coburg
and Gotha)
1844-1900

Helena
Princess
Christian
of Schleswig-
Holstein
1846-1923

Louise
Duchess
of Argyll
1848-1939

Arthur
Duke of
Connaught
1850-1942

Leopold
Duke of
Albany
1853-84

Beatrice
Princess Henry
of Battenberg
1857-1944

GEORGE V *m* Mary of Teck
1865-1936   1867-1953
King 1910-36

Louise
Princess Royal
1867-1931

m Alexander Duff
Duke of Fife
1849-1912

Victoria
1868-1935

Maud
1869-1938

m Haakon VII
of Norway
1872-1957

Mary
Princess Royal
1897-1965

m Henry Lascelles
6th Earl
of Harewood
1882-1947

Henry
Duke of
Gloucester
1900-74

m Alice
Montagu-Douglas-Scott
b. 1901

George
Duke of Kent
1902-42

m Marina
Princess of
Greece
1906-68

John
1905-19

William
1941-72

Richard
Duke of
Gloucester
b. 1944

m Birgitte
van Deurs
b. 1946

Alexander
Earl of Ulster
b. 1974

Davina
b. 1977

Rose
b. 1980

George
7th Earl
of Harewood
b. 1923

m (1) Marion
Stein
b. 1926
div. 1967

(2) Patricia
Tuckwell
b. 1926

Gerald Lascelles
b. 1924

m (1) Angela
Dowding
b. 1919
div. 1978

(2) Elizabeth
Collingwood
b. 1924

David
Viscount
Lascelles
b. 1950

James
b. 1953

Jeremy
b. 1955

Mark
b. 1964

Henry
b. 1953

Edward
Duke of
Kent
b. 1935

m Katharine
Worsley
b. 1933

Alexandra
b. 1936

m Angus Ogilvy
b. 1928

Michael
b. 1942

m Marie–Christine
von Reibnitz
b. 1945

George
Earl of
St Andrews
b. 1962

Helen
b. 1964

Nicholas
b. 1970

James
b. 1964

Marina
b. 1966

Frederick
b. 1979

ROYAL FAMILY

The Country Life Book of the

ROYAL FAMILY

GODFREY TALBOT

WILLIAM MORROW AND COMPANY, INC.

New York   1981

First published in the U.S.A. in 1981 by
William Morrow and Company, Inc., 105 Madison
Avenue, New York, N.Y. 10016

Originally published in 1980 by Country Life Books
and distributed for them by
The Hamlyn Publishing Group Limited
London · New York · Sydney · Toronto
Astronaut House, Feltham, Middlesex, England

ISBN 0 688 00564 0
Library of Congress Catalog Card Number 80-9001

Filmset in 11 on 12pt Poliphilus by
Keyspools Limited, Warrington
Colour reproduction by
Culver Graphics Limited, Lane End
Printed and bound in England by
Hazell Watson & Viney Limited, Aylesbury

Contents

Author's Note

The title and the first paragraph of this book tell what it is about: a family of royal people and their part in the story of our times. A richly illustrated story.

There is little call, therefore, for the traditional Introduction – except perhaps for immediate assurance that 'The Crown' in these pages will not emerge as an outworn symbol but as a lively and attractive focus of democracy. The appeal of the Royal Family is unceasing. Much of the world envies Britain in having a monarchy, one that works. It is indeed a piece of luck that we still possess this ancient yet adaptable institution, particularly that Queen Elizabeth II is the leading *embodiment* of the institution. She fulfils the need – so staple now, though scarcely confessed, in an age of graceless ferment – to have someone decent and constant to look up to, a steadying Universal Representative such as no party-elected President or Prime Minister can provide.

The text I have written dwells more on modern times than ancient history. But naturally the starting point is in origins, in the thread of several reigns preceding those of the House of Windsor. For they lead to the main narrative, which concerns Palace People we know and remember today. Here are human beings of a variety of ages and kinds and occupations. The story does not stop at kings and queens. The full circle of the wider Royal Family is presented. And, without refusing the Throne its magic, something of the *machinery* of the Monarchy is disclosed – through some of the men and women who principally sustain it. The whole book is personal – and about personalities.

This opening Note gives opportunity to acknowledge indebtedness to both celebrated chroniclers and self-effacing courtiers for guidance and counsel as I wrote. I am fortunate in having experienced from a professional observer's front seat many of the events described, and in having seen the Royal Family at work for a long time. But of course not everything told in this book has been within my personal ken, and so I am beholden to earlier writers and to people close to the Family or associated with historic events who have been good enough to talk to me of their memories.

Aspects of the leading figures in the House of Windsor's annals are preserved in innumerable books. A few stand clear above the ruck. Lady Donaldson's account of the failed *Edward VIII*, for instance, is compelling; and I have found special rewards in information and understanding in Lady Longford's *Victoria, R.I.,* and the classic *King Edward VII* by Sir Philip Magnus. There is rich lore in Mr James Pope-Hennessy's *Queen Mary*. For years I have had recourse – with pleasure, instruction and great envy – to Sir Harold Nicolson's *King George V*. And it would have been almost sinful, certainly foolish, to put pen to paper without a grounding in Sir John Wheeler-Bennett's masterpiece, *King George VI, His Life and Reign*. Deepest bow to him.

In seeking factual accuracy and fair assessment, I have resorted considerably to friends in the Royal Households, and have found generous help. But none of the consultants, I must quickly add, bears responsibility for the content and interpretations of the text. The opinions, and any errors, are mine.

I wish I could have thanked in print everyone with whom I talked, but many have asked for anonymity. Some people may and must be mentioned, however, with my own gratitude and that of publisher, photographers and picture-researchers.

The gracious permission of Her Majesty The Queen was given for the reproduction of a number of pictures (sources of illustrations are noted elsewhere) and for the taking of photographs at her own houses specially for this book. From Her Majesty Queen Elizabeth The Queen Mother similar kindness must be warmly acknowledged. Her Grace the Duchess of Beaufort at Badminton was generous in recollections of her aunt, Queen Mary. Help from the offices and estates at Windsor, Sandringham and Balmoral was unstinted.

Indebtedness to the Lord Chamberlain's Office – to the support and patience of Lieutenant-Colonel John Johnston, CVO, MC, Assistant Comptroller, and his courteous staff, and to advice from Sir Oliver Millar, KCVO, FBA, FSA, Surveyor of the Queen's Pictures – is gladly set down. The office of Her Majesty's Private Secretary has always been more than co-operative; and a valued mentor when textual fallibilities loomed was Mr William Heseltine, CB, CVO, the Deputy Private Secretary. I am in debt also to the Press Secretary at Buckingham Palace, Mr Michael Shea, and to Mrs Michael Wall, CVO, Assistant Press Secretary.

To my publisher, Mr Robert Owen, editorial director of Country Life Books, and himself a sage author, a full salute. In the mining and manufacture of this book he has worked at the coalface as well as at the pithead.

Finally, a semantic aside. I have built no Hadrian's Wall in my sixty thousand words about *Britain*. But it may be that eagle-eyed zealots of the Northern Realm can find that I have somewhere said 'English' as a variant of 'British' because it sounds so nationally natural and comes trippingly on the tongue and the pen. No more than that. The alternative word is no slight to Scotland, the land to which our story owes so much. With like assurance, let me disarm any critics taking watch in Wales or umbrage in Ulster.

So, enough of Introduction. Turn over the pages, reader, and walk at large through the years and the palaces. Meet the people.

George ÿ First

PART ONE

Windsor Heritage

The Reason Why

TO MANY READERS, to listeners to radio and viewers of television, the word 'Windsor' at once suggests either a royal castle or a king who abdicated. This book does not concentrate on either, though both have places in it. It is the story of the *House* of Windsor, of Britain's Royal Family through a number of generations, and especially from the time, early in the twentieth century, when Windsor was proclaimed the dynastic surname. For historical background, there is a look at earlier times too: in fact, at three royal centuries which lead us into the threescore most recent years which are our main concern.

It was in 1917, during the First World War, that the Royal House changed its name. Bitterness, war-weariness and frustration were in the prevailing mood of many people in Britain at that time. The war was bogged down; we seemed far from winning; loss of life in the deadlock of the Flanders trenches was appalling; and the Germans had become a terrible foe.

On the home front, one of the reactions to the situation was a crop of jingoistic witch-hunts, spurred on by press propaganda and innuendo. Gangs of citizens had been going round the streets in a hysteria of xenophobia, cursing the archfiend Kaiser, kicking stray dachshunds and smashing shops with German names. There was a desire to lash out at anything suggestive of the hated Hun, and this led even to some questioning about the monarch, King George V. Fed perhaps by rumour and unease which had spread from within the borders of our ally, Russia, where pacifist revolution had toppled the Tsar who was the King's cousin, doubts were aired in certain quarters over the resoluteness of the British Throne. It was apparently not enough that the banner of the Kaiser, who also was a cousin of King George, had been removed from the royal chapel of the Knights of the Garter at Windsor. Suggestions were made that something should be removed from the King himself – his surname. For was not his name 'Coburg'? Surely that was German? Might it not be therefore that the British Sovereign himself had sympathy with the enemy?

The notion was absurd and the questioning was from a small minority. Nevertheless, King George – always sensitive to criticism, faultlessly patriotic wartime leader though he was – read and worried over the reports. He was surprised and hurt by them. He accepted that his family name and some of the titles of his relatives in Britain did not sound exactly home-grown, so he took advice on whether it might be wise to remove any uncertainties by making an alteration of the name by which he and his kin should henceforth be called. As a result, in the middle of that third year of the war he issued a solemn and official declaration that his House and Family were to bear a new name – 'Windsor'.

The human story of that event will be told, in its place, later in this book. First must come its setting in history. No dynasty is an island; and a reign is an arbitrary passage of time in the stream of the generations. We know why in 1917 the German dignities were ruled out. It is necessary to know how they rolled in.

Therefore, the look back.

George V's granddaughter, our reigning Queen Elizabeth II, is descended not merely from the royalty of the First World War but from a far succession of sovereigns which transcends nationality.

OPPOSITE *George I, the first of the Hanoverian sovereigns, pictured in the role he loved, that of a European soldier.*

RIGHT *Queen Anne presided over England's Augustan Age. She was the last of the Stuart monarchs, the 1701 Act of Settlement carefully excluding her Catholic half-brother from the succession.*

She is heir to fifteen centuries of seething history, in fact, and her line is remarkably enduring. The ancestry has been traced fifty generations back to a semi-mythical Cerdic, the Saxon chief who founded the Royal House of Wessex four hundred years before Alfred the Great.

The full genealogical tree of the House of Windsor turns wide and far even within what is today the United Kingdom. The Queen and her family are successors, through the years, of ancient princes of England, Scotland, Wales and Ireland as well as of the distant Danes and Saxons, Normans and Plantagenets, Lancastrians and Yorkists, Tudors, Stuarts and Hanoverians. Zigzag, the ancestral line is followed to the present Royal Family.

But here we need a recall, to trace the path, only to the old Hanover line and the reign immediately before it – that of Queen Anne, early in the eighteenth century. For it was when she died that there entered the Georgian kings. It was religion that brought them in: England required a Protestant Throne.

Anne, last of the Stuart sovereigns, was a devoted Protestant, though daughter of the Roman Catholic James II. She was married to Prince George of Denmark. Her personal life had little glamour but her reign of a dozen years has a firm and fine stamp in history: she presided over England's Augustan Age. Its domestic politics were dirty, but Anne's era shines because of its flowering of artistic decoration, its legacy of classic architecture, its literary figures – Pope, Swift, Addison and Steele – and the military and diplomatic distinction which was brought to it by the triumphs of the great Duke of Marlborough.

The age of Blenheim was also the age, incidentally, in which another Duke, Buckingham, created, on grounds where a mulberry garden had been established in James I's time, a building which was called Buckingham House and which was the beginning of the Buckingham Palace we know today. There is still one mulberry tree in the Palace grounds and it bears fruit every year.

Great houses and their occupants were grand indeed in Anne's day. But the Queen herself and her way of living were hardly grand, though she did build a fine set of State apartments at the Palace in which she made her home, St James's. Her personal life was grey and gout-ridden and ultimately barren. She was mother of a whole series of stillborn and puny babies, and none survived her. She worried over the question of the Succession, family loyalty at first inclining her to the view that she should be followed by James Stuart, the son of her father's second marriage, though later she tacitly recognised the Hanoverian claim.

In any case, England's legislators were addressing themselves to the problem even before her accession in 1702, for the majority of the people wanted to ensure a Protestant succession, passing over Catholic heirs, the Stuart line. The damage which James II's Catholic bias had done still rankled. Clearly, as time went on, the next choice of monarch was going to be between Anne's Jacobite half-brother, James – the Old Pretender who was waiting in the wings – and the next-best acceptable connection, a ruler from the small principality of Hanover in north Germany who was a descendant of the first James – and a Protestant. Religion decided it. The vote went to the now German connection, the Act of Settlement of 1701 carefully excluding the senior line of the Stuarts.

On Anne's death in 1714, therefore, the next monarch came from Hanover, though not the person originally expected. The law had decided that the Crown was to go to a granddaughter of James I of England and niece of Charles I – Sophie, the Electress of Hanover, the next Protestant heir after Anne. But because that lady died two months before Queen Anne did, there came to England and the Throne her son, George Louis, who therefore became

King George I of Britain, the first of the Hanoverian sovereigns.

His accession began the German line of the Royal Family, replacing what had been an Anglo–Scottish monarchy (though one cannot but interject that Scotland will enter our royal story again, later and enchantingly, with the lady who is today's Queen Elizabeth The Queen Mother).

This King George I was neither polished nor popular. He was a man who had spent a good deal of time soldiering – in a small way, but relishing his experience in the European wars of Marlborough's time. The new monarch spoke little English and spent only part of his time in his kingdom. He reigned until 1727, a king by Act of Parliament. He does not glow in history, but perhaps has been over-maligned: the complete failure of the Jacobite rebellion of 1715 points to the stability of his crown. A dull and unsympathetic foreigner, no doubt, but he possessed a more sure political touch than some of his Hanoverian successors. And it is worth noting that it was he who made Kensington Palace a favourite royal home. In his tidy German way he laid out its gardens in the attractive form we know today – what is more, he opened them to the public.

After him came his much-lampooned but generally more popular son, George II, politically inept but militarily able, the last British monarch to lead his troops into battle, defeating the French at Dettingen in Bavaria in 1743. It was in his reign that there came a last Jacobite throw: the vain bid for the Throne by the Young Pretender, Prince Charles Edward Stuart, who in 1745 marched down from Scotland into the middle of England but failed to press on to London. King George had been ready to pack up and go when Bonnie Prince Charlie turned about and retreated to the Northern Realm. Back there, at Culloden, the Prince's forces were cruelly crushed by a son of the King, the Duke of Cumberland.

The longest reign by far of the Georgian century, the eighteenth – the era of Walpole and the Pitts, Clive of India and Wolfe of Quebec, Wesley of Methodism and Hargreaves of the spinning jenny – was the fifty-nine years of George III, English-born grandson of George II, who came to the Throne in 1760 and died in 1820 at the age of eighty-one. Bouts of derangement clouded his later years and eventually brought in his son (the future George IV) as Prince Regent.

George III – son of Frederick, Prince of Wales, and Augusta, a princess of the Saxe-Gotha dukedom – has been summarised in history as the Mad King who lost the American colonies, but that is not the whole story. There were times when, much more than a useless royal umpire, he played a brief brave innings for the Crown in the long political cricket matches of cunning Whigs and Tories. Nor were the controversial demands made in his name to the colonists across the Atlantic wholly shameful.

Our own Prince of Wales of today, Prince Charles, a student of history, is a stout defender of this stigmatised ancestor of his, protesting at the way the Whig bosses belaboured him. Pointing out that the king was a literate and much-loved country gentleman, a model of civilised domesticity who bought Buckingham House for Queen Charlotte, His Royal Highness has stressed that the King's mind was not dangerously unhinged until he was attacked by physical illness late in life. If only Royal Tours had been in the pattern of those days, if only the home-loving monarch could have *visited* the American rebels, Prince Charles suggests, they might have understood him and the realities of the quarrel a great deal better.

This third George was brave as well as kind. When, in 1803, Napoleon began massing his troops at Boulogne to attack England, His Majesty wrote to the Bishop of Worcester: 'Should his troops effect landing, I shall certainly put myself at the head of mine . . .

TOP *An engraving of Buckingham House entitled 'A View of the East Front of the Queen's Palace, St James's Park'. Built by the Duke of Buckingham in the eighteenth century, the house was bought by George III for Queen Charlotte. It was largely rebuilt by John Nash to George IV's orders. In James I's time a mulberry garden flourished on the site and there is still a mulberry tree in the garden of Buckingham Palace today.*

ABOVE *A cartoon by Gillray depicting a reconciliation between George III and the Prince of Wales (as the Prodigal Son) after one of their innumerable disagreements. Members of the Royal Family were often savagely lampooned in the popular press.*

OPPOSITE *Gainsborough's portrait of Queen Charlotte, consort of George III, which hangs in the private rooms at Windsor Castle.*

OPPOSITE *William IV in 1833: a portrait by Sir David Wilkie. Another of George III's sons, he was succeeded by his niece Victoria.*

ABOVE *Windsor Castle. Founded by William the Conqueror, it has been a fortress and a home of kings for centuries and is a favourite – and fitting – residence of the family which today bears its name.*

should the enemy approach too near to Windsor, I shall think it right the Queen and my daughters should cross the Severn, and shall send them to your episcopal palace.' (This was the courage of a monarch comparable to another brave Sovereign well over a century later: King George VI, who when enemy invasion in the Second World War seemed very near was himself determined to stay and fight the Germans, but who had armoured cars waiting, secretly at that time, in the Royal Mews at Windsor, to send, if necessary, his Consort and the two Princesses to the West of England.)

But because of the eternal fascination of eccentricity, George III remains popularly remembered by such apocryphal anecdotes as the one about him shaking hands with an oak-tree branch in Windsor Great Park and making a speech to it under the impression that it was Frederick the Great. He was indeed mentally disordered in his last years, and he died, in a seclusion and restraint which sadly had become necessary, in 1820.

Which brings us to 'Prinny', the extravagant George IV, gifted and full of style and wit as a young man but a fat voluptuary as an old king. He was as renowned for immorality as his father had been for rectitude. A costly show-off, but an intelligent patron of the arts and as a collector of pictures second only to Charles I. His seventeenth-century Dutch and Flemish masterpieces alone are worth a dozen Brighton Pavilions.

His Regency and his reign were outstanding for their fashions, furniture and architecture. He gave Windsor Castle the outlines and appearance we know today, and the magnificent Waterloo Chamber is a monument to his effectively grandiose manner. Most of the Chamber was built in the reign of his successor as King, William IV, but it was George IV who conceived the whole commemorative scheme of the room and its specially commissioned portraits to recall, vividly and permanently, the men who led the triumph of the allied countries over Napoleon. He was an indefatigable employer of architects and builders, not only at the Castle but in many other parts of Windsor, including Royal Lodge, today the out-of-town house of Queen Elizabeth The Queen Mother. He also got the great John Nash to alter old Buckingham House, where fourteen of his father's fifteen children had been born. Typically, George IV decided to rebuild rather than alter, so creating an enormous and elegant royal Palace, fit for a king indeed. However, this monarch who conceived it never inhabited it, for it was not completed until after both king and architect were dead. The Palace had a splendidly ornate gateway which is today a London landmark elsewhere, for what we know

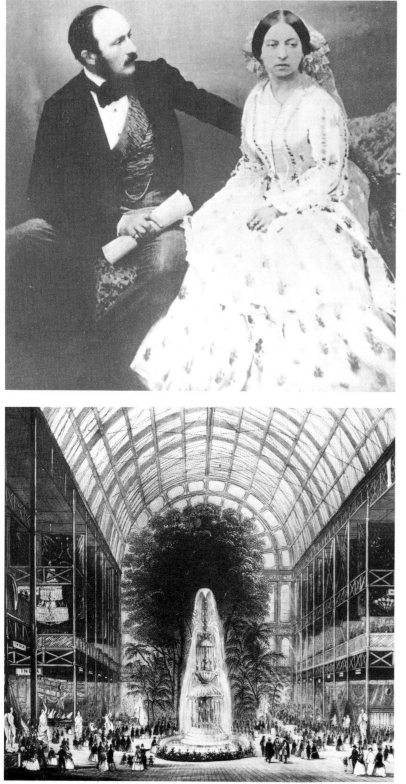

TOP *Queen Victoria and her beloved Prince Consort in 1854.*

ABOVE *The scene inside the Crystal Palace during the Great Exhibition of 1851. Planned by Prince Albert, who followed its tremendous success with intense interest, the exhibition was a turning point in the public's appreciation of his considerable abilities.*

ABOVE *A painting by Sir George Hayter of Victoria and Albert's wedding in the Chapel Royal, St James's, in 1840. She had been Queen for less than three years. Albert was a prince from the German duchy of Saxe-Coburg-Gotha and her first cousin. Their personalities were complementary and the union a success.*

now as the Marble Arch was constructed as Buckingham Palace's front gate. It was moved to its present free-standing situation, at the north of Hyde Park, in Queen Victoria's time. The arch is a victory monument, an imperial symbol. .

Never an inspiring ruler of Empire, early a debauchee (in reaction to a father's strict upbringing) and notoriously an embarrassing sight at the end, the fourth George has however left his mark as a romantic royal forebear through whom the name of Regency is blazoned upon one of England's most spirited and elegant periods.

Next upon the Throne, for a short seven years, was another son of George III: William IV. He was a dull son but not one of the notoriously disreputable ones. With him came a great change from the fandangos and free-spending of his brother. Nobody was pavilioned in splendour in William's time. Like some of his successors in the twentieth century, he made the Royal Navy his career, but was famous in the Service for abruptness rather than ability. To say that he was warm-hearted, well-intentioned, and woefully blundering is not unfair. An eminently forgettable monarch by comparison with most others. Understandably, because of the situation he had inherited from his brother, he was inordinately debt-conscious. He tried hard to get rid of Buckingham Palace. Clarence House was his home when he was King, as it had been when he was a royal Duke.

He is no doubt best remembered as uncle of Victoria, the almost unknown little princess of Kensington Palace, daughter of the fourth son of George III, who had become next in line for the Throne, and whose mother, the Duchess of Kent, he heartily disliked. Indeed, his overmastering ambition as monarch was to keep alive until the middle of the year 1837, long enough to see Princess Victoria reach eighteen, at which point she would be 'of age' and could rule as Sovereign *alone*, without the domineering parent. He made it by twenty-seven days.

Grandmother of Europe

And so – Victoria.

The Great White Queen, great-great-grandmother of both Queen Elizabeth II and Prince Philip the Duke of Edinburgh, may be reckoned by strict pedigree to have been the last monarch of the House of Hanover. However, since she had grown up isolated from the surviving members of her late father's family, and since the hitherto linked Crown of Hanover did not pass to her, it could be argued that the start of her reign ended Britain's run of Hanoverian sovereignty – the four Georges and William, all with Continental wives. By that token, it was *she* who really began a new dynasty, English-orientated at last, eighty years before Windsor became the official name of the Royal House.

But in fact Victoria's arrival did no such thing as sever German links. On the contrary, her mother, her governess and her guardian uncle Leopold were all Germans, Coburgs, and she always considered herself a member of that House, as did the son who many years later succeeded her. What is more, she married, in the year 1840 and before she had been Queen three years, a prince from the German duchy of Saxe-Coburg-Gotha.

Handsome cousin Albert, her adored Prince Consort, was the man. His character and the Queen's are worth a moment's thought. Albert was serious, reserved, industrious, careful, considerate, conscientious. He would rise with the lark to work on his papers, and when not still at his desk late at night, he liked to retire early. His young wife, on the other hand, though seemly and dutiful, was demonstrative and quick with words – sometimes words of flaring anger, though she *was* often amused and showed it. *She* would happily stay up and dance till all hours. Theirs were two complementary natures, meshing felicitously. Opposites, but in good partnership.

We know a lot about Queen Victoria as a human being, thanks to the outpourings in her journals and letters. We know her early spontaneity and bounce; we know the stubbornness and inflexibility, the devotion to past tradition which caused her name to be used as an adjective meaning old-fashioned. Yet the truth is that she was more advanced and liberal than many of her ministers – on racial prejudice for instance (she became angry if anyone said 'nigger'). She did not want females entering politics, and yet backed Nurse Florence Nightingale's storming of the male hospital wards.

As monarch, quite simply there was never a Sovereign like her and never an epoch to compare with the vast Victorian Age which brought to Britain the apogee of temporal power and imperial glory. Most of the years of that hard-working age – though they had their grey areas of hypocrisy and working-class hardship at home and the limited but grim wars of the Crimea and the Transvaal overseas – were years of prosperity and peace. It was the golden age of Melbourne and Palmerston, Gladstone and Disraeli, Tennyson and Dickens, Gilbert and Sullivan, Dr David Livingstone and Dr W. G. Grace.

It was the age of the Railways, and Royal Trains, marvels of

OPPOSITE *An early State portrait of Victoria. Little known on her accession, she had a reign of over sixty years which came to symbolise Britain's power and glory.*

LEFT *An enlargement of a miniature of George II.*

BELOW *Zoffany's painting of George III, Queen Charlotte and the six eldest of their fifteen children. They are dressed in Van Dyck costumes.*

THE ROYAL FAMILY OF GREAT BRITAIN 1897.

OPPOSITE *George III in his coronation robes. The portrait was painted by his Scottish court painter, Allan Ramsay.*

ABOVE *Queen Victoria pictured with three generations of her family in the White Drawing Room of Buckingham Palace.*

engineering. It was a time of unprecedented and fundamental change in society, science, and social wellbeing. It brought a great flowering of commercial and colonial might. It was also the age of agitation for Irish Home Rule and Votes for Women, the great era of the Industrial Revolution – and also one of its ultimately explosive products: trade unionism. Overseas, the Dominions solidified – Canada, Australia, New Zealand. By the time her own and the nineteenth century's end came, wide areas of the world were coloured British red on the map and their inhabitants by the million paid fealty to Victoria as Empress. Her reign was the longest span in the nation's royal history. She gave her name to a civilisation. The Head of State and the country itself were uniquely conjoined. For more than sixty years this woman *was* Britain.

No one ever began a reign more briskly. The little Princess Victoria had been dominated by her mother; she had slept in the Duchess of Kent's bedroom every night till she became Queen. Then, instantly, the mother was set aside and the eighteen-year-old girl, suddenly a perfect dynamo of quiet energy, within three weeks of becoming Sovereign had firmly and quite unmistakably established herself as the ruling First Lady of the Realm and had moved out of Kensington into Buckingham Palace, huge empty shell though the house had become. To her, the sentiment 'not fit to live in' was a spur; orders went out to sweep and furnish rooms. She staged a big dinner and a concert in the place forty-eight hours after taking up residence there.

Soon she was making her presence felt in other houses also. In Windsor, of course, and before long in far Scotland too. Early in the reign she discovered the Highlands and fell in love with them for ever. To her delight, Albert built a fine turreted home beside the Dee; and between them they smothered the inside of it with tartans. 'Our dear paradise' was what Victoria called Balmoral Castle.

But Buckingham Palace was the powerhouse, headquarters of the monarchy for the first time, and the Sovereign's dwelling place. The Queen redesigned and enlarged it for her growing progeny (she got part of the money for this work from the sale of her Regency Uncle's Brighton Pavilion). Large families bloomed in the nineteenth century, and Victoria herself was eminently prolific. Nine children were born to her before the premature death, from typhoid in 1861, of the Prince Consort, worn out at the age of forty-two by self-imposed cares of government and hard-driving devotion to the sciences and arts of the country to which he had come and of which he was in fact an inspiring leader. Public mistrust had been directed at Prince Albert at first, because of his German connections and his political influence at the Queen's side. But groundless

21

ABOVE *Mother of the Empire, Grandmother of Europe.*

OPPOSITE *Queen Victoria, Prince Albert and their nine children. This commemorative postcard was published after the old Queen's death in 1901, by which time she had been a widow for forty years.*

suspicions had been largely dispelled after the success of the famous Great Exhibition which he had planned, and after his death there dawned on the nation a remorseful appreciation of how wise a counsellor he had been.

To Victoria the loss was devastating. Grief-stricken beyond consolation, bereft at a stroke of a husband and adviser on whom she had daily clung and depended, the Queen withdrew from the public scene, abandoned Buckingham Palace altogether, and for years lived in mournful retirement, enveloped in widow's weeds, the mists of Windsor Castle and the remoteness of her Osborne House on the Isle of Wight. This Teutonically overdone withdrawal, as it became protracted, built up streams of public complaint and criticism. England experienced a period of rare republican sentiment. But Her Majesty's eventual emergence and longevity abolished that; recognition and loyalty were regained; and by 1887, the year of her dazzling Golden Jubilee, her popularity was widespread, despite the international disquiet which the closing years of the century were bringing. She was a goddess in a golden frame, focus of pride in the achievements which the Victorian era had brought, and an object of unparalleled sentimentality.

And still she lived on and on, increasingly revered, symbol of

British greatness – even if now that greatness was beginning to be eroded – and when the *Diamond* Jubilee came, the little old lady rode in her carriage through beflagged and crowded streets awash with gratitude and affection.

Queen Victoria had long since become matriarchal as well as monumental. Mother of Empire, but Grandmother of Europe too. Her family circle was enormous, and when her own children grew up and married they too had numerous offspring. The Queen could count thirty-seven grandchildren and nearly eighty *great*-grand-children at the end of her life. They were almost all 'Royalty' of course, for Victoria's ever-widening circle was adorned with crowns and coronets. When betrothal times came, it was often not so much a matter of personal choice as of assiduously organised foreign alliances which made the matches. The picture indeed was worlds away from the healthy pattern of today's royal scene, in which dynastic unions are not sought and hearts overrule hierar-chies. (Nowadays it is becoming almost the rule rather than the exception that princes and princesses marry commoners.)

So, as Victoria's years went by and the Queen had two, and then three, generations of her own to supervise, an extraordinary international web of royal relatives was woven, its strands running to and from the ever-concerned Presiding Mama. The entwining of Continental dynasties and names was compounded beyond all precedent until most European Royal Families stemmed from the Queen and Albert. Their descendants came to reign as kings and queens in Germany, Norway, Sweden, Spain, Greece, Romania and Yugoslavia. Victoria was Grandmother of Europe.

The Queen's eldest daughter – Vicky, the Princess Royal – became the Empress Frederick of Germany and, ironically, as it proved, the mother of that Kaiser who was to preside over the Enemy Powers against which Great Britain fought in the First World War. Had it not been for that German Emperor cousin, King George V might never have changed his name. But for the 1914 Hate of William, the House of Windsor might not have been born.

The other routes of royal descent – other than the basic German ones – are almost as fascinating (and all are best followed by studying a well-laid-out genealogical chart). Along them are found, among her granddaughters alone, Queen Maud of Norway, Queen Sophie of the Hellenes, Queen Marie of Romania, Queen Victoria-Eugénie of Spain (who, with her husband, King Alfonso XIII, was so nearly killed by a bomb as they returned to their palace in Madrid after their wedding ceremony), and that ill-starred Tsarina, Alexandra-Feodorovna, consort of Nicholas II, Tsar of Russia, who, with the Tsar and their family, was assassinated at Ekaterinburg in 1918.

But the Grand Trunk Route of our story, leading from past history to the present House of Windsor, runs not from the Urals or across the Channel, but within the United Kingdom – and brings us to Victoria's eldest son, the future Edward VII, born in 1841, the 'naughty Bertie', Albert Edward, who as Prince of Wales was a source of parental worry and who as both Heir and later as Sovereign has left an engaging if at times errant imprint on history. His love of high living, his famous infidelities, his lordly but winning skill as a diplomat when at last he wore the Crown and became something more than royal bon viveur – all this gave him appeal and tolerant respect. He was a king whose times wore a gaiety and sophistication never to be seen again. Indeed, compared with the eleven months of flashy parties of another self-indulgent Edward who briefly reigned two generations later, Edward VII's period had grandeur.

THE LATE EMPRESS FREDERICK.

H.M. KING EDWARD VII.

H.R.H. THE LATE DUKE OF ALBANY.

H.R.H. THE LATE DUKE OF EDINBURGH.

H.R.H. DUKE OF CONNAUGHT.

HER LATE MAJESTY QUEEN VICTORIA, PRINCE CONSORT, AND FAMILY.

H.R.H. PRINCESS CHRISTIAN.

H.R.H. THE LATE PRINCESS ALICE.

H.R.H. PRINCESS HENRY OF BATTENBERG.

H.R.H. DUCHESS OF ARGYLL.

396.D.

BEAGLES' POSTCARDS

ABOVE *Frith's painting of the wedding in 1863 of the Prince of Wales, later Edward VII, and Princess Alexandra, the eldest daughter of Christian IX of Denmark; her sister, Marie, became Empress of Russia and mother of the last Tsar. The Prince had rejected a number of princesses before marrying Alexandra, whose beauty and generosity soon made her a popular figure. At the time of the wedding Queen Victoria was in mourning for Prince Albert. She viewed the ceremony in St George's Chapel, Windsor, from a secluded gallery.*

OPPOSITE *Prince George (later George V) at the age of five. Much of his childhood was spent at Sandringham, where his brother and three sisters helped to form an affectionate family group. In 1877 the Prince joined Britannia at Dartmouth, having passed his entrance examination for the Navy.*

PART TWO

Victoria and Edward VII

Problem Prince

WELL BEFORE the closing decades of his mother's reign and the nineteenth century, well before he had become the portly King Teddy retaining the rogue whiskers, rich cigars and rakish Homburg hats, Prince Albert Edward, destined to be Heir to the Throne for more than half of that century, was an established national character. Everybody was aware not only of the large, resplendently uniformed figure of the ceremonial duties and the foreign missions but also of the larger-than-life off-duty Prince epitomising the man about town's grand manner and grand fallibilities. The public knew about his graciousness and gusto, and also his large appetites – for food, drink, tobacco, card parties, shooting, horseracing, and beautiful ladies. A Prince of Pleasure, and a Royal Problem. Such was the future Edward VII.

He was, at least, a problem and a constant anxiety to the royal mother whose severe character and strict way of life was in such contrast to his own.

Not for the first time in royal history, nor the last, the son's behaviour was in part a reaction to lack of understanding, secluded education and confined upbringing parentally dictated. Albert the Good had sought to put this Bertie in a strait-jacket. The Prince of Wales's earnest father (whose precepts were forever right in Victoria's view) laid down for the young man an unpalatable pedagogic course of learning over which the Consort watched with the misconceived zeal of a prison warder. Private tutoring, rigorous programmes of study at home, term-long but tiresome attempts to control the nice, affectionate but never intellectual Bertie within the scholarly confines of Edinburgh and Oxford and Cambridge – all were disastrous. Nor were the student journeys in Europe and the Middle East any better: temples bored him, and when he dodged them his teachers sighed but succumbed to his charm.

After the shock of his father's death, restrictions on the twenty-year-old Prince were not at once lifted, but he gladly ended formal education then and proceeded to gain a variety of experience in his own way. He travelled widely, officially perforce and on private pursuits too. He began to taste and like the social life of witty and well-to-do people outside the royal circle. But he did not neglect public duty, genially tackling in his mother's place such important official functions as he was permitted to undertake after she had become a widowed recluse to the world outside her own family. Victoria, however, did not allow him, until her very last years, to play any part in Statecraft or get to know the office work of monarchy – an obstinacy which doubtless sped the restless Bertie into his enjoyed but often irresponsible private behaviour.

In 1863 the Prince married a beautiful Danish princess, 'Sea-King's daughter from over the sea', Alexandra, whose father was Christian IX of Denmark and whose sister became the Empress mother of Russia's last Tsar. Bertie was twenty-one and Alexandra eighteen. The lovely young Princess of Wales was at once nationally popular. Decoratively and with dignity, she carried out together with her husband many engagements which ordinarily would have been undertaken by the Sovereign.

Soon, Edward and Alexandra had a family of their own. Children of the marriage arrived early and in rapid succession: Prince Albert Victor (Duke of Clarence), Prince George Frederick Ernest Albert (the Duke of York who was to become King George V), Princess Louise (who married a Scottish landowner and became Duchess of Fife), Princess Victoria (the

unmarried one) and Princess Maud (later to be Queen of Norway). Before long they had plenty of cousins – one of them, the elegant Princess Alice Countess of Athlone, far outliving her generation to survive spiritedly into the twentieth century's eighth decade – and all brought up to regard with awe the remote and already legendary Grandmother Victoria.

As to Bertie, the Prince of Wales, his children stood somewhat in awe of *him*, their large and ebullient father; they found his chaffing a little frightening and beyond their comprehension, fond and devoted parent though he was, and specially tender towards the second boy, 'Georgie', whom he later was at pains to introduce to the business of kingship. For this son was the sailor Prince who, on the death of his elder brother in 1892, came at twenty-six years of age into the direct line of succession to the Throne. When that change in the Succession occurred, Queen Victoria had reached the age of seventy-one and seemed immortal. And Bertie, her now middle-aged son, seemed eternally in the wings, forever Heir-in-Waiting.

But he, the Prince of Wales, was a prominent figure of the times in more ways than one. He did not neglect the official duties. But there was also his gregarious social life, the amorous liaisons, the gay theatregoing, the gaming and the rumbustious sporting style, aspects of his behaviour which revolted some of his contemporaries. To many people as the years rolled on, however – and the Prince's nature did not suddenly alter when he became King Edward VII – the very weaknesses tended to give spice and popularity to the image of the man.

Nor in fact did the Prince of Wales's extramarital activities damage the bonds of sympathy and respect which existed between him and the faithful wife Alexandra, who was as domestic as her husband was convivial. He remained a kind and generous partner; and the Princess, later his Queen, enduringly good-looking and ornamental, was an understanding and forgiving wife – perforce maybe. Increasing deafness weakened her ability to enjoy a full social life, and her aesthetic outlets were limited. She was no connoisseur, no amasser of pictures, preferring to surround herself with knick-knacks and small animals. She collected lapdogs whilst her husband collected ladies. . . .

Households and Houses

Let us look at the setting of our scene . . .

Fascinating though the human story is, we must, before going any further, put the Kings in the context of the Court, pausing to widen our focus and take what the old novelists used to call 'a peep behind the scenes'. For monarchy, even in the rich-living days of Edward VII, was never all beanfeasts and baccarat. It has owed much to its backroom men, the quiet but essential chiefs of staff of royal households, pillars of the constitution.

The Sovereign is always the star and, very naturally, the personality of the man who became King Edward VII is what has most attracted writers of memoirs and histories. But no account of him as prince or monarch – no report on any leading figure of the

ABOVE *Edward VII's study, which he always used when he lived at Marlborough House as Prince of Wales. This photograph was taken in the 1890s.*

RIGHT *Sir Arthur Bigge, Lord Stamfordham, attends George V as he works in the garden of Buckingham Palace during the First World War. Lord Stamfordham was royal Private Secretary for thirty years and his grandson, Sir Michael (now Lord) Adeane, was to hold the same office under Queen Elizabeth II for twenty years.*

OPPOSITE *Great White Queen with son and daughter-in-law: bejewelled symbols of country and empire.*

Royal House – would be complete without acknowledgement also of the work and the machinery behind the lofty and sometimes lonely office of Sovereign. The hours spent at the study table are mandatory, the meetings and audiences essential, the round of public engagements an immutable part of the business of modern constitutional monarchy. All of which needs much talented help. This was as well recognised in the nineteenth century as it is today. King Edward had no illusions at any time that he could do without his support troops.

The continuity of the work of the British Crown – whatsoever king or queen may reign – is assured by the devoted and highly professional labours of the personally appointed officers in royal employ, a succession of unobtrusive, able, hard-working, respectful but far from obsequious senior servants of the Throne. And, personally the nation's successful Number One Public Servant though she herself is, Edward's great-granddaughter, the Queen Elizabeth II of today, knows this too. The officials inside Buckingham Palace, however much they mantle their work with a cloak of beautiful manners and what seems effortless ease, constitute the world's most efficiently run Household.

The Lord Chamberlain, chief of a busy department, is the head of Her Majesty's Household; but in the continuous work of the monarch, the key position is that of the Private Secretary – who is not and never has been named as one of the Great Officers of State but is nevertheless the person who in day-to-day affairs is prime adviser and vital liaison officer to the Sovereign. He is the least publicised, most self-effacing but most influential of the Silent Men of the Palace.

Any appraisal of the monarchy, any lifting of the lid of the royal headquarters, must pay tribute to such men.

Sir Francis Knollys was Edward VII's devoted Private Secretary, a fellow spirit, friend and confidant for forty years. With more sedateness and renown, Sir Henry Ponsonby had sagely served Queen Victoria for over thirty years. Spanning three reigns, the great Sir Arthur Bigge, who became Lord Stamfordham, was for more than half a century a perfect aide and counsellor to the Royal Family, his service stretching from the Victorian age to the years of the Queen's grandson. George V was quite forthright about him: 'He taught me to be a king.'

There is an unbroken line in Secretaries as well as in Sovereigns. Lord Adeane, who (as Sir Michael) served for long years as Private Secretary to the present Queen and followed the eminently literate Sir Alan Lascelles (who himself had served in three reigns), is a grandson of Lord Stamfordham. And Lord Adeane's son Edward is now at the Palace, having become Secretary and Treasurer to a king-to-be, our own Charles, Prince of Wales.

Michael Adeane was on retirement succeeded by the Deputy Private Secretary, Sir Martin Charteris (now Lord Charteris of Amisfield), who in turn handed over the principal office to his own right-hand man and present holder of the post, Sir Philip Moore. Sir Philip, scholar and sportsman as well as diplomat – as so many of his predecessors have been – was appointed to the Queen's service

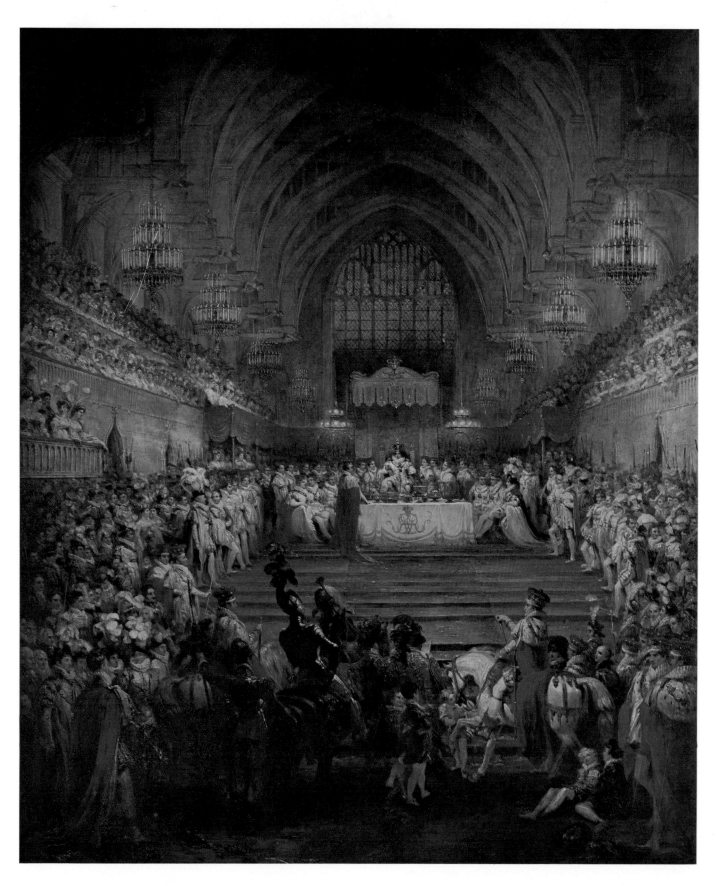

OPPOSITE *One of the great murals by Laguerre in royal Marlborough House in London, created by Duchess Sarah, wife of the famous Duke who was John Churchill. The pictures show his military triumphs.*

ABOVE *The scene at the coronation banquet of George IV in Westminster Hall in 1821. The King's Champion is in the foreground. Following ancient custom, the Champion has ridden into the hall in full armour to read a ceremonial challenge. This was the last coronation banquet to be held in Westminster Hall. In fact, according to contemporary accounts, the occasion did little credit to the historic room and dissolved into a dissolute party.*

ABOVE *A portrait of the first Duke of Wellington by Sir Thomas Lawrence, one of a group commissioned by George IV to hang in the Waterloo Chamber at Windsor Castle. The Chamber was built as a memorial to Allied triumphs over Napoleon; it recalls the grand yet exquisite taste of an extravagant sovereign.*

TOP *John Wootton's picture of George II's family out for a picnic above the Thames at Henley. This picture was painted in about 1743 when picnicking was becoming an increasingly popular pastime.*

ABOVE *Sir David Wilkie's painting of Queen Victoria's first Council at Kensington Palace on 20 June 1837. The Queen praised the picture at first but later came to detest it.*

in 1966 in his prime, already bearing a distinguished record in the Civil Service both at home and overseas. He progressed from Assistant to Deputy, and then – when Martin Charteris retired in 1977 and was appointed Provost of Eton – he became the chief Secretary.

These were, these are, the invisible men of the machinery of monarchy and State, experienced, exceptionally informed and discreet, utterly loyal yet not afraid to speak frankly in interpreting the outside world to their employer within the Palace. It was Stamfordham the royal Private Secretary who in 1923, having talked with elder statesmen, advised George V that a House of Commons man and not a peer should succeed the dying Bonar Law as Prime Minister, thus bringing the appointment of the then relatively unknown Stanley Baldwin instead of the exceptionally qualified and expectant Lord Curzon. It was Edward VIII's Private Secretary, Major Alexander Hardinge, who, in the finale of the Abdication Year of 1936, placed on his royal master's desk the warning and subsequently controversial letter which spelled out bluntly the facts of the nation's attitude to the King's attachment to the then Mrs Simpson, dispelled Edward's illusions, and brought to a head the constitutional crisis which ended in the departure of the eleven-month monarch who became the Duke of Windsor.

Today, much of the work which the Queen has to deal with every day is channelled through the Private Secretary, the Deputy Private Secretary and the Assistant Private Secretary, themselves the heads of a vital department at the Palace. These men are responsible for Her Majesty's official programmes of engagements and her vast correspondence as well as the masses of official papers. And the Queen certainly needs help. She has to cope with well over fifty thousand letters a year addressed to her personally (some of them from ordinary but anxious citizens and beginning with a straightforward 'Dear Queen').

The Private Secretaries provide the link between the Sovereign and the Government of the day and all the Ministerial offices and Whitehall departments – and they are also the link with the governments of the fourteen Commonwealth countries of which the Queen is Sovereign. They are the royal visit and overseas tour organisers, speech-writers, watchdogs-at-elbow during any royal walkabout, immediate go-betweens of exemplary skill and tact, essential to the transactions of the Throne.

Though the public is rarely conscious of *them*, the Secretaries have one extra task in the present Age of Publicity: they have to see that the public are properly conscious of the official activities of the House they serve. Which is to say that, through the Palace Press Secretary's office, they must oversee the presentation to 'the media' of all the factual information needed about the work of the Queen and other members of her family.

The royal Households – and there are a dozen of them in the Windsor family today in addition to the Queen's own Household – are a complex of workers ranging from the principals who are close companions of those whom they attend to the youngest footmen ever to carry a plate at a State banquet. They are a thread running

OPPOSITE *Winterhalter's picture of Prince Albert in splendid pose. Adored by Victoria, he died in 1861, leaving the Queen inconsolable.*

RIGHT, TOP *The trick bookcase in the Smoking Room Library at Marlborough House – fun for Edward VII's guests when he was Prince of Wales.*

RIGHT, BOTTOM *Marlborough House was Queen Mary's home in busy widowhood. This was her writing desk, placed in her bedroom.*

33

through the Royal Story, a thread which will appear again in this book.

Not only Households, but houses – the residences where royal employers and employees live and work. They too form a thread. The official list of palaces is long and full of variety. It has to include royal buildings as distinct from royal dwellings: St James's Palace, Westminster, Whitehall, Hampton Court, Greenwich, the Tower of London and the Dutch House at Kew, and Scotland's Stirling and Linlithgow. What we are concerned with, however, are lived-in palaces such as Holyrood in Edinburgh and Kensington in London, with Clarence House which is Queen Elizabeth The Queen Mother's home, with Balmoral and Birkhall and Mey, with castles such as Windsor and country mansions such as Sandringham in Norfolk, loved by every generation of the family which bears the Windsor name. The residences themselves tell most evocatively in their stone and brick the changing tale of royalty; and they attract public interest which never flags.

At this point – for we are yet in the nineteenth century – still another dwelling comes in. Not Buckingham Palace, which old Queen Victoria had long since abandoned and which was becoming a habitation only of damp and mould, but Marlborough House, which became the first official home of the Prince of Wales, her son and heir, when he married. This was the house which Alexandra adorned as the Wales's children were born and grew up; this, in the following reign, became the home of their second son, the future George V, when he was the next Prince of Wales. And Marlborough House is specially remembered as the home of Queen Dowagers.

It stands in the heart of London between the Mall and Pall Mall, not many yards east of St James's Palace, on the site where it was built by Sir Christopher Wren in the reign of Queen Anne. It bears the name 'Marlborough' because it was put up for John Churchill,

the first and greatest Duke of the noble line; but it was almost entirely the creation of Sarah, his formidable Duchess, the lady who attained such unique intimacy with Queen Anne when she was one of the attendant Ladies of the Bedchamber. Duchess Sarah chose Wren as architect because she had fallen out with Sir John Vanbrugh who was building the great Palace of Blenheim in Oxfordshire for the glory of her husband; but eventually she quarrelled with old Sir Christopher too and supervised the completion of the house herself.

Royal occupation of Marlborough House began early in the nineteenth century with the handsome young German Prince Leopold of Saxe-Coburg-Gotha (that House again!) who in 1816 married Princess Charlotte, the only daughter – and at that moment the Heiress Presumptive to the Throne – of the future George IV. Charlotte died in childbirth the next year, and afterwards Leopold used Marlborough House as his London base until he was elected King Leopold I of the Belgians (the famous Uncle Leopold who from Brussels pressed so much dogmatic advice upon the young Queen Victoria). Next, the house was the home of the gentle Adelaide, consort of William IV, in the days of her widowhood. It was in the mansion's most elegant rooms that Queen Adelaide staged a wedding banquet in salute to Victoria and Albert when they had left town for a Windsor honeymoon.

It was after Adelaide's time that the house was settled on Edward VII, as Prince of Wales, and subsequently on his son. When King Edward died and that son moved to the Palace as the new King, George V, the widowed Queen Alexandra then returned to Marlborough House and lived there (when she could tear herself away from Sandringham to London) in a retirement of inactivity enlivened chiefly by bursts of generous support for charities and the companionship of a variety of canine pets (the elaborate headstones of her dogs' cemetery are still a feature of the garden). In turn another

RIGHT *Princess May of Teck. She was engaged to Prince Eddy, the heir to the throne, for a short time before he died of typhoid in January 1892. In 1893 she married Prince George, the Duke of York, in the Chapel Royal, St James's Palace. A great-granddaughter of George III on her mother's side, she exhibited qualities which met with Queen Victoria's approval and seemed an ideal partner for the 'Heir to the Throne'.*

BELOW *A wedding picture of the Duke of York (the future King George V) and Princess May (the future Queen Mary).*

LEFT, TOP *Kaiser William II in 1891. Like George V, he was a grandson of Queen Victoria. He became Emperor of Germany in 1888. Seemingly close to his grandmother and the British Royal Family, he was still capable of precipitating events that led to the First Great War.*

LEFT, BOTTOM *Four royal generations at the christening of Prince Edward (later Edward VIII and the Duke of Windsor) in 1894.*

ABOVE *Queen Victoria arriving at St Paul's for a service of thanksgiving on the occasion of her Diamond Jubilee in 1897. Every part of the Empire was represented in the magnificent procession. By then the Queen had almost become deified by her age.*

ABOVE *The order of service for Queen Victoria's funeral, bound in purple velvet, and tickets for the memorial service.*

RIGHT *Sailors pulling the coffin of Queen Victoria to the funeral at Windsor in 1901.*

widow, Queen Mary, with her considerable collection of antique furniture, went into her long residence at the house following the death of King George V in 1936.

The late Queen Mary was the last royal occupant – and how different a lady from the turbulent Sarah, first mistress of Marlborough House! The house had been changed, added to, modernised and refurbished by successive possessors, but it was, and it remains, essentially the same finely proportioned and sumptuously furnished Wren mansion as it was nearly three centuries ago.

Today, however, the building is no longer a residence. It is an office, a meeting hall. In 1959 Queen Elizabeth II gave it as the Conference Centre and administrative headquarters of the Commonwealth, the unique worldwide association of countries of which Her Majesty is acknowledged Head. Officials ply their telephones there with classic chandeliers coruscating above their heads; multi-racial committees sit around the tables of bygone banquets; and, displaying medleys of modern national costume and modish lounge suit, international receptions buzz and boom in the salons once adorned by the quiet grace of royal dowagers. But the grandeur of the house's first great years is still to be seen unimpaired, and a prime attraction is the famous series of huge Laguerre wall paintings which excitingly depict the Duke of Marlborough's battlefield triumphs long ago.

A century and a half after those battles had passed into history,

another and very different example of wall decoration was executed at Marlborough House. It is still to be seen in a first-floor room called the Smoking Room Library – a name which, like the wall in question, conjures up the flavour of a laughing, vibrant Bertie, Victoria's son who as Prince of Wales used the room for forty years. The room is a piece of fun. It is furnished with bookcases, well filled; but one inside wall has a 'jib', a disguised door flush with the shelves around it and covered entirely by what look like well-bound old volumes but in fact are spoofs, merely leather spines with nothing behind them save the door. And the imaginary titles on the spines are examples of elementary Edwardian humour: *Warm Receptions* – by Burns, *Lamb on the Death of Wolfe, Payne's Dentistry, Spare that Tree* – by Y. Hewett, and so on.

During Edward's occupancy of the Library the trick door had no visible handle on the inside, so that when it was closed there was no telling that it was a door at all. It could be opened from within only by finding the correct book spine, titled *Tricks on Travellers*, which had a small tab of leather attached. When this was pulled, it released the door latch. Jib doors were a period joke in many great houses. This one is now a permanent fixture at Marlborough House; and on visiting the room and seeing it one can imagine the Prince, wreathed in cigar smoke and wheezing with laughter, exhibiting the trick to his visitors.

Permitted callers at the house nowadays may also catch sight of

LEFT *The crowned Edward VII with Queen Alexandra on 9 August 1902.*

ABOVE *An invitation to the Coronation dinner of Edward VII – but the Crowning was postponed by His Majesty's illness.*

another survival, from royal residence of a later period. This is a small elevator which was installed to help Queen Mary – Edward's daughter-in-law she was – to reach her first-floor apartments during her final wheelchair years in the early nineteen-fifties. The lift is a panelled box, stark but shining, just big enough to contain Her Majesty's equipage with scarcely an inch to spare.

Upright, economical and steady is that little lift – just like old Queen Mary herself . . .

Turn of the Century

Queen Mary was neither a queen nor an old lady in the nineteenth century. It was in that century of Queen Victoria and the future Edward VII that she came into the immediate Royal Family. The year was 1893 and she was in her twenties, Princess May of Teck, daughter of a German duke and a descendant on her mother's side of Hanoverian George III. But she was British-born, at Kensington Palace, and for the most part brought up in this country. She had been engaged to Albert Victor, Duke of Clarence, that elder son of the Prince of Wales and Princess Alexandra. But he died suddenly in 1892. A broken thread was rejoined soon afterwards, however, when she married his brother Prince George, the prince who had become Duke of York and was to be the next Prince of Wales and Heir to the Throne a decade later, and who eventually succeeded as the fifth King George.

George and May (later, her full and formal name of Mary took over) had a very splendid wedding, its scenes a kaleidoscope of European royalty. An outsider, looking through a window at the glittering mass of them all, would have had difficulty in sorting them out, particularly hard put to know which was the Prince and which his cousin from Russia, for the last Tsar – Tsarevitch then – was present, looking almost like a twin of the bridegroom.

The firstborn son of the marriage of George and Mary arrived promptly in 1894 – 'David' to the family, but christened with six other names preceding that one: Edward, Albert, Christian, George, Andrew and Patrick. Queen Victoria was quick to point out that with this birth Britain had three direct Heirs as well as the Sovereign alive. Forty-two years later that baby was himself Sovereign, Edward VIII, unsettling and unforgettable as the King Who Abdicated.

But in the 1890s, the years of David's early childhood, any shaking of the Throne was unthinkable. Many royal cradles were being rocked, but never the Crown. Solid and imperial Victoria, nearly deified by her own longevity and the material prosperity of her realms, was in her last golden years, now having emerged into public view and popular veneration, an unparalleled and undoubted Head of State.

OPPOSITE, TOP LEFT *Queen Mary, when Princess of Wales in 1906, giving Prince George, later Duke of Kent, a piggyback ride.*

OPPOSITE, TOP RIGHT *Queen Alexandra in 1904 with one of her numerous pet dogs. This one she named Little Marvel.*

OPPOSITE, BOTTOM *King George V – as he later was – with some of his young family on the Sandringham estate early in the century.*

ABOVE *The Prince and Princess of Wales with all their children in 1906 at Abergeldie Castle, near Balmoral.*

The euphoria of Victoria's Golden and Diamond Jubilees had not been able, however, to conjure away the dark clouds edging into the national outlook at home and already changing the international picture. Hard though it was to realise the fact, the British Empire was past its zenith, and for its people there was no smooth coasting into the next century. Amid social and industrial unrest at home, criticism of colonialism's seamy commercial side was swelling; and inevitably the rivalry of European powers was beginning to erode Britain's world supremacy.

Kaiser William – Victoria's grandson had become German Emperor in 1888 – still came over on enjoyed visits, and from the British side the Prince of Wales and others of the Royal Family went over to Germany from time to time on trips both domestic and formal, manifesting personal warmth and ceremonial cordiality. Nevertheless, German militarism and harsh colonial expansion, spurred by this same Kaiser's vaulting ambition, were an increasing anxiety for a whole decade even before they became a very real and near menace to the peace of Europe and the world.

It was not only the growing German army which was altering the picture and the balance of power. Englishmen were, rather contemptuously, familiar with photographs of Prussian soldiers goosestepping up and down Potsdam. But now British sea supremacy was clearly going to be challenged, and that was a very different matter. An ominous weapon was being forged to oppose the British Navy: a German High Seas Fleet. The first keels of this modern Armada were already laid down, and before long a succession of dreadnoughts were gliding down Baltic slipways.

Meanwhile, in the last year of the old century, Britain was herself humiliatingly at war, in South Africa, and was being made painfully to realise that the bandoliered burghers in the slouch hats were no pushover. So the dawn of 1900 was not altogether rosy. The year saw the agony of Ladysmith and Mafeking, and the bloody Boxer Rising in China. There was change and challenge on the home front too. A hitherto unknown force was established in the House of Commons: an Independent Labour Group. And another phenomenon – far from unknown was this one – entered politics at Westminster: an ex-war correspondent-cum-soldier named Winston Churchill, Member of Parliament at twenty-five and trailing clouds of glory from escapades in four continents.

In the Royal Family, lives were ending and lives were beginning. Queen Victoria's own course had not long to run. She was now weak and unwell, however determined the spirit with which she received an old friend or from her chair pinned a medal on the chest of a war hero summoned to quiet Osborne. She had lost exact count of all the new arrivals in her family and the nobility: she was living in the past and not the future – and would have no reason to remark, in that year 1900, the birth of a baby, royal then only through her Scottish blood, who was destined to become Britain's best-loved royal Consort and Queen Mother: Elizabeth Bowes-Lyon.

The end of Queen Victoria's life came in the first month of 1901. With the family at his grandmother's deathbed on the evening of 22 January was William. The German Emperor had hurried to England the night before, had been met by the Prince of Wales – wearing Prussian uniform – and with his uncle had crossed to the Isle of Wight at dawn. At noon Victoria had a moment of consciousness, saw her son, put out her frail arms from the bedclothes and said 'Bertie'. The Prince embraced her and broke down. After that, she went into a final coma until, as the message to the bowler-hatted reporters at Osborne's gates put it, she 'breathed her last, surrounded by her children and grandchildren'. She was eighty-one.

ABOVE *Prince Edward (later Edward VIII) in 1909.*

OPPOSITE *One of King Edward VII's shooting parties at Sandringham. The day's wholesale 'bag' is laid out before the King's assembled family and friends.*

The Kaiser in later years made a point of telling his English relatives how he had been the one to help the doctor to support the tiny figure propped up on the pillows. It is said that for the final two hours William stayed with his right arm about the Queen's shoulders without changing position, for his left arm was withered. Certainly his cousins admitted that on that visit William had behaved in an exemplary manner, dignified in his sorrow and never thrusting himself forward till the closing bedside hours. When Bertie, King at last, went to London next morning for the Accession Council which proclaimed him Edward VII, he asked the Kaiser to take charge at Osborne. And it was William who, the Queen in her will having forbidden undertakers, measured the last Hanoverian for her coffin.

Shock and grief reigned in Britain for days. Although a public announcement that she was sinking had been made two days before, the death of Queen Victoria was a stunning blow to the nation, and to many people almost beyond comprehension. Most had lived their entire lives under her reign, so that her passing was like the end of a world. She had become something permanent, both an idol and a human epitome of conscientious work, a guardian of morals, a civilisation's foundation stone. Now she was gone, and a sense of security had vanished with her. Would life ever be the same again?

Mourning was widespread. In icy weather, people knelt in the fields alongside the railway track as the special train conveying the body made its slow way from Portsmouth to the London station bearing Victoria's name. There followed a procession through city

streets draped in purple, and another train journey from Paddington to Windsor. At Windsor station a team of Royal Artillery horses waited to pull the coffin on its gun-carriage to the Castle for the final entombment. But when the funeral party from the train arrived, one of the horses, chilled by a long wait in the bitter cold, suddenly reared and snapped the traces. Moments of panic ensured, but brisk commands from a royal Secretary and a quick-thinking director of naval intelligence from the Admiralty who was on the spot (no less a person than Prince Louis of Battenberg, father of the late Earl Mountbatten of Burma) produced ropes quickly made from knotted harness and the communication cord ripped out of the royal train. With this improvisation, a team of straw-hatted sailors who had been furnishing a guard of honour on the spot grounded their arms, took to the tow-lines, and marched a hundred-strong up the steep and slippery slope from the station to the main road and on to the Castle, hauling the gun-carriage. Thus was established the funeral tradition of royal coffins on their gun-carriages being drawn by marching men of the Royal Navy (and in this fashion honour was recently paid, at *his* funeral in 1979, to that great-grandson of Queen Victoria, Louis Mountbatten – for the murdered earl was buried like a king and a gun-crew of a hundred bluejackets drew his coffin through the streets of London to Westminster Abbey).

Of course, life in England in the years following Victoria's death in 1901 could not be the same as it had been. Not with an essentially different monarch as Head of State, a king at once so new, so old, so extrovert. His style was in such contrast to his parent's, no matter how much he tried in public affairs to follow her example of duty. And Edward VII knew, as his subjects knew as they now took stock of the years past, that the Victorian years had been as unmatched and unmatchable as the mother's own life had been. When she had succeeded to office, she had taken over a Throne tarnished by the conduct of her uncles – and in her sixty-three years' reign had restored it out of all recognition, making it a symbol of public honour and private virtue. She had presided, moreover, over an era as revolutionary in its own setting as the Atomic Age. It had seen steam, electricity, wireless signals, the internal-combustion engine and the embryonic flying machine progressively annihilating distance. The nation had grown in population too: two million it had been at the time of William from Normandy, eight million in the days of George from Hanover, and now it was thirty million.

This was the land Prince Albert Edward took over, becoming King Edward VII in his sixtieth year and a grandfather. He was faithful always to the memory of his mother, but mindful too, broad, bluff Englishman though he might be, that he was a Coburg son of a Coburg father. He rolled his 'r's like a Teuton and had possessed since birth, quartered with those of England, the Royal Arms of Saxony on his insignia. Though as monarch he took the name of Edward, not Albert, his father's family name was his. Dynastically, he was the first, and the last, Sovereign of the House of Saxe-Coburg and Gotha.

In the context of other reigns, Edward's can be quickly told, luminous though he was as a king. He worked hard to build upon

the foundations of service his mother had laid, but many of her affections and obsessions could not be his. He lost little time in disregarding Victoria's wish that her beloved island home, Osborne, should be kept in the family. None of the family would live there and he emphatically wished to be done with the dull house. So he gave it to the nation as a Royal Naval college and convalescent home.

Another thing he wished to dispose of was the memory of John Brown. He was swift on this too. He ordered the removal or destruction of all the statues and busts of Victoria's extraordinarily privileged Highland servant, loved by his mistress and loathed by her family.

The actions were typical of a bustling and forthright man, a robust royal personage whose character as a human being as well as a holder of office had been so well known to the public long before he came to the Throne. This time it was no isolated figure who was wearing the Crown; it was a widely popular person. Edward's image and link with ordinary people was enhanced, for one thing, by his passionate enthusiasm for the Turf, his horseracing appearances and successes. As Prince, he was an owner who had twice won the Derby: in 1896 with Persimmon (whose statue in bronze can be seen at Sandringham today) and in 1900 with Diamond Jubilee. Nine years after that, in the owner's last year as monarch, came a third victory with the famous Minoru.

To some sections of his subjects, King Edward was a sovereign who administered recurrent shocks by undisguised personal indulgences in pleasure. But he gave the whole nation a very

particular shock, of a vastly different kind and certainly unwillingly, early in his reign. For he nearly died on the eve of his Coronation.

In May 1902 the long-drawn-out war in South Africa came to an end, and the Westminster Abbey ceremony to crown the new monarch was fixed for 26 June. But, with only forty-eight hours to go before the great event, the King – never a life-insurance agent's good risk – became desperately ill. He was found to be suffering from not only straight appendicitis but perityphlitis, necessitating an emergency operation at once – and this in the days when appendicectomies were pioneer ventures, very serious surgical tasks. The Coronation, for which unprecedented preparations had been made, had to be postponed. Its final dress rehearsal was hurriedly turned into a service of prayer for the Sovereign's life.

Happily, the life was saved. To everyone's joy – astonishingly, considering that Edward was no fit man, his ample frame having suffered for years from large intakes of food and drink and tobacco fumes – the operation was an immediate success and the patient's recovery very rapid indeed. Within two weeks he was completely out of danger and full of his old zest. The postponed crowning was fixed for 9 August.

ABOVE *Nine reigning kings followed Edward VII's coffin through the streets of Windsor in May 1910 for his burial at the Castle.*

OPPOSITE *The nine kings. Standing (from left to right): Haakon VII of Norway, Ferdinand of Bulgaria, Manoel of Portugal, William II of Germany, George I of Greece, Albert of the Belgians. Seated: Alfonso XIII of Spain, George V, Frederick VIII of Denmark.*

Though most of the dignitaries who had assembled in London from all over the world had had to go home and were unable to attend again, so shearing the ceremony in the Abbey of some of its public interest and splendour, the ancient rite, shortened anyhow so that the Sovereign should not be fatigued, duly took place to the accompaniment of popular rejoicing. The King himself was in good form. On the morning, before starting out from the Palace, he called his grandchildren to see him in his robes, did a little skip for them, and said 'Am I not a funny-looking old man?' But at the ceremony His Majesty was solemn and dignified, manifesting an air of purposeful dedication. He was much moved by the ritual. When his son George, the Prince of Wales, had knelt before him and declared his allegiance in the ancient words, the King laid on him a detaining hand, drew his Heir towards him, clasped his hand and kissed him on each cheek with spontaneous parental emotion.

46

During his years as King, Edward never ceased to enjoy his family and his wider social life, but he did not at any time fail to pursue energetically the exercises of State. He embarked, sometimes with Queen Alexandra attractively accompanying him, upon a series of overseas visits, personally promoting international friendliness. This was becoming more and more difficult as far as Germany was concerned, partly because the Kaiser nephew now felt that Uncle Bertie was unbearably patronising, and the pair eventually became incurably antipathetic to each other. Cordial relations between Britain and the swelling Fatherland were kept up publicly for several years yet, but inevitably there was a shift of amity away from Germany and towards a new alliance with Russia and especially with France. King Edward was popularly credited as the inspirer, if not the architect, of the *Entente Cordiale*. All of which, not unnaturally, upset the jealous Germans, whose clouds of suspicions were only temporarily dispelled by the State Visit which the King and Queen paid to William in 1909.

In the spring of the next year the King, his attacks of bronchitis having become more and more damaging, died in his sixty-ninth year.

Viewed in the light of history, Edward VII's more debatable personal attributes have tended to obscure his kingly diligence and serious political endeavours, his strenuous efforts to be a soothing, albeit realigning, Uncle of Europe. He did not himself sway the destiny of nations – politicians had by his time shed the tutelage of

kings – but his own contacts, his innate courtesy and disarming panache during his travels undoubtedly helped to improve understanding between differing peoples. In the nine troubled years of his reign, he was the last monarch to play any really personal part in shaping foreign policy, and, although his activities became increasingly curtailed by uncertain health, he proved a more able Sovereign than many had expected. And he was an admired stylist and sportsman to the end, the endearing 'King Teddy'. On the day of his death, 6 May, he insisted on getting up, dressing in his frockcoat instead of the informal rig which the valet had laid out, lunching almost as he normally would, and then lighting the usual large cigar. His last word, later that day before collapsing into the coma of death, was to express joy on being told that his horse had won at Kempton Park. He had insisted that, whatever his state, he must be informed of the result.

Half a million people filed through Westminster Hall to pay their silent tribute as the body of their late Sovereign lay for three days in State, high on its catafalque. An even greater crowd watched the funeral procession in which the gun-carriage was immediately followed by mourners of a master and a monarch – Edward's faithful fox terrier and nine reigning kings.

There followed also a sorrowing son – 'I have lost my best friend and the best of fathers', he had written in his diary – the prince who was now King George V, with twenty-five tumultuous years and a world war ahead of him.

PART THREE

George V and Queen Mary

Twilight of Peace

THE NEW SOVEREIGN was not yet forty-five years old. Middle-aged. But in the eyes of many people at that time, George V was a youngster of a King, for they had long been accustomed to much older monarchs.

Nor was he very well known. Most of his early life had been spent unexcitingly, in the country at Sandringham or closeted with governess or tutor in the London house. Even when he had emerged into the outer world he was exposed not to public perusal but the more private perils of the ocean, for he was thrust into the boisterous experiences of a naval cadet and eventually of a hard-driven midshipman sailing the world in a British man-o'-war. And he loved seagoing. In 1892 however, because of the death of his elder brother, it had been necessary for him to alter his life, switch careers, and exchange the chosen profession of fulltime officer of the Royal Navy for the inescapable routines of Heir to the Throne. As Duke of York, with his wife and future Queen beside him, he made a series of overseas tours, an Imperial ambassador instead of a seaman. He was created Prince of Wales in 1901.

Visits to foreign Courts, public engagements at home, deskwork in his study and, at his father's suggestion, a beginning of acquaintanceship with official papers – all these exercises were punctiliously carried through by the boy who had been 'Georgie' and was now a dutiful adult Prince, himself a father of a family, the Quiet Apprentice on the path to sovereignty.

This man who became George V was never a showy or scintillating personality. Sincere and dependable utterly, but probably more shy, more inflexible, more conservative, more Victorian even than his grandmother. The style of his reign, therefore, was in immediate contrast to that of his father. His Court in fact became the antithesis of Edward VII's. It was a Court of reaction, faultless as the quarterdeck of a martinet. And, presiding over it, a monarch who was correct and kindly but inordinately self-effacing.

Yet this was a king who proved to be a loved national patriarch, first of a line of enthroned democrats, a rock of calm sense and firm leadership. He was the pioneer of *representative* kingship, speaking

and acting for the nation. People gradually began to feel that here was an unpretentious Head of State with whom they could be identified. It was perhaps because he had been a working seaman, knowing what it was to be backaching and footsore and palm-blistered, that he had an innate *rapport* with the great mass of his people who worked with their hands. A Father-figure.

But in May 1910 that stature was still to come. The crowds who watched the untried son walking in the cortège of King Edward were yet to know the guiding goodness of George V. There was a clue, could they have seen it, standing on the working table of his London home. It was a few well-known lodestar lines, copied out in his own laboured hand on Marlborough House headed writing paper and framed: 'I shall journey through this world but once. Any good thing, therefore, that I can do, or any kindness that I can show any human being, let me do it now; let me not neglect or defer it, for I shall not pass this way again.'

OPPOSITE *The King-Emperor and his consort at the magnificent Coronation Durbar held in Delhi in 1911. The Imperial Crown of India was made for the occasion and has never been worn since.*

RIGHT *Princes Henry (born 1900) and George (born 1902). With Prince John (who lived from 1905 to 1919), they were the King's younger sons.*

The text had been before him for a long time; and he had been doing his own generous, hard-working best for nearly ten years – keeping count of the labour of it in his own diary too (he had inherited the habit of journal-writing from his grandmother). When he and his wife, royal Duke and Duchess representing the King his father, had gone out to Melbourne to open the first Parliament of the Commonwealth of Australia, the voyage had become an eight months' world tour during which, as he recorded, they travelled 45,000 miles, 33,032 of which were by sea and 12,000 by land. They laid 21 foundation stones, received 544 loyal addresses, presented 4,329 medals and shook hands with 24,855 people at official receptions alone.

There were many other journeys after that one. But now, at the start of his reign, solemn domestic affairs of State anchored George V in London. His Accession was formally proclaimed by the Earl Marshal and his tabarded heralds from the balcony of Friary Court, St James's Palace, three days after his father's death. Across the road, two teenage naval cadets stood at the salute and watched the ceremony from over the garden wall of Marlborough House. They were the new Sovereign's two elder sons, Prince Edward and Prince Albert, whose parents were also looking down on Friary Court, but from behind a curtain of the boys' bedroom in the house. It would not have been seemly for the King to be observed watching the opening salute to his own grandeur.

Marlborough House was still the family home. Not until very much later did they move along the Mall to take up residence in Buckingham Palace in the rooms that had been those of King Edward and Queen Alexandra (who had themselves not been able to live in the long-neglected Palace for well over a year after *their* accession). When eventually they did go to the Palace the place was at last possessed of private apartments fit for a family to live in. Queen Alexandra had had a long struggle to put life and good looks, electricity and adequate furnishing, into a mansion unin-habited and untouched for fifty Victorian years. She and King Edward had not had years enough there, however, to do anything about the disliked East Front of the Palace added for Queen Victoria in 1847 – the one that faces down the Mall and is seen by the public – and it was not until 1913 that Sir Aston Webb built the present façade in Portland stone, to make the royal dwelling 'a cynosure instead of an eye-sore'.

The new Sovereign and Consort of that time, King George and Queen Mary, needed plenty of room for their family. They had six children, all born between 1894 and 1905: five boys and one girl. The last child and youngest son died young. So our history follows the remaining four Princes of this generation.

The children of George V, in order of arrival on the scene, were: Prince Edward, who was subsequently Prince of Wales, King Edward VIII and Duke of Windsor; Prince Albert, subsequently Duke of York and King George VI; Princess Mary, subsequently the Princess Royal, who married Viscount Lascelles who became the sixth Earl of Harewood; Prince Henry, subsequently Duke of Gloucester; Prince George, subsequently Duke of Kent; and Prince John, the youngest, who suffered from attacks of epilepsy and so was brought up apart from his brothers and sister, and who died in 1919 at the age of thirteen. The little boy's grave is in Sandringham churchyard.

But Sandringham, as thousands of tourists now able to visit the house and grounds know, has many memorials that are happy ones. The whole area, unsheltered though it may be from the cold east winds sweeping in from the North Sea, has a redolence of generation after generation of pleasant country living. This great rambling Jacobean-style house in Norfolk, most intimate and most affectionately regarded of the royal residences, then and now – the fact that Her Majesty The Queen has since 1977 opened it to the public does not alter its standing as one of the Family's favourite homes – was to George V 'the place I love better than anywhere else in the world'.

Even before he became King in 1910 he felt like that about Sandringham. For seventeen years he and his wife, Duke and Duchess of York and then Prince and Princess of Wales, had contentedly made their home in York Cottage, an old-fashioned villa in the grounds of 'the big house'. Except for the eldest, all their children had been born there. When the Prince and Princess became King and Queen they kept the Cottage on for many years, living in it rather than in the Sovereign's rightful home, Sandringham House itself, and being quite happy to do so. This

LEFT *York Cottage, on the Sandringham House estate, was George V's Norfolk home for many years both before and after his accession. He described Sandringham as 'the place I love better than anywhere else in the world'.*

OPPOSITE *Two cousins extraordinarily alike: Nicholas II, Tsar of Russia, and George V, in the uniform of a German cuirassier. The photograph was taken in 1913 during a visit to Berlin for the wedding of the daughter of another cousin – the Kaiser, William II.*

was fortunate, because George's 'Motherdear', Queen Alexandra, did not move out of the main house in 1910 when Edward the King died and she became a dowager, the Queen Mother. Indeed she stayed there for the rest of her life, another fifteen years. Members of the Household of the new Sovereign and Consort, George and Mary, incredibly crowded as they all were in York Cottage (the Sailor King's grey parrot and all, a privileged bird addicted to hopping along the royal breakfast table and crashing its beak into the boiled eggs of his master's guests), felt that Queen Alexandra could never quite bring herself to look upon her son and daughter-in-law as King and Queen. At any rate, so far as Sandringham House was concerned, she had no doubt at all about her right to be there. Her view, rightly, was that the house had been built and paid for by her husband and was not a State palace or a possession of the Crown. It was quite different from Marlborough House which she used in London, for Sandringham was personal property and therefore hers. It did not occur to her that her son either needed it or ought to have it.

And her son, the new King, contentedly let it be so.

He was not pretentious or possessive, and most restrained when it came to putting his views. Over and over again his personal diary

demonstrates his character. Perhaps never more so than on the day of his Coronation, which took place in June, 1911, a magnificent occasion of ancient ritual and modern pageantry. It had all the splendour and beauty of Abbey pomp and processions through the London streets. Escorting the King and Queen in their golden coach which had been first used by George III one hundred and fifty years before, Nation and Empire were on parade in full dress – the Empire now including the new *Dominions*: Canada, Australia, New Zealand, the Union of South Africa. All sent their leaders and their cohorts of soldiery. Among the chief figures at the Westminster ceremony walked two great captains of arms, the best-known British generals, Lord Roberts and Lord Kitchener, each holding aloft a Sword of State. Kitchener, coming to the height of his fame, was commanding the fifty thousand troops who lined the processional route in the heart of the capital city.

It was a tremendous, resounding day, an epic of anthems and trumpets, of thundering guns and marching men. The monarch at the centre of it all, a King richly adorned and gravely submissive, was clearly very deeply moved by all that took place. And yet, when that night he wrote his journal before going to bed, the diary was as unemotional a log as ever: '... Overcast and cloudy with some

showers and strongish cool breeze, but better for the people than great heat ... May and I left B.P. at 10.30 with 8 cream-coloured horses ... Service in the Abbey was most beautiful, but it was a terrible ordeal .... Worked all the afternoon with Bigge & others answering telegrams. Our guests dined with us at 8.30. May and I showed ourselves again to the people. Wrote and read. Rather tired. Bed at 11.45.'

George V was not given to any excess of drama in writing, but no one who had dealings with him was in any doubt that he was nevertheless a sensitive man who was deeply involved in and deeply emotional about all the historical ceremonial which touched himself and his family – including that revival from ages past which the bravura of David Lloyd George conjured up at Caernarvon Castle a month after the Coronation, the Investiture of David, the seventeen-year-old Prince of Wales. Nor did the King's domestic austerity affect the splendour of the Courts, the full-dress levees, over which he and Queen Mary regularly presided at Buckingham Palace. He had nothing but enthusiasm for traditional forms of royal display, especially if they could in his view help the cohesion and peaceful government of his subjects overseas.

Having visited the vast country as Prince of Wales, he had a special interest in India, and when he ascended the Throne was much concerned over the fierce tides of disruptive nationalism which were rising in the subcontinent. It was at his insistence that he and the Queen, at the end of 1911, sailed away to make the last great State Progress of a British Sovereign in Imperial India. The centrepiece of the tour was a fabulous Coronation Durbar in Delhi. Brushing aside advisers' doubts about the safety of the visit, His Majesty rode, high-minded and heavily uniformed, through the streets of the new capital city, and Bombay and Calcutta, exalted as King-Emperor. Over-decked and in vain as that sun-baked enthronement may seem to have been, it was nevertheless a statisfying pageant of the old Raj, an occasion of Princes in Homage never matched in the annals of the panoplied East.

Back in England in 1912, the King faced a different picture. His own country was racing wondrously out of the horse-drawn era into the age of the motor car and other exciting conveyances, and the first flying machines were beginning to shudder into the air from grassy aerodromes. But socially and constitutionally, the prospect was, for the average man-on-the-ground, anything but glittering. Industrial unrest was rife, and the contagion for a long coal strike spread from the miners to the dockers and railwaymen. Lloyd George in-

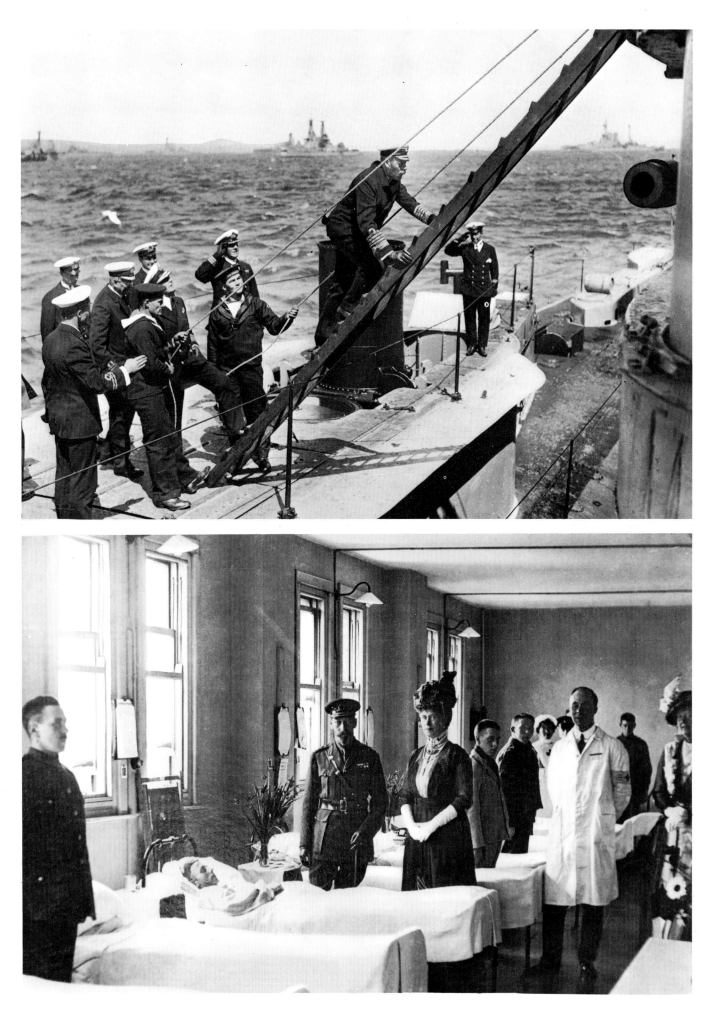

OPPOSITE, TOP *George V, Sailor-King, was always at home and happy at sea. He was rarely out of touch with the Royal Navy. Here he is visiting the Fleet during the First World War.*

OPPOSITE, BOTTOM *Thousands of war casualties – and members of medical staffs – were visited in hospitals by Their Majesties.*

ABOVE *The desolation of Ypres in 1917. The Ypres salient was the scene of great battles and great loss of life.*

LEFT *The House of Windsor proclaimed.*

BY THE KING.

A PROCLAMATION

Declaring that the Name of Windsor is to be borne by His Royal House and Family and relinquishing the use of all German Titles and Dignities.

GEORGE R.I.

WHEREAS WE, having taken into consideration the Name and Title of Our Royal House and Family, have determined that henceforth Our House and Family shall be styled and known as the House and Family of Windsor:

AND WHEREAS We have further determined for Ourselves and for and on behalf of Our descendants and all other the descendants of Our Grandmother Queen Victoria of blessed and glorious memory to relinquish and discontinue the use of all German Titles and Dignities:

AND WHEREAS We have declared these Our determinations in Our Privy Council:

NOW, THEREFORE, We, out of Our Royal Will and Authority, do hereby declare and announce that as from the date of this Our Royal Proclamation Our House and Family shall be styled and known as the House and Family of Windsor, and that all the descendants in the male line of Our said Grandmother Queen Victoria who are subjects of these Realms, other than female descendants who may marry or may have married, shall bear the said Name of Windsor:

And do hereby further declare and announce that We for Ourselves and for and on behalf of Our descendants and all other the descendants of Our said Grandmother Queen Victoria who are subjects of these Realms, relinquish and enjoin the discontinuance of the use of the Degrees, Styles, Dignities, Titles and Honours of Dukes and Duchesses of Saxony and Princes and Princesses of Saxe-Coburg and Gotha, and all other German Degrees, Styles, Dignities, Titles, Honours and Appellations to Us or to them heretofore belonging or appertaining.

Given at Our Court at Buckingham Palace, this Seventeenth day of July, in the year of our Lord One thousand nine hundred and seventeen, and in the Eighth year of Our Reign.

GOD SAVE THE KING.

LONDON: Printed by EYRE AND SPOTTISWOODE, LIMITED, Printers to the King's most Excellent Majesty.

troduced a revolutionary palliative called Unemployment Insurance, but neither that piece of legislation nor the team efforts of the now substantial group of Labour members in the House of Commons did much to help the negotiations of the new trade unions. It seemed impossible to take the heat out of workers' grievances. Poverty brought protest to English streets. More serious still was the running sore of Ireland. The issue of Home Rule was at explosive point in the Parliament of Westminster as well as in Ulster.

Another focus of disorder in the years between 1910 and the outbreak of the Kaiser's War in 1914 was the campaign for Votes for Women. Dedicated suffragettes were on the march. They advanced inexorably from shouting down political speakers to horsewhipping Winston Churchill, clawing policemen, smashing shop windows, dropping bombs into pillar-boxes and chaining themselves to the railings of Downing Street. One woman committed suicide by throwing herself under the hooves of the King's horse in the 1913 Derby to win a martyr's crown.

Within the Royal Family's circle, too, at least one member was starting to turn patterns of behaviour upside down. King George's eldest son, the impulsively up-and-coming Prince of Wales, having emerged from a segregated life of tutors, naval colleges, and a few months as a midshipman, went up to Oxford for a time, and at Magdalen – in contrast to the pattern of college life laid for his grandfather at Cambridge fifty years before – lived as much as possible the existence of an ordinary undergraduate. It was not easy, but the coltish Heir to the Throne made a number of friends in social classes other than his own, as well as among young aristocrats, and is reputed to have deflated certain taunting socialist republicans by singing 'The Red Flag' to his own banjo accompaniment. His years of non-compliance were beginning.

The young Princes were being brought up in conventional royal style without university forays. The second son, Albert – another 'Bertie', in name but not in character – passed through the Royal Navy's Dartmouth training, though with some classroom diffi-culty; the younger Prince George followed later through the College and towards the Senior Service; and the path of Prince Henry was through Sandhurst to a career in the Army.

At home, the Family's life went its orderly way under the strict watch of a King and Queen whose styles and standards had not altered in twenty-five years. Their character was impeccable, but unbending too. When their children were toddlers they were a fond and understanding father and mother. Then, as the years went on and successions of severe governesses and tutors ruled their young, they gradually and without intention became out of touch with offspring growing to young manhood. They never gave children's parties. Kind and loving still, they nevertheless found it hard to bridge the generation gap and were unskilled as communicators even in their own sitting rooms. Whilst to the nation King George was a caring father-figure, to his sons he seemed more like a crusty fag-master. He knew it, and now and then he tried not to be so. Lacking any knack of relaxed fatherhood, and having been himself brought up in obedience to and even fear of a father, he would attempt to alter his ways by occasional bursts of rough jocularity, which made matters even more strained and embarrassing. The deep and enduring shyness in the make-up of both King George and Queen Mary was no doubt at the root of the brittle family situation.

Moreover, the King now had not much time for lowering his domestic fences. Barriers between classes and nations were going up instead of down all over the world, it seemed. There was little contentment in the air. Barbed camps of bigotry were being fostered.

OPPOSITE, LEFT *David Lloyd George, famous wartime Prime Minister. When pictured here, before 1914, he was Chancellor of the Exchequer, notable for introducing old age pensions and unemployment insurance.*

OPPOSITE, RIGHT *A suffragette tries to sell her paper to police officers outside Bow Street court. From 1910 to 1914 militant suffragettes struggled to obtain votes for women, often through acts of violence.*

RIGHT *The year 1924 brought the first Labour government in British history. Here the King, with Queen Mary and suitably uniformed, was meeting Mr Stephen Walsh, his new War Minister.*

All sorts of sadnesses and disasters were making the news. One of the shocks was the loss of the 'unsinkable' liner *Titanic*, holed by a huge Atlantic iceberg off Newfoundland on her maiden voyage in 1912. The same year had brought the chilling story of the death of a hero, Captain Scott of the Antarctic.

The gravest of stormclouds were banking up over the continent of Europe, and to those who cared or dared to survey the scene the thunderclap of war was an inevitable outcome. In a clash of ambitions, great nations were feverishly arming and ranging themselves in sinister coalition.

Germany's was the most frightening of the mailed fists. Yet an exchange of Anglo-German official visits continued almost until the moment of the cloudburst. Emperor William had eagerly come over to attend the unveiling of the Victoria Memorial outside Buckingham Palace, keeping up his ambivalent love-hate relationship with his grandmother's country. To the end, this Kaiser, head of a now overbearing Fatherland, could not believe that if he and his Austrian ally went to war, England would oppose him in battle and not allow France and Russia to be crushed.

King George could exercise little influence over the crescendo of events in Europe. The final explosion was triggered by the murder of the heir to the Austrian throne at Sarajevo in the June of 1914. Austria made this an excuse to declare war on Serbia; Germany declared war on Britain's now mobilised allies, Russia and France, and brutally invaded Belgium; and on 4 August a state of war between King George's country and Kaiser William's country came into being. The Foreign Secretary, Sir Edward Grey, watching the dimming of Whitehall's gaslamps that night, uttered a phrase that became famous: 'The lights are going out all over Europe. We shall not see them lit again in our lifetime.' The First World War had begun.

All over Britain, the one European country which had been militarily unprepared, indignation at the German assault burst out in a matter of hours, bringing to the surface a deep-seated patriotism which without any conscription sent men flocking to the recruiting offices. And on that August night, when our ultimatum to Germany expired, it was to the Palace that the cheering crowds in the London streets instinctively turned. At midnight they were in dense mass outside the railings, calling out for the man who by history and tradition was their trusted representative in time of trial. When the King came out to face them he had beside him the Queen and the young Prince of Wales.

Meanwhile, at the Admiralty, Winston Churchill had sniffed battle and already deployed the King's warships. As always, he squared his shoulders gladly to the challenge of action. And presently a tiny British Expeditionary Force of putteed soldiers slipped across the Channel singing 'It's a Long Way to Tipperary'. Before long those regulars, joined by great numbers of volunteer comrades, were to find themselves in a devastation of mud and blood, advancing and then retreating to dig in desperately along lines of sodden trenches which ran from the Swiss border to the sea.

On the night when the Four Dark Years of conflict began, the British King, with one son Prince Albert already away in the Navy at sea, with his Court mobilised, and with his people feverish to defend 'little Belgium' and not yet imbued with Edward Grey's fatalism, wrote in his diary a few words which calamity had not robbed of habitual truth and terse factual reporting: 'War with Germany. Terrible catastrophe, but it is not our fault. Please God it may soon be over and that he will protect dear Bertie's life. Bed at 12.'

The prayer could hardly have been simpler, the entry more sincere. He went to war with faith and no illusions.

ABOVE *On the occasion of their Silver Wedding in 1918 Their Majesties were photographed at Buckingham Palace. The war was continuing, and the King's anniversary message was one of sympathy for the sorrows of his people.*

LEFT *In 1922 Princess Mary, the only daughter of George V, was married to Viscount Lascelles, who became the sixth Earl of Harewood. A wedding-day group on the Palace balcony.*

War that Changed a Name

Cataclysmic periods of history bring unexpected by-products. A new title for the British Sovereign's family was presently to be among them. The First World War, the war of 1914–18, was the earthquake from which the royal House of Windsor was officially born. The name was begotten out of anguish and quandary.

The trauma of that first Great War began in the first months of the fighting; and the cheering crowds of August 1914 were soon to realise, as dire casualty lists were posted, the cruel weight of the machine which the Germans had long been preparing. With a series of hammer blows, the enemy swept through Belgium and forced back the French and British troops. The Allies counter-attacked and frustrated the German plan to annihilate the French armies, but the Battle of the Marne only made certain a long static war in the shell-torn devastation of mud which was called the Western Front. War names became synonymous with misery: Ypres, Arras, Neuve-Chapelle, Verdun, Vimy Ridge, Messines, the Somme and eternal Passchendaele. The words stood for sickeningly costly gains, shattering bombardments and inconclusive Big Pushes in France and Flanders. British 'Tommies', however resilient the bittersweet humour which sustained them, had gone to earth and as the years went on were living and dying in a vast system of trenches and craters at times waist-deep in stinking water.

By 1917, too, America was still not quite sure about being in the war, Russia was cracking internally and becoming near-useless as a fighting ally, the failure of our Gallipoli landings against the Turks had left nasty scars and frightful Anzac casualties, submarine attacks were playing havoc with our shipping, German zeppelins

RIGHT, TOP *The marriage of Lieutenant Lord Mountbatten, later the first Earl Mountbatten of Burma, to Miss Edwina Ashley in 1922. The wedding was attended by all the Royal Family.*

RIGHT, BOTTOM *A rare photograph taken at Glamis Castle, the Scottish seat of the Earl of Strathmore, and showing the Duke and Duchess of York before their engagement in 1923. Lady Elizabeth Bowes-Lyon, today's Queen Elizabeth The Queen Mother, is seated in the centre with the Duke behind her. On his left is the Earl (Lady Elizabeth's father) and on his right the Hon. David Bowes-Lyon.*

LEFT *The Duke of York and Lady Elizabeth Bowes-Lyon: their official engagement photograph, 14 January 1923.*

OPPOSITE *A popular wedding picture taken on the day the Duke of York married Lady Elizabeth. The parents of the couple are with them.*

had been bombing Britain for two years, Field Marshal Lord Kitchener had been drowned at sea when a battle-cruiser sank, and, in our own islands, there was the Sinn Fein Irish rising. The nation was deep in gloom and sorrow. Had the public known of the lingering seriousness of the King's injuries, suffered when his horse reared and fell on him during one of his assiduous visits to the armies in France, there would have been further anxiety – and less questioning.

Questioning there certainly was – and a search for scapegoats, for someone to blame for the way things were going. The witch-hunts, unreasonable but hardly unnatural, were a symptom of the same fear and frustration which had gripped sections of the population in the first hate-the-enemy campaigns of 1914, over two years before, and were now one consequence of a people's continuing hurt and desperation at the tragic stalemate of a war which seemed never-ending. Calumny spread, and spared nothing, not even the Head of State.

Looking back on those demonstrations of doubt from the viewpoint of the present day, with *two* world wars experienced, it is not easy to understand the wild lashing-out. But the fact is that civilian conduct in the first German War lacked the patience and steadiness which characterised Home Front morale in the second war. Malign suggestions were tossed around at all and sundry, including the Monarch, unjustified though it was to snipe at a man who was essentially a dedicated, God-fearing English squire with

two sons in the war – for the Prince of Wales, 'David' to the family and now in his twenties, was a staff officer in France, itching to get to the trenches, and Prince Albert, 'Bertie', as a serving sublieutenant in the Royal Navy, had been in action at the Battle of Jutland.

The rumour-mongering and questioning of 1917 had the political and military leadership as general targets, but presently became concentrated on the German origins and names of the King and his relatives. The inquisition which had begun feverishly so soon after the start of the war had already scandalously unseated – solely because of his German birth – the loyal and brilliant sailor and First Sea Lord, Admiral Prince Louis of Battenberg, who was a cousin of the King.

The forced resignation of Prince Louis, then the long-serving and exceptionally skilful chief of the Royal Navy, had greatly distressed the King by the sheer injustice of it. It had also pained Winston Churchill, First Lord of the Admiralty (who, however, lived to see the equally distinguished son of the Admiral – Lord Louis, who became Earl Mountbatten of Burma – appointed to highest rank in the Navy and the nation's Defence Staff after the *next* World War). And now, in 1917, malice struck at the monarch himself. Brief stirrings of republicanism, unknown in Britain for half a century, and distorted by certain cheap newspapers, caused whisperings that the King had a pro-German streak – and this brought out royal anger at the very thought of it.

There was one particularly resented sneer. The writer H. G. Wells, at his most waspish after a Socialist rally celebrating the overthrow of the monarchy in Russia, publicly remarked that England was struggling through adversity 'under an alien and uninspiring Court'. King George in his sentient modesty was perfectly aware that his own circle was no focus of high intellectual endeavour, but on reading the Wells slight he rasped out an immediate riposte which became famous: 'I may be uninspiring but I'll be damned if I'm an alien.'

He had become determined, nevertheless, to look into the name business. He did so quite firmly, but reluctantly. It was not that he felt guilty or that he was lukewarm in war effort because he was fighting his first cousin. It was simply that fairness to others, even fairness to insidious hate-rousing propagandists in his own country, was part of his nature. It had not occurred to him that the Germans had ceased to be human overnight.

His common sense, however, dictated that advice should be sought, especially when he discovered that some of his subjects – and these were some who were sincere and not rabble-rousers – felt it was improper, when we were struggling for our lives against the Germans, that our own Sovereign, symbolic leader of a Britain opposing a loathed Hohenzollern, should bear the designation Saxe-Coburg-Gotha.

The King was not sure that strictly he *had* a surname. He had never used one – understandably, because no royal surname operated

in Britain. He belonged to a branch of an old German family of course, and his Queen was a Teck; but even the Royal College of Heralds said they were not certain what His Majesty's own name was. Not 'Guelph', they thought, and not 'Wipper' or 'Wettin' either – which were names associated geographically and dynastically with the Guelphic Saxe-Coburg family, and in any case were unfortunate labels if given English pronunciation. But yes, the College of Arms agreed, some members of the monarch's family in Britain did have unpopular names like Schleswig-Holstein. No clear ideas were forthcoming, however, even when the politicians as well as the family-tree pundits were brought into the consultations and asked for alternatives. All sorts of cumbersome and unpropitious titles – 'Tudor-Stewart' and 'Fitzroy' amongst them – were put up and in turn rejected.

But now the King had firmly decided that a new name *must* be taken. And at length there came, as in so many problems through the years there has come, a solution from the Royal Household. For it was Lord Stamfordham, that soundest of Private Secretaries, who suggested 'Windsor'. The name was so natural and native, so proper and foursquare in English history that it was at once gladly accepted.

On 17 July 1917 a royal statement was approved by the Privy Council, and its terms were made public in the form of a solemn Proclamation garnished with the traditional flourish of words and a good sprinkling of 'heretofore' and 'whereas' and 'henceforth'. The

substance was His Majesty's decision that 'Our House and Family shall be styled and known as the House and Family of Windsor' and that all British-based descendants in the male line of 'Our Grandmother Queen Victoria of blessed and glorious memory' were immediately to relinquish 'All German Titles and Dignities'.

So Coburg and Hanover and Brunswick were swept away, and in came names with a good United Kingdom ring about them. The King's two brothers-in-law, the Duke of Teck and Prince Alexander of Teck (Queen Mary's brothers), became the Marquess of Cambridge and the Earl of Athlone. Prince Louis (the deposed Admiral) and Prince Alexander of Battenberg, cousins of the King, became the Marquess of Milford Haven and the Marquess of Carisbrooke, with the new family name of Mountbatten.

Thus was the royal style anglicised by George V 'in the eighth year of our Reign'; thus a dynasty was christened; and thus the Windsor tapestry began to be woven. It was a soothing change. The strange thing, perhaps, was that so right a name as 'Windsor' had not been used before.

Across the battle lines, the German Emperor was predictably not amused. His reaction, spiky as his moustache, was that he would be looking forward to the next performance of Shakespeare's *Merry Wives of Saxe-Coburg-Gotha*. And in England, the German-born but very English Prince Louis, on hearing that it had been officially proclaimed that he was titled Battenberg no longer, wrote in the visitors' book of a house where he spent several days: 'Arrived Prince Hyde. Departed Lord Jekyll.' Hostilities never subdued the Mountbatten family sense of humour – and that grandfather of Prince Philip's possessed it abundantly.

Meanwhile, the war ground on. It seemed grimmer than ever in 1917, and the outlook gave no promise of brighter news from the front. Altering a royal name had not altered either the weary stalemate or the weight of shellfire on the Western Front. But what King George's pronouncement had done was implacably to blazon

the determination of British monarch and British people to conquer a tyranny. The King, though no chauvinist and a hater of war, was said to have turned pale with anger many times on reading gruesome dispatches from the front and reports of enemy atrocities. He urged his mother Queen Alexandra to keep heart and faith that we should win in the end. 'I shall never submit to those brutal Germans', he told her. Secretly, he must have wondered at times whether he might be the last as well as the first 'Windsor'.

The moments when Britain appeared nearest to defeat occurred in fact in the year that eventually brought victory, 1918. Then were courage and faith most needed. On the Continent, not only armies but ancient institutions such as monarchies were being swept away, victims of the disillusion of despairing soldiers at the front and dedicated pacifist socialists behind the breaking battle lines. Bad news came from all directions, but for the British monarch the tidings that came from Moscow were shockingly grim. A signal arrived out of now republican Russia telling of the murder by the Bolsheviks of the Tsar and his entire family. This was personal bereavement for the King, but served only to strengthen his will to conquer on the Western Front, however unlikely any such success seemed early in the year. Germany's massive Spring Offensive of 1918 broke through the Allied lines. But British, French, Anzac and Canadian counterattacks, joined now by the armies of the United States, not only stemmed but turned the tide after a few weeks. A spent enemy had made his final throw. It was at last the khaki uniforms, not the field-grey ones, which swept forward. Triumph was in sight.

By October the German Government was putting out feelers for armistice terms. Early in November a Socialist Republic and the abdication of the Kaiser were proclaimed from the Reichstag steps in Berlin. The deflated William, emperor no more, was allowed to escape from his own country's and the Allies' vengeance, and was admitted into neutral Holland as a private and protected exile.

OPPOSITE *When King George opened Wimbledon's Jubilee Tennis competition in June 1926 Queen Mary received France's Mlle Suzanne Lenglen, six times singles champion in the post-war years.*

RIGHT *George V at the helm of his racing yacht* Britannia *in 1925.*

BELOW *Golf was one of several sports enjoyed after the war by the Duke of York, here seen in action against Frank Hodges, leader of the Miners' Union, on a course in the Rhondda Valley in 1924.*

Two days later, at dawn in the coach of a train in the French forest of Compiègne, the Armistice was signed. Fighting ceased along the whole Western Front 'at the eleventh hour of the eleventh day of the eleventh month' of 1918.

The First World War was at an end. In London a riot of jubilation and thanksgiving lasted for a week. The King – with staunch Queen Mary, straight-backed and toque-topped at his side – drove in an open carriage through the crowded streets and was deafeningly cheered. On horseback he reviewed a huge parade of convalescent soldiers in Hyde Park and was nearly pulled off his horse when men broke ranks and rushed forward to shake his hand. No doubts encircled him now. He had become the nation's symbol of endeavour and triumph, a stainless priest of victory held in unalloyed affection by his people. Romanov and Hohenzollern cousins and their monarchies had gone, but Windsor remained. The British crown and its wearer, the institution and the man, were alike solid and secure.

None knew better than the Head of State, however, that an exhausted country would soon be expecting a reward of tonic and ease after all the sacrifices; and, pray though he did, he was aware that no magic stroke would bring it. The bells of thanksgiving rang out bravely enough after the bugles of truce, but they did not peal away the truth that the flower of the nation's young, leaders for rebuilding the future, had been slaughtered on the battlefields. The emaciating sacrifices had not created a new earth, and there was no new heaven just round the corner.

Aftermath

The King was fifty-three when the war ended, and was looking old beyond his years. Queen Mary was a well-preserved fifty-one. The Prince of Wales was twenty-four, Prince Albert nearly twenty-three, Princess Mary twenty-one, Prince Henry eighteen, and Prince George sixteen.

LEFT *Engagement photograph, 1935, of the Duke of Gloucester and Lady Alice Montagu-Douglas-Scott, now Princess Alice, the dowager Duchess. Her mother, the Duchess of Buccleuch, is on the left.*

OPPOSITE *Balmoral in the evening sun: three new views of the Castle. More a home than a fortification, it is to Scotland what Sandringham is to England: private house and holiday retreat. Balmoral was the realisation of a dream of Queen Victoria, and its building, between 1853 and 1856, was supervised by the Prince Consort. Victoria called it her 'dear paradise' and the house still reflects her taste, which extended to tartan carpets.*

The family – except the Prince of Wales who was in Canada on the first of his Empire tours – saw His Majesty lead the nation's tribute to the 900,000 war dead at the tall Cenotaph in the middle of London's Whitehall in 1919. The ceremony took the form of a memorial service at the foot of the monument on 11 November, exactly one year after the fighting had stopped. The Cenotaph was at first built of wood, to the design of Sir Edwin Lutyens. It was reconstructed in stone during the following year, and stands in Whitehall still. Indeed, although some voices are raised regularly protesting that the ceremony opens old war wounds and should be allowed to die, it continues to be the scene of the crowded annual service on Remembrance Day – 'Armistice Day' is no longer the name, for the Cenotaph now commemorates the dead of *two* Great Wars. Wreaths are placed when November comes; but, except on this one day of official remembering each year, the Cenotaph has become a largely unremarked piece of the London scenery. Gone are the days when men removed their hats from their heads as they passed the monument on foot or in a bus. (Gone are the hats too, for that matter.) Nor does the whole nation now pause at the eleventh hour on 11 November, for the observing of the Two Minutes' Silence on the stroke of eleven a.m. continues only at the central shrine and at the church services of that anniversary morning. But in 1919 the Observance was total.

In 1920, on the second anniversary of the Armistice, there took place not only the wreath-laying and the service of prayer at the monument in London's famous street of Government offices but also the burial of an Unknown Warrior in Westminster Abbey. Unidentified by name or rank, his remains had been taken from a grave in France to be buried among England's kings. George V, accompanied by his two eldest sons, acted as one of the pallbearers and walked in procession behind the gun-carriage bearing the coffin from the Cenotaph to its place near the west door of the Abbey.

Soon, the King was grateful to resume at least some of his old peacetime routines in both protocol and personal pursuit. He held formal receptions at the Palace once more, and the pageantry of the Guards in the full glory of scarlet tunics and bearskins was seen when he drove out to open Parliament in State. He was able to see Balmoral again – he had not visited it for six years – and there was more time for Sandringham and the country life he loved. Queen Mary was busy again in London with her passionate and knowledgeable collecting of Chinese Chippendale and jade, the prime decorations of her extensive house-furnishing. She could concentrate now on her expert petit-point needlework, having spent the war supervising the rougher stitchings of the national Women's Guild, heroines of the Balaclava helmet and knitted scarf industry which inspired the song 'Sister Susie's sewing shirts for Soldiers'.

The Queen accompanied her husband on most of his activities, though not, if she could avoid it, on board ships. She loathed the sea as much as he loved it. The King was never more animated and happy than when at the helm of his racing yacht *Britannia*, with a great spread of sail above him, his crew of thirty fellow enthusiasts around him, deck aslant and lee gunwale under water as the vessel went tearing through the scudding Solent during the competitions of Cowes Week.

But there was more to the peacetime years than bright ceremonial and sailing. Post-war pleasures were overclouded for everybody. However strong was the anxiety to get back to normal – to forget troubles and cheer Hobbs hitting centuries, Joe Beckett knocking out Bombardier Wells, Bolton Wanderers scoring Cup goals, Charlie Chaplin making the first comedy film classics and *Chu Chin Chow* breaking records at His Majesty's Theatre – life was chiefly a thing of work-chasing worry, and the world would never be the same again. Politics and industry were in painful disarray, and Prime Minister Lloyd George's 'Land Fit for Heroes' just a dream. Disappointment was the aftermath of war.

And not only in Britain. Continental Europe even had a fresh war, Greece against Turkey. In 1921 during the period of that

ABOVE *The King George IV Gateway from the lawns beside the Long Walk. The battlemented towers of Windsor were built during reconstruction work carried out at the Castle by Wyatville between 1820 and 1830.*

OPPOSITE, TOP *Broadlands, the Hampshire home of the late Earl Mountbatten of Burma. The present Queen and the Duke of Edinburgh spent part of their honeymoon here in 1947. The house was opened to the public shortly before Lord Louis's death in 1979.*

OPPOSITE, BOTTOM *The view from the Green Drawing Room in the Queen's own apartments at Windsor Castle. This unique photograph shows the gardens below the little-known East Terrace.*

67

conflict there was born (on the dining-room table of a villa in Corfu) a boy named Philip, son of a Greek general, Prince Andrew. This was the Prince Philip who three decades later was to be Britain's 'First Gentleman' and Consort, the man who brought the name of Mountbatten into the Royal House.

In 1922 Philip's father, Prince Andrew, was pretty unjustly put on trial for his life in Athens by the Greeks, smarting under defeat by the Turks; and King George V, who was related to the Greek royal family, managed to send in a rescue ship to bring the Prince and his family to safety – the infant Philip, future Duke of Edinburgh, included.

All the same, the Sovereign could hardly have had much time to think about Greek babies just then. Turmoil in his own kingdom was preoccupation enough. As so often, Ireland was proving the grievous sore. Anti-British Sinn Feiners formed themselves into a National Assembly called the Dáil and, forced underground, illegally proclaimed an independent Republic. Guerrilla zealots of the movement, the first Irish Republican Army, fought fierce gun battles in the streets and in every possible way resisted the troops, the armed police, and especially the harsh police auxiliaries who had been recruited largely from daredevil ex-Service misfits and were called the Black and Tans. In 1921 the British Government was forced to seek agreement with the Republicans, with the result that the Irish Free State, given Dominion status within the British Commonwealth, was shakily founded and the South was divided from the six counties of the Protestant North.

The King, deeply disturbed at the break-up of part of the United Kingdom, had brushed aside warnings of personal risk and crossed to Belfast to open in person and earnestly to address the first session of a new Ulster Parliament under the Government of Ireland Act. He hoped that peace and amity on both sides of the border would follow, but it was not to be. The ardent Republicans were not appeased by the new status, and civil war ravaged Dublin. Violence continued – as it continues in even more bitter and concentrated pattern today in the North – and the extremist De

Valera came to political power in 1932. By then the South was well on the road to complete separation, a wholly independent Eire.

On the English side of the Irish Sea, meanwhile, the coming of peace brought no lasting calm or surge of prosperity, but only an increasing unemployment problem and mounting public dis-satisfaction with Ministers' management of both foreign affairs and industrial strategy. Lloyd George and his Coalition Government had to go, and in 1923 a pipe-smoking country gentleman named Stanley Baldwin became Prime Minister at the head of a Conservative administration. He was defeated eight months later, and at the beginning of 1924 Britain for the first time had a Labour Government, an unprecedented experience for the King as it was for his people.

His First Minister now was a former clerk and son of a farm labourer, James Ramsay MacDonald from Lossiemouth in Scotland; the new Lord Privy Seal was a trade union organiser who had been a Lancashire mill hand, J. R. Clynes; the Home Secretary was an ex-foundry worker, Arthur Henderson; and the Secretary of State for the Colonies a sometime engine-driver, J. H. Thomas. It was characteristic of the King's sense of duty and his honest efforts to be impartial that, unfamiliar though he was with leaders of such kind, he treated them as though they were blue-blooded to a man. He knew that they had become experienced politicians. He recognised their intelligence and seriousness; he was willing to look for their potential as statesmen and was hopeful that their sense of responsibility would increase.

In short, the King treated the Labour men with kindness, sympathy and co-operation from the start. He was at pains to know them personally, to be useful to them with experienced advice when they came in audience, and to give them guidance on matters of protocol. They, for their part, though a little awkward in his presence at first, warmed to the genial reception they received and liked the quiet kindness of the man in whose name they and their administration had been called upon to act. Somewhat against the grain, they even took trouble to meet the Sovereign's meticulousness

OPPOSITE, TOP LEFT AND RIGHT *The Duke and Duchess of York in the twenties. Prince Albert is in RAF uniform and wears his pilot's 'wings'.*

OPPOSITE, BOTTOM *The East Front of Buckingham Palace, one of the most photographed buildings in the world – a picture from the nineteen-forties, when the sentry-boxes were outside. Nowadays they are inside the forecourt, so no longer overwhelmed by camera-happy tourists.*

ABOVE *Parents and grandparents at Princess Elizabeth's christening on 29 May 1926. At the time no one imagined that this child, the present Queen, would occupy the Throne.*

RIGHT *The Music Room at Buckingham Palace. Designed by Nash, the decor includes eighteen columns of deep-blue scagliola with gilt Corinthian capitals and very fine immense chandeliers. This room overlooks the garden of forty acres and one of the most extensive lawns in the world. It has been the scene of many royal christenings.*

over what he deemed to be correct clothing by buying or hiring suits of tailed Court dress – though, fearing the laughter of their followers, they jibbed at knee breeches.

The King wrote to his mother: 'They have different ideas to ours and they are all socialists, but they ought to be given a chance and ought to be treated fairly.'

He readily took to his well-spoken new Prime Minister, and indeed seemed from the very beginning to see more sound qualities in him than many other people did, including some of his own colleagues. Unfortunately, Mr MacDonald, seasoned public figure though he was, after a short time began to worry judicious observers by an inclination, or so it seemed, to spend as much time in drawing rooms as in debating chambers. His manifest basking in the Sovereign's friendliness displeased many Labour followers. He found it hard to resist giving himself airs. Though he worked hard and with some success for general disarmament and the settlement of a disturbed Europe, the problems proved too much for him and, deserted by the Liberals, his Government fell after ten months and Mr Baldwin and the Tories returned to power. But in 1929 'Ramsay Mac' was back in office for a second time. Two years later, with the country in deep financial crisis and nearly three million people out of work, he resigned once more – only to return to Number Ten Downing Street as head of an emergency 'National Government' composed of representatives of all parties, a coalition charged with the task of attempting to find shelter from the economic blizzard and lessen the shame of the Depression.

Mr MacDonald had taken the task of leadership this time at the insistent request of the King. Throughout the post-war years George V was as much in day-to-day concern over the state of the nation as his politicians were, and did not hesitate to put forward opinion and appeal over matters on which he felt deeply. One of

these problems was the mounting total of the unemployed (even by 1920 the total had passed the two million mark) and the meagre amount of State aid for people out of a job. In 1921 he had sent a typical letter to the Secretary of the Cabinet urging that there should be more concentration on work schemes such as road-building and forestation. Giving subsistence money was not enough, and in his view the amounts of the weekly dole payments were not enough anyhow. 'It is impossible', the royal message said, 'to expect people to subsist upon the unemployment benefit of fifteen shillings for men and twelve shillings for women.' Could not the Government treat the situation 'with the same liberality as they displayed in dealing with the enormous daily cost of the war?'

Just as he had placed his faith and his counsel in the service of Stanley Baldwin during the earlier troubles culminating in the National Strike of 1926 – His Majesty had declined personal intervention then but had warned against Churchillian extremes of provocation – so the King in 1931 worked with a mixed assembly of Ministers as they fought to bring the nation back from the brink of bankruptcy. MacDonald gave up as leader after four grim years, during which his bland association with the Liberals, the Conservatives and the King brought to him the final break with the Labour Party which he had helped to found. In 1935 Baldwin was at the wheel again.

It was during those post-war years of worldwide slumps and realignments that the King, though zealous to succour both his politicians at home and his own family life around him, was anxious also to keep fast the straining ties of Empire. And for this he dispatched his not unwilling eldest son on a further series of long tours abroad – during the Eastern journey alone he travelled fifty thousand miles. On these official missions, the smiling fair-haired Prince of Wales established a popular image all over the world.

OPPOSITE *A scene near the Stock Exchange during the General Strike of 1926. The public transport system had come to a standstill; commuters hitched lifts whenever they could.*

RIGHT *King George and Queen Mary were not frequent travellers overseas, but on reaching Continental sunshine they enjoyed themselves. Here they are with Prince George and friends.*

The King himself always preferred to stay at home in Britain rather than embark on State Visits overseas. He did however go to great lengths in entertaining elaborately many other Heads of State when they came over at his invitation to London. To them he was a cheerful host, certainly more relaxed than with his own family. For a man whose nature was reserved, whose temper was often short and whose outlook was not the widest, he managed remarkably well with less august overseas callers too. When the American Charles Lindbergh made his dramatic solo non-stop flight across the Atlantic in 1927 (New York to Paris in thirty-three hours) and was given an audience at the Palace, the royal entourage wondered how the shy monarch and the staunch republican would get on. They need not have worried. The aviator, a prickly young Isolationist who hated crowns and thrones, confessed after the talk that the British Sovereign had been such a jovial interrogator that he found it natural to regale him with all the details of his pioneer crossing. And the King's diary said: 'A very nice boy and quite modest.'

Modesty was one of the pleasant qualities of George V's second son, Bertie, the stay-at-home one, quietly content to be 'also-ran' to the mercurial David. This was the son whose unassuming nature was in accord with his own. But the royal father was anxious to 'bring Bertie out' and help him to combat his hesitations of speech in public and the innate shyness which had not been dispelled by his wartime service in Navy and Air Force and a subsequent course of study at Trinity College, Cambridge. He had enjoyed a largely informal visit to East Africa in 1924 and 1925, but now a big official test was arranged. Although the King was well aware that his eldest boy was the one who was the Golden Tourist, and was happy about the success which the Prince of Wales's breezy manner and easily switched-on charm had achieved during his visits, it was the second son Albert, now Duke of York, who at the beginning of 1927 left for Australia to open the first Parliament to meet at Canberra, new Federal capital of the Dominion, and to make a six months' official tour of the Antipodes.

On that formidable exercise in royal duty overseas, the still nervous and highly strung Duke made the first firm steps towards confidence in public – largely because he had acquired delightful support. For already the future King George VI had beside him his wonderful wife. The nervous but determined Prince Bertie had courted Lady Elizabeth Bowes-Lyon for two years. She accepted him in 1923 and they were married the same year. The new Duchess of York, destined to be a shining thread in the fabric of modern royal history, was a charmer from the beginning, as she was to be in the half-century of sterling service as Queen Consort and Queen Mother which – though none knew it then – lay awaiting her strength and her smile.

Her husband was the first of George V's sons to marry. The next to do so was the fourth in age, Prince George the Duke of Kent, who took as his bride in 1934 the elegant Princess Marina of Greece. In the following year came the wedding of Prince Henry the Duke of Gloucester, third son, to a Scot, Lady Alice Montagu-Douglas-Scott, pretty daughter of the seventh Duke of Buccleuch. The King's daughter, however – Princess Mary, the Princess Royal – had been the first of the children to leave home. She was married in 1922 to a Yorkshire landowner, Viscount Lascelles, who became the sixth Earl of Harewood.

All the marriages were popular public occasions. But the most shining matrimonial event of those times, also in 1922, was a wedding that was not only royal but the social event of a decade, a picture-book extravaganza at St Margaret's, Westminster. It was the wedding of the brilliant royal cousin 'Dickie' Mountbatten, then Lord Louis and a handsome naval lieutenant, to the

Bertie
1929

74

glamorous and highly intelligent Edwina Ashley, heiress to the fortune of a millionaire grandfather, Sir Ernest Cassel, an Anglo-German financier who had been a great friend of King Edward VII. The Prince of Wales, looking extraordinarily young and slightly overpowered by his Admiral's uniform, was best man. It was all very star-studded. King George and Queen Mary and Queen Alexandra attended; royalty came from all over Europe.

The old Victorian pattern of 'royals marrying royals' had been broken, all the same. It had been quite happily demolished, in fact, in the year after the war when there took place the wedding of the popular Princess 'Pat' of Connaught, a granddaughter of Queen Victoria, to Admiral Alexander Ramsay – technically a commoner though the son of an earl – and the Princess resigned all claims to being a Royal Highness. For the remaining fifty-five years of her life she was 'plain' Lady Patricia Ramsay.

Small though the signs were, barriers of archaic formality surrounding the monarchy were beginning to be breached during the twenties and thirties of the century.

New Blood

To King George and Queen Mary the marriages of the three sons brought more than ordinary parental joy. Ever since their family had emerged from the nursery stage they had found it difficult to have any close companionship with them. No real *rapport* existed: the generation gap inside the Palace seemed unbridgeable. Formality reigned at family gatherings. No parties were given for the young people. The Queen was shy, as unbending with her own offspring at home as she was when on public duty. She was never bred to romp and frolic – though she was not without a sense of humour. And the King, kind and domestic person though he was, had not moved out of the nineteenth century when it came to confronting teenagers. To be censorious with his growing-up boys was a natural reflex; he never began to understand, never ceased to criticise the altered conventions and standards of behaviour which had come in with the post-war years. He used to try to amend this failing by bursts of rough chaffing, but they only made matters worse. His sons were afraid of him. Even when the Princes attained manhood his often querulous disapproval did not stop – until those marriages came. Then the situation altered rosily.

The arrival in a family circle which had become cold and isolated of three lively daughters-in-law from worlds outside the Court caused a distinct relaxation of manner in the King and Queen in their homes. The geniality and unembarrassed affection which the sons and daughter had known when they were very small, but not since, was shed on them once more because it was released upon their wedded partners. In the King the change was most happily marked. And in return he himself was loved, no longer feared, by his own.

The Duke of York's bride, the uninhibited Lady Elizabeth, daughter of the Earl and Countess of Strathmore, at once captivated her father-in-law when she danced like a breath of Highland air and shaft of sunshine into the hitherto hidebound Court and cloistered Palace life. That was no surprise to Queen Mary, who from the moment of meeting the girl from Glamis, before ever she accepted her son's proposal, had taken a great liking to a charming young lady who so naturally combined spontaneity and sense of duty. All through her life, the undemonstrative Queen Mary maintained a relationship of special affection for the younger woman whose standards were often her own and whose endearing ease in public

OPPOSITE *The Duke of York as soldier and Highlander in 1929.*

TOP *Three generations in front of the miniature Welsh cottage at Royal Lodge, Windsor, which was given to Princess Elizabeth (on the right) by the people of Wales when she was six.*

ABOVE *Armistice Day, 1933. The Duke and Duchess of York in procession from St Giles' Cathedral, Edinburgh. They are led by the chief of the Scottish Heralds, Lord Lyon King of Arms.*

and in facing new situations she admired though could hardly by nature emulate. As to the King, the love he gave to his first daughter-in-law lifted his spirits, mellowed his views, and contained in it something of the same sort of devotion which throughout his life he extended to his 'Darling Motherdear', Queen Alexandra (who died at Sandringham in 1925, well into her eighty-first year, almost as old as Queen Victoria had been).

Elizabeth Bowes-Lyon had – as the Queen Mother of today still has – the touch of gold in human relationships, and it was almost effortlessly that she not only enhanced the life of her husband but by her influence fashioned the new warmth between her husband and his father, an accord of confidence and encouragement. King George had always felt more akin to his second son than to his eldest, the personable but iconoclastic David, the Prince of Wales. And now, towards the married Bertie, the affection was almost wistful when the father wrote to him: 'You are indeed a lucky man to have such a charming and delightful wife as Elizabeth. I trust you will have many years of happiness ... You have always been so sensible and easy to work with ... Very different to dear David.'

And Elizabeth, the new Royal Duchess, inspirer of this release of sentiment, reciprocated the King's feelings. Unlike his own children, she was from the start never afraid of him, and not once in the twelve years of being his daughter-in-law did she have any experience of the well-known tetchiness which never altogether deserted him. In her own words written later in life, 'He was so

dependable – and could be deliciously funny when he was in the mood.'

A measure of this fond relationship was the happiness of the King at the birth of the Duchess's first baby on 21 April 1926 – Princess Elizabeth Alexandra Mary of Windsor, today's reigning Queen Elizabeth II. She was the first grandchild in the male line.

For the prematurely old monarch, however, domestic felicity was never for long undisturbed. He was plucked from it by the cares and councils of the General Strike which came two weeks after the Princess's birth. He was also denied family life's full enjoyment by his own frail health, the progressive physical weakness which became seriously worrying to his Queen, his children and his doctors. He had suffered from chesty colds since he was a small boy, and soon after the war attacks of bronchitis developed. Through these his constitution had noticeably begun to fail in 1925, the year after he had painstakingly marked a national milestone by opening and making his first broadcast speech at the great British Empire Exhibition staged in Wembley Stadium.

He was so stricken, weak and bedridden at the beginning of 1925 that for a whole fortnight he was unable to hold a pen and write the nightly log in his leather-bound diary – which was for him a depressing failure and deprivation, and for those about him an indication of the seriousness of his condition. The death of his loved and lovely mother, late that year, was a weakening sorrow too, though by then he was up and about, on the surface much as usual.

Indeed, with care his health did improve. In the next two years he was able to confront with at any rate an appearance of robustness the continuing political and industrial troubles of his country. He also resolutely fulfilled heavy programmes of public engagements, laying foundation stones, opening county halls and a number of bridges as well as the Mersey Tunnel, inaugurating London's first airport on the grass of Croydon, attending Wimbledon and the Cup Final and as many other varied sporting occasions as his days could possibly stand.

But in November and December of 1928 he became even more gravely ill than before. 'Unable to give due attention to the affairs of Our Realm', as his royal warrant put it, he appointed six Counsellors of State to act in his stead. Propped up in bed, he was barely able to sign the warrant. A pleural abscess had developed, weakening the King's heart. An operation was performed just in time to save his life, but he was in a critical condition for many days. Crowds waited outside the Palace gates to read the doctors' bulletins posted there each day. Churches were kept open day and night for intercessions.

Again he recovered, very slowly this time. Not until February 1929 had he turned the corner sufficiently for Queen Mary to take him to a house named Craigwell on the outskirts of Bognor in Sussex for several weeks of convalescence. He was not a patient patient: boredom and irritableness retarded progress. One of the things which cheered and improved him most was a series of visits by a lively three-year-old Princess Elizabeth, who would chatter beside him as he was wheeled out in a bathchair and dig castles and sand-pictures along the seashore for the entertainment of the old gentleman she knew and loved as 'Grandpapa England'.

One of the nicest stories of the early childhood of the Princess – the present Queen – reports a remark she made one Christmas at Sandringham when, with the family, she was listening to, and mishearing, carollers singing 'Glad tidings of great joy I bring to you and all mankind'. The small girl's comment was: 'I like that. And I know who Old Man Kind is – it's Grandpapa.'

OPPOSITE *The welcome given to the Jubilee procession by the London crowds in the last months of the King's reign deeply touched his heart.*

ABOVE *The West Terrace of Sandringham House. Although these formal flowerbeds are gone, the house remains essentially unchanged.*

In the spring of 1929 'Man Kind' was better enough to return to London, and in July he was able with the Queen to attend a national service of thanksgiving for his recovery. But his operation wound was unhealed, and this contributed to a reverse which he suffered a few days after that service in Westminster Abbey. Strangely enough, the setback was triggered by a friend, none other than that former railwaymen's leader, Jim Thomas, the down-to-earth Cabinet Minister who was notorious for possessing neither awe nor aspirates. He was the member of the Labour Government whose company His Majesty used to find particularly congenial, though the two men were poles apart in background and manner. A real friendship had developed. The King had never come across a socialist (or any other) statesman so frank and so irreverent in talking to a monarch. Thomas's bluntness was disarming, and the Sovereign was amused rather than offended when his Minister told him that his princely sons were reluctant to pay visits to Balmoral because it was 'such a bloody dull 'ouse'. But now, in May 1929, the Minister unwittingly caused damage when he was received at the Palace, for his latest crop of ribald jokes made the King laugh so much that he burst open the wound abscess below his ribs and suffered a relapse. Soon his condition was once more occasioning anxiety. In the ensuing months two more operations were necessary. But again he recovered.

King George's final years, in the first half of the thirties, were plagued by the inherent bronchitis. But he brushed aside medical advice in persistently refusing to go abroad for even a week or two of Mediterranean warmth and sunshine. He worked on, in his own land, taking things more quietly than he had ever done but worrying over the papers on his desk as much as ever he had. There was plenty of cause for concern. The country had barely avoided complete economic collapse. Massive loans from foreign bankers had not eased the chronic unemployment situation or erased the shame of the Hunger Marches and the Great Depression.

Abroad, Germany's even more ghastly post-war slump had given birth to a Fascism more terrible than Italy was experiencing under the strutting Mussolini. The anti-Semitic, anti-democratic Brown Shirts of Hitler were on the march, trampling down the law, the League of Nations and anything else which stood in their militaristic path. For a second time in less than twenty years Germany was flagrantly rearming and presently gobbling up weak neighbouring territories. The black and crooked cross of National Socialism was putting half Europe under menacing shadow.

However much British appeasers declared that Adolf the Führer had really no evil intent and that war would not come again, King George V had no illusions: he clearly saw the dangers of both Nazi ambitions and France's outdated Maginot Line fixations. Yet again in his lifetime, Germany was boiling to aggression and no doubt about it. And in Russia the Soviet hierarchy had inherited the harsh Imperialism of the Tsars.

'What will people think of such fuss in these anxious times?' His Majesty had growled when he surveyed the plans – which Queen Mary had willingly encouraged – for a national celebration in 1935 of his twenty-five years on the Throne.

What people *did* think was that it was well worth while; and on the day of the royal Silver Jubilee, a gloriously sunny May the Sixth, beflagged London fairly exploded with enthusiasm as the King and Queen drove to give thanks in St Paul's Cathedral. The open landau of the Sovereign and Queen Consort was preceded by the carriages of the Duke and Duchess of York and their children the two Princesses, Elizabeth aged nine, and now a four-year-old sister, Margaret Rose, with her; and the Prince of Wales arrayed in the full scarlet of the Welsh Guards. It was all a brave and happy sight.

Towns and villages far and wide spent the day in jollifications to salute the anniversary. Then at ten in the evening the King pressed a button in Buckingham Palace to light a huge bonfire a mile away in Hyde Park. This was a signal for two thousand other beacons to burst out, making chains of light crisscrossing the whole country. People danced round the flames singing patriotic songs and standing to attention for 'God Save the King'.

The King was surprised and moved. Why, he asked in his diary, should such a never-to-be-forgotten day take place at such a time of national difficulty and world danger? 'I'd no idea they felt like that about me', he wrote. 'I'm beginning to think they must like me for myself.' It was the right answer. He had become a focus of stability and reliability in a darkening scene; the demonstrations of regard for him must have warmed a weak old heart which was destined to beat for only another eight months. Soon after the period of the Jubilee celebrations the final decline of his health began. He was too frail to attend the 1935 service of November remembrance at the Cenotaph, and his grief at the death of his favourite sister Princess Victoria in December seemed to lessen his will to live.

But he did manage to make his Christmas Day broadcast, from a small ground-floor room at Sandringham House, and he insisted on doing it 'live' as usual, with his family listening nervously in the next room. It was he who in 1932 had started the now traditional Sovereign's Message via the BBC microphone to nation and Commonwealth. Those little fireside talks 'on the wireless', the measured voice conveying the sincerity of the speaker, were milestones in the early history of public broadcasting which had begun in 1922. He did not know it, did not try to be it, but the King was a perfect radio talker. There was a nice rumbling depth in the phrases, and a bit of bronchial grating too, but no trace of the guttural Germanic of his forebears and a few of his family contemporaries. The tones were warmly resonant and paternal, bringing the caring personality of the man into millions of homes by the very sound of him.

He used to broadcast because he felt it his duty, not because he liked doing it. He was always glad when what was for him an ordeal was over – and was far from impressed when told on one occasion by an obsequious Minister that 'you have been permanently recorded for posterity as you spoke, Sir. How wonderful if we'd had a recording of Queen Elizabeth I.'

His Majesty's reply was a gruff 'Damn Queen Elizabeth'.

Broadcasting – in sound only, for regular public-service television, in which the British Broadcasting Corporation led the world, did not come until late in 1936 – was the outstanding scientific achievement of George V's era. The reign had also seen tremendous developments in other fields. Australia was brought within three days' flying time of the United Kingdom, for example; advances in electric power banished a gaslit world; motor-car owning started to be popular; and a matchless railway system had its crack expresses steaming along, even then, at a hundred miles an hour. Literature and music and the theatre flowered too in that quarter of a century, its giants including Chesterton and Belloc, Shaw and Galsworthy, Elgar and Delius, Frank Benson and Ellen Terry. Sport had its Hobbs and Sutcliffe, a jockey named Steve Donoghue was the lion of the racecourses, and an Englishman, the imperishable Fred Perry, actually won the men's singles at Wimbledon – three times in a row.

A Rip Van Winkle from Edwardian times would have been astonished to find how the appearance of human beings had changed by the end of King George's reign. Hourglass waists had been released and muffs rebuffed; giddy girls called flappers wore their hair bobbed and lavishly lipsticked their mouths; they danced the Charleston in the shortest of skirts and in backless bathing costumes swam unsegregated from their boyfriends. Men had turned away from silk hats and high-crowned bowlers to free-and-easy soft caps and trilbies; Oxford bags and loud plus-fours flapped round male legs.

Not that the King altered *his* style, however. It was in his nature to regard sartorial changes as the eccentricities of a raving world, and he himself kept to the fashions of his youth: hard hats, stiff collars, waistcoats, watch-chains, narrow trousers creased at the sides, spats and cloth-topped boots. It was reputed that he used the same collar stud for fifty years. He had a cautious suspicion even of some of his era's technical advances, including miracles of communication which had entered the nation's life. Though he was glad enough to use it to keep in touch with that loved sister Victoria on any day when he had not seen her, he was inclined to regard the telephone as a diabolical invention for lazy people. Queen Mary never used the instrument at all.

It was well that the King's ways did not alter. His moral strength, and in the end his repute and his value to his country, lay in the quality of unvarying dependability, the rocklike common sense and enduring fairness which he exemplified. And his probity prevented his prejudices from hurting anyone but himself. He left behind his sterling character as well as his stamp collection. In his old-fashioned decencies resided a national asset and anchor.

The anchor chain was slipping, clearly and quickly, as the New Year began, and from Sandringham a stand-by warning went out to the family. The Sovereign's life was moving peacefully towards its close. So they gathered to Queen Mary's side: the Prince of Wales, now forty-one years old; the Duke of York (forty) and his Elizabeth (the Princesses Elizabeth and Margaret were at that time nine and five); Princess Mary, who was thirty-eight (her firstborn son, the present Earl of Harewood, was almost thirteen); the Duke of Gloucester, aged thirty-five; and the Duke of Kent (thirty-three),

ABOVE *George V died at Sandringham on 20 January 1936. Here his coffin is borne to the train for London, followed by his sons. His body had lain in state in the chancel of the little church at Sandringham where it had been guarded by estate workers.*

OPPOSITE *A glimpse of the Palace of Holyroodhouse, Edinburgh, the official residence of the Sovereign in Scotland.*

whose first child, the present Duke, was barely three months old.

On 20 January 1936, members of the Privy Council assembled in the King's bedroom where His Majesty lay gravely ill. The Lord President read aloud a proclamation setting up an emergency Council of State. At the end, the King said 'I approve', but even with help his hand was unable to manage a signature at the foot of the document. Finally, with a faint smile of apology to those around the bed, he made the mark of his initials. But no further word came. The voice which less than a month before had been heard sounding a brave note of hope around the nations was silent now. It was his last broadcast; and now he was in his last hours. Just before midnight on that cold Norfolk night the King died in the presence of Queen Mary and the children. He was seventy years old.

When the news of his passing was announced, a sense of loss and uncertainty was widespread throughout the country, for Britain's respected Head of State had become not only a symbol of all that was dutiful and decent but an earnest of continuity in a decaying world. The now widowed Queen Mary, sixty-eight years old, wrote in her own diary: 'The sunset of his death tinged the whole world's sky.' It was a time of darkening. King George V's own twilight months had been saddened by the shadows which the bellicose Dictators were already casting across the Rhineland and far Abyssinia.

Moreover, within the family it was also known that in His Majesty's mind there was a small though worrying cloud of a more intimate kind, centred on his popular eldest son and heir, David the Prince of Wales – Prince Charming in the eyes of the public and an admired figure to his relatives, but in fact a charmer who was proving unsure and erratic, a man whose nature, so unlike his father's, betrayed a leashed restlessness and rebellion against the regimen of his parents. David was loved but David was alarming. His personal style, his friends and interests, were already disturbing. His father and mother had for some time known about his 'latest friendship' with an American married woman. The King had always done his best to bring up this vigorous son to be ready to give his whole mind to the responsibilities of sovereignty which were his destiny.

But how would that Prince shape now that the supreme torch of service was coming to his hand? What sort of monarch was about to leap on to the stage?

It was a question hardly yet breathed as the nation mourned the loss of the first of the Royal Windsors.

PART FOUR

Edward VIII

Enter Beau Geste

THE ACCEDING SOVEREIGN chose to be called Edward VIII.

'Great Expectations' was surely the title of the new page in the royal story that was beginning now. Here was the Golden Boy become King, cynosure of glamour and goodwill in the popular mind, a leader and spokesman to bring hope to young people and his own disillusioned post-war generation. This would be not only a shining new reign but a supercharged new regime. As a world traveller, entrancingly and informally in tune with the times, the man coming to the Throne had captured hearts and imaginations. The broad smile, the hair a boyish buttercup-yellow, the athletic stride and sympathetic mien, the facile amiability – all were most winning. A brave new era was dawning, an affectionate sportsman-adventurer was now in charge. Welcome, Beau Geste!

The possibility that the new King Edward might not prove to be as good as that was not in the world's consciousness at all at the beginning of 1936. There was no thought that he might not be what was needed, that he might disrupt and fail. And indeed only soothing calmness and quiet conformity marked the sombre hours which opened his reign.

In that room of death at Sandringham Queen Mary had set the key. Her grief concealed as always beneath an undemonstrative shyness and iron self-control, she had been the first of those at the bedside to move when King George had breathed his last. Rising to her feet, she took the hand of her eldest son who had been Prince of Wales until a few minutes before, and, stooping in obeisance, she kissed it. The husband who had been the centre of her life for forty years was dead, but the King lived – for the King was now her son, the eighth reigning Edward. To him now went her whole allegiance. The continuance of sovereignty and the unselfish obeying of its demands were the guiding precept of her life.

The body of her husband rested for thirty-six hours before the altar in Sandringham Church. Men of the royal estates, tenants and gamekeepers, kept continuous vigil beside it. They were mourning a loved Squire. Then the coffin was taken to London, where it lay in State for four days in Westminster Hall. A million people filed slowly past the catafalque to pay their last tribute. At the four corners of the platform, Household troops in relays stood motionless

with heads bowed, keeping watch day and night without interval – except for twenty minutes, before midnight on the second day, when the new King and his three brothers took the soldiers' places and, incognito, themselves stood guard over their father's coffin.

Windsor was the scene of the final obsequies. The crowds in the London streets on the funeral day itself were so dense that the cortège was two hours late at St George's Chapel, where the body of the late Sovereign was laid to rest.

Solemn ceremonial over, it was now the new Sovereign's turn to face the responsibilities of his inheritance, the business of reigning as constitutional monarch of an ancient realm at an uneasy and fearful stage of its history. Edward VIII was an unmarried – though not in-experienced – forty-one-year-old King, but looking and behaving as though at least ten years younger than that. All the duties were his now: the audiences, the reading of boxes full of documents of State, the overseeing of the royal residences and lands, the public engagements, consultations with Government ministers, the desk work at all hours with necessarily importunate secretaries.

He had devotedly done many strenuous tours of overseas duty in

OPPOSITE *The future Edward VIII photographed wearing the Garter regalia in 1911, the year of his investiture as Prince of Wales.*

RIGHT *The young Heir Apparent with his mother, brother 'Bertie' (the future George VI) and sister Mary (later Countess of Harewood).*

ABOVE *The Prince of Wales was a tireless ambassador for Britain. In 1922 he was striving to cement ties with India in the face of a Gandhi-inspired boycott of his tour.*

LEFT *The unconventional Prince of Wales balances on the cow-catcher of the royal train and quizzes the engineer at a halt during his Canadian tour of 1919.*

ABOVE *Prince Edward receives the homage of African chiefs at Accra. He was visiting the Gold Coast (now Ghana) on his way to South Africa and yet another royal tour in 1925.*

LEFT *The young Prince was as popular at home as he was abroad and worked hard in the interests of the younger generation. Here he attends a Scouts and Cubs' rally at Alexandra Palace in 1922.*

the years before, but gone now was the leisure which, when he was Prince of Wales, had allowed him the days of flying and fox-hunting, the hard-riding point-to-point competitions, the jaunts round his Canadian ranch, the nightclub frolics, and the golf and the gardening. No longer could he easily retreat from the Palace and the conventions of his family to the place which he had made into his own private country home, Fort Belvedere. This was an eighteenth-century fancifully castellated folly near Virginia Water and the edge of Windsor Great Park, which he had modernised and had come to love as his special get-away house. 'The Fort' was the spot where he had regularly shed all formality, had dug his garden, played his bagpipes, directed the house's furnishing and meal-preparing, and danced away his week-ends with the international jazz-set friends of his own – not of his family's – choosing.

But not now. It was King's work to which he had to bend; and for some months he seemed to tackle it with conscientiousness and consideration, maintaining as much of the old styles and traditions as his spirit would allow. In certain matters, it is true, he did at once start 'letting in the twentieth century' which he felt his father had long held back. He halved the period of Court mourning, trimmed formality at the Palace, sometimes grabbed an umbrella and walked to a meeting instead of riding in the waiting limousine. He ordered a streamlining of the estates management at Windsor and Balmoral, and – almost his first act – abolished what had been Edward VII's and George V's 'Sandringham time', which had always meant that every clock in the Norfolk houses was half an hour fast – to encourage punctuality, his father had said. In London he instituted outdoor receptions for débutantes instead of the old Presentation Courts.

On the whole, however, there did not seem any sensational change in the royal scene during the first months. Official engagements were punctiliously fulfilled, including the inauguration of the huge Canadian War Memorial at Vimy Ridge in France. It was characteristically impulsive of the new monarch, however, that he invited all eight thousand Canadian veterans who had attended the ceremony to a garden party at Buckingham Palace on their way home.

He observed annual custom by taking the salute at the Trooping the Colour ceremony on Horse Guards Parade; he presented new colours to battalions of the Guards regiments in Hyde Park (and appeared remarkably undisturbed when a madman threw a loaded revolver at his horse as he rode back along Constitution Hill from that parade). But by the summer of that 1936, after six months as King, he had had enough of work and of walking well-worn paths. Impatience to be free of irksome duties could be curbed no longer. He was going off on holiday in his own way, to do what he liked, whatever anyone thought. So August was not spent on the northern grouse moors. Instead, he went cruising – with friends.

It was the chartering of the large yacht *Nahlin* and that summer's royal voyages down the Adriatic and Aegean coasts which brought before the eyes of most of the world – though not for months yet into the awareness of the public in England – the existence of Mrs Wallis Simpson; a married lady from Baltimore, USA, already once divorced. This was the person who was not only to alter the King's entire life but to bring an undreamed-of crisis in the history of the British Crown.

As the Royal Family had uneasily come to know, the prince who was now Edward VIII had met Mrs Simpson five years before and had become so increasingly warm in his feelings towards her that by the time of his Accession in 1936 he could scarcely bear to be

ABOVE *Prince Louis of Battenberg, created first Marquess of Milford Haven and given the family name of Mountbatten to counteract anti-German hysteria in 1917. A son-in-law of Queen Victoria, he was the father of Earl Mountbatten of Burma and grandfather of Prince Philip. He died in 1921, the year of this portrait.*

RIGHT *A family gathering portrayed in the Drawing Room at Glamis Castle. The young Lady Elizabeth Bowes-Lyon, future consort of George VI, is in the foreground with her favourite brother, David. Her parents, the Earl and Countess of Strathmore, are taking tea at the nearby table. Later, George VI and Queen Elizabeth often stayed at Glamis. Princess Margaret was born there.*

without her companionship. He had even brought her into St James's Palace to stand beside him, though half hidden, at a window, to watch the heralds proclaim him as Sovereign at the start of his reign.

The British people generally were in ignorance of the affair, and indeed through most of that fateful year – extraordinary though this may sound today when newspapers and television hold almost nothing to be private or sacred – the BBC and the press kept silent on the subject of the royal attachment and its portents. But in foreign countries, and particularly in America, newspapers and magazines had been gleefully alive to the situation; and when it was known that among the guests on board the *Nahlin* was Mrs Simpson, the yacht was the object of excited journalistic pursuit. Whenever the King and his companion landed at any of the ports they were dogged by crowds of reporters, cameramen and tourists. In America and on the Continent photographs of the smiling couple in brief and casual holiday attire were published, and the accompanying stories left no doubt about the earnestness of 'the Royal Romance'. Only the readers of the uniquely circumspect British papers were kept in the dark. Most members of the general public at home – almost until the time when the affair had its sensational outcome at the end of the year – did not know that their monarch was deeply in love with an American lady, and indeed had hardly heard of Mrs Simpson at all.

Back in Britain after the cruise, the King communicated virtually nothing to his mother and his family about the situation. He had in fact become a changed person, often irritable and thoughtless when he was with them – which was seldom. They felt cut off from him, for he was spending most of his personal time with an assortment of what his relatives could only regard as cocktail-party friends. And always with Mrs Simpson (before long to divorce Husband Number Two). She was a smart and intelligent forty-year-old socialite, briskly and brightly entertaining, well groomed and well informed; she talked with an attractive Maryland drawl – and she was a very good listener to the King's views.

The Royal Family, especially the Duke and Duchess of York, had not failed to see their loved and admired David becoming more and more drawn to her whilst he was Heir; and now, as King, far from ending the attachment, he clearly was totally bewitched. Affectionate and impressionable himself, his life was centred on one person: Wallis. His devotion to her gradually took precedence over his devotion to his country and his job. For what he wanted, come what might, was a future with her. The tragedy was his myopia to the consequences.

So it was that, as the year advanced, King Edward's periods of self-indulgent social life encroached upon the time which constitutional duties demanded. To the family he became almost a stranger; and meantime Court Circulars from York House and even Balmoral announced guest lists that had an incongruous ring. It became difficult for his relatives to get to see the King, even to talk to him on the telephone. No longer was there a smiling Uncle David to pop in and visit the little Princesses, Elizabeth and Margaret, now aged ten and six, at their parents' home, Number 145 Piccadilly. The Duke and Duchess missed his calls and his company. The fact was that it was to his Wallis now that he was pouring out his hopes and his plans.

Stanley Baldwin, the Prime Minister, anxiously sought an audience to discuss the state of affairs now inescapably coming to notice. Yes, he was told, the King's wish was to marry Mrs Simpson. A life together with her was what he wanted. For Edward VIII there was no one else in the world. Affectionate and patriotic still, well intentioned and sincere, the King was nevertheless found to be boyishly immature in his outlook, obsessively in love and either unable or unwilling to see the difficulties which would stand in the way of a marriage between the person he was and the person Mrs Simpson was. He spoke lightly of a sharing of the Throne, of 'special arrangements', of ideas of morganatic marriage. It took a long time for him to see that divorce was a bar to Mrs Simpson being Queen, and that he would have to give up a kingdom for a wife. But in the end it was clear. And so was his purpose.

Exit, Uncrowned

The dramatic events of the last few weeks of 1936, as they moved to the climax of abdication, are now well over four decades back in history. They are a story that has been told over and over again. But the final sensations of the finish of that Eleven Months' Reign not only enthralled the public then but continue to exercise fascination as a subject for books, plays and television series. Some of these products have stressed preconceived views. Edward VIII is extravagantly believed by some people to have been an uncaring quitter (which he was not) and by others a romantic knight who was thrown out of his native land by a prudish Establishment headed by a fuddy-duddy Premier (which is just as false). The truth

OPPOSITE *A happy family occasion for four generations. Great-grandmother Queen Mary and grandfather George VI pose with the infant Prince Charles and his mother after the christening in December 1948.*

RIGHT *Prince Edward demonstrating his expertise as a horseman in 1924.*

H.R.H. THE PRINCE OF WALES.

H.R.H. THE PRINCE OF WALES.
IN A MERRY MOOD.

H.R.H THE PRINCE OF WALES.

H.R.H. THE PRINCE OF WALES.
IN JAPANESE COSTUME.

90

OPPOSITE *The Prince of Wales was an immensely popular figure and something of a leader of fashion. Postcards of him proliferated, depicting the sailor, the sportsman and the man about town. The Japanese costume was not adopted for a fancy-dress party but for the Prince's visit to the Far East in 1922.*

ABOVE *A formal moment during the one year in which 'David' was sovereign King, Edward VIII. He is with the Royal Heralds after his State Opening of Parliament on 3 November 1936.*

is that the decision to resign was his own, firmly and sadly and irrevocably taken.

The facts can be simply set down.

During that autumn the King seemed to his friends, his family and his Household to be more concerned with his domestic and personal affairs than with his official life. But he did not abandon work and duties – and perhaps he embraced them as therapy postponing the great decision he would soon have to make. He still fussed erratically about modernising the royal estates and 'stuffy' London formalities (and, rushing his fences as ever, caused some distress by hasty and hurtful staff economies). He went down to South Wales, saw the hardship which lack of jobs was causing in the mining valleys, and vowed: 'Something must be done.' But he could not do anything himself to implement his speech: his own momentous step into unemployment was not many days away, and he knew it. His intentions had already been made clear enough to the Prime Minister, Stanley Baldwin.

On 3 November he drove to Westminster and carried out the State Opening of Parliament for his first and last time. His attendance at the British Legion Festival of Remembrance in the Albert Hall and the wreath-laying at the Cenotaph in Whitehall on 11 November proved to be his final ceremonial duties.

On 13 November His Majesty's Private Secretary, Major Alexander Hardinge, was constrained to lay before his employer an urgent letter telling him that the silence of the British press on his relationship with Mrs Simpson and his intention to marry her could not be maintained for many days longer, and also that there was a real possibility that the Government might resign over the constitutional situation. For the divorcée could not be Queen. Hardinge urged that Mrs Simpson should go abroad without delay (in fact, she did go, earnestly offering to be the one to make renunciation, shortly before the departure of the King), otherwise there might be a dissolution of Parliament and a General Election on the issue of the King's personal affairs. This could only damage the Crown, 'the cornerstone on which the whole Empire rests'.

The King was dumbfounded and dismayed at this letter. Here was the truth on a plate. It made his course painfully clear, for, whatever his weaknesses, the notion of harming his country was abhorrent to him. Meetings with Mr Baldwin spelled it out: he could not eat his cake and have it. Parliament, people, and the Dominions were against a divorcée beside the Throne, were against a Sovereign's morganatic marriage. The King had to go.

Early in December, at last, the whole startling story broke in the British newspapers and on the wireless. To the public it was a bewildering and at the same time spellbinding bombshell. Ten days later Edward VIII renounced the Imperial Throne and abdication was official and final. On 11 December, by night and by British warship, he left the shores of his native land to begin a chosen exile. But not before he had made a poignant broadcast from his old room in one of the towers of Windsor Castle. This was the famous farewell in which he declared that he could not discharge his duties as King 'without the help and support of the woman I love'. Winston Churchill, royalist and romantic, had helped with the phrasing of the speech, and there was an unmistakable Churchillian sound to the words with which the departing 'Prince Edward' (as he was announced with Reithian solemnity by the BBC's Director-General) commended to his subjects his brother and successor, who possessed 'one matchless blessing, enjoyed by so many of you and not bestowed on me – a happy home with his wife and children'.

He was saluting the new king, George VI, for the Heir

INSTRUMENT OF ABDICATION

I, Edward the Eighth, of Great Britain, Ireland, and the British Dominions beyond the Seas, King, Emperor of India, do hereby declare My irrevocable determination to renounce the Throne for Myself and for My descendants, and My desire that effect should be given to this Instrument of Abdication immediately.

In token whereof I have hereunto set My hand this tenth day of December, nineteen hundred and thirty six, in the presence of the witnesses whose signatures are subscribed.

SIGNED AT
FORT BELVEDERE
IN THE PRESENCE
OF

OPPOSITE, TOP *The smile of the Prince Charming the world knew – before his accession.*

OPPOSITE, BOTTOM *By 1936, when this photograph was taken, there was much speculation about the relationship between Edward, now King, and an American married lady, Mrs Simpson. Foreign newspapermen were particularly assiduous in their pursuit of the couple and had plenty of opportunities when the King and Mrs Simpson went on an Adriatic cruise together in August. The British public were not allowed to see such pictures as this.*

ABOVE, LEFT *Stanley Baldwin was the Prime Minister who had to deal with the constitutional crisis which the King's friendship with Mrs Simpson threatened to create. On 16 November 1936 the King told him that his intention was to abdicate and marry Mrs Simpson.*

ABOVE, RIGHT *The Abdication document, issued from the King's country retreat, Fort Belvedere, near Windsor, and witnessed by his three brothers, the Duke of York, now to have kingship thrust upon him, the Duke of Gloucester and the Duke of Kent.*

Presumptive had become, however reluctantly, the next Sovereign. The Duke and Duchess of York were already King and Queen, immediately in Edward's stead; the Coronation Day in six months' time which should have been his was now to be theirs. Edward VIII was the King Who Was Never Crowned, his encounter with destiny uncomfortably short-lived. He had reigned for 325 days, and in that time his conduct had all but killed his charisma. Against the odds, his going sent no convulsions through the British Throne.

The abdication trauma scarred his kin more than it did the Crown and the country. It brought the greatest personal distress to Queen Mary (now removed from Buckingham Palace and beginning what was to prove a residence of over sixteen years in Marlborough House). She did not weep: it was not her way to show her feelings, save in rare private outbursts. But she was appalled and humiliated that a son of hers should have abandoned his post. She recognised, though did not forgive, his submission to a consuming personal obsession; but, once the renunciation of the Throne was a fact, Her Majesty without a moment's hesitation transferred her loyalty to the unassuming and understandably dismayed Bertie upon whom David the Defector had thrust an utterly unsought Crown. 'The person who needs sympathy is my second son', were her words. 'He is the one making the sacrifice.'

A sacrifice it unquestionably was, forfeiting the quietness of a loved family life to become the nation's Unremitting Servant. George VI gave his life for the upholding of kingship. And the brother whose action brought upon Bertie the rigours of supreme office in fact survived him for nearly twenty years (he died in 1972 and was buried at Windsor). Soon after the abdication the new King made him Duke of Windsor – the only time the family name had been used for a dukedom – and reconferred on him the title of Royal Highness. The style, however, was never given to his wife, though Mrs Simpson became the Duchess when Edward married her in June 1937, quietly and privately in a loaned château in Touraine. On a personal level, they lived to enjoy thirty-five years of wedded happiness, taking up residence in France. To those who

visited them, a handsome and elegant couple, rich and rootless, growing old gracefully. To the history books of the future, perhaps, two admired but unenvied outcasts existing in semi-obscurity after their meteor flash across the world scene.

What remains a remarkable fact is that when Edward VIII finally left home and country and gave up his heritage in that chill December of 1936, after creating the most serious and potentially catastrophic constitutional crisis Britain had known for centuries, the event was over and done with straight away, leaving hardly a ripple on the surface of the lives of ordinary people.

A few hours after he had gone, the abdication which had dominated the headlines was suddenly a story no more. The nation settled thankfully down to its new Sovereign and Consort, to its Christmas shopping, to the nuisance of the Nazis, the remote Civil War in Spain, the strutting Duce and a stricken Haile Selassie, the football season and the English winter.

Swiftly and totally, a King was eclipsed . . .

OPPOSITE *On 3 June 1937, at the Château de Candé in France, the former King married the lady for whom he had renounced his throne. This honeymoon photograph of the Duke and Duchess of Windsor was taken in the grounds of Castle Wasserleonburg in Austria.*

ABOVE *The Duke of Windsor only occasionally broke his self-imposed exile in France to return to Britain. Meetings with his mother were therefore rare.*

RIGHT *On this occasion both the Duke and the Duchess were visiting England, thirteen years after the Abdication crisis had stunned the nation.*

ABOVE *A picture taken immediately after the Coronation of King George VI on 14 May 1937. The King and Queen Elizabeth are wearing their Coronation robes and crowns. In regalia too are the Princesses, eleven-year-old Elizabeth and six-year-old Margaret.*

OPPOSITE *A charming studio portrait of Queen Elizabeth and her two daughters. It was taken in December 1936, the month of the Abdication which was totally to alter the family's way of life.*

PART FIVE

George VI and Queen Elizabeth

Restoration

THAT THE ABDICATION was a tragic episode in the royal story is indisputable; and widespread sympathy went out to Edward in the hour of his dilemma. But the long view of history may be that the nation, with his going, had a narrow escape from trouble, and that he was the most awkward as well as the most attractive Sovereign of the twentieth century. Perhaps his resignation from public life was a blessing in disguise, for he had been tried as a monarch and found wanting. To be well-meaning, to have bursts of energy and capricious enthusiasms was not enough. Charm was not talent. Sound judgement and sensibility to advice were qualities needed, but these were not present.

In a way, he never grew up. His blind *tendresse* towards the power-drunk leaders of Hitler's Nazi Germany was a chilling index of ingenuousness.

With his departure and the advent of his brother as George VI, Britain lost an erratic iconoclast and gained a steady traditionalist who re-endowed the Crown with respect and stability. But that was all in the future. As the year 1937 began the character of the new reign had barely started to show and the benefits of the change were far from fully discerned. What the nation did know however was that, instead of being the *pied-à-terre* of a wayward bachelor, Buckingham Palace (housing its third Sovereign within twelve months) was now the home of a close and exemplary family, manifestly happy in their domestic life together.

Although business of State at once cut heavily into the monarch's domesticity, his home and family – especially the incomparable support of his wife – were comfort beyond measure for the brave but still nervous and hesitant Duke of York who had become King George VI three days before his forty-first birthday. He was appalled by the Abdication which precipitated him into kingship. Up to that time he had spent his life in the shadow of a mercurial brother and was unprepared for supreme office. In earlier years he had faced adversity in nursery and classroom, had battled against ill-health in wartime – though he served and saw action in the Navy and later won his wings in the Royal Air Force – and now he was up against much greater struggles, all in the limelight which plays upon the Throne.

Congenital diffidence and stammering speech were amongst his personal troubles. He met these difficulties head-on and did not shirk showing his hesitations in public. It was typical of his courage, his dogged determination to shake clear of his reign's daunting start and at once face his duties with all the reserves in his power that, although he had been too exhausted to go before the

microphone and give the Sovereign's Christmas Message from Sandringham two weeks after his accession, he did continue his father's seasonal tradition a few days afterwards. Speaking 'live', the worrying pauses notwithstanding, he broadcast a New Year's address in which he dedicated himself and his Queen to the service of the peoples of the Empire and Commonwealth.

In his speech difficulties, as in all his problems, his Consort brought to him her tireless help. No monarch ever stood less alone. Her Majesty the Queen, with her serenity and smiling aplomb, was beside him at his life's testing moments, giving him confidence from her own calm and reassuring nature. From their early days of marriage she had been his speech-teacher in private, had gone through quiet rehearsals of scripts with him, had pressed him not to give in to what had previously seemed an intractable stammer, and had sat unruffled at his side as he made his brief addresses. Several

ABOVE *In his Duke of York days the King was a 'horseman' at a Surrey country fête.*

OPPOSITE, TOP *Enthusiasm for George VI's Coronation was fervent. Even the rain failed to dampen the spirits of these London East-enders, who were intensely proud of their decorative efforts.*

OPPOSITE, BOTTOM LEFT *As Duke of York, George VI had been the first member of the Royal Family to enter the Wimbledon Championships, at which, a left-hander, he played in the men's doubles in 1926. Partnered by Sir Louis Greig, he was defeated in the first round.*

OPPOSITE, BOTTOM RIGHT *The Duke of York's Boys' Camps were always a cherished memory of the King. He relished his relaxed days there.*

years before he became King, she had persuaded him to work with Lionel Logue, an Australian therapist practising in London's Harley Street, under whose advice and teaching the royal client made himself able to relax more, control his breathing and allow the words to flow more smoothly.

Now, as King, he was painstaking with his practising. He sat in his study in Buckingham Palace, in a lounge suit and with a crown on his head, rehearsing over and over again for the Sovereign's Speech from the Throne at his first State Opening of Parliament – and using the text of his father's last speech at that recurring occasion. When the day came, he got through the ordeal passably well. He never in his life completely lost the speech hesitation (it was hardly noticeable, incidentally, in private conversation) but the trouble decreased during the most important years of his reign and he always felt that he was in control of it, except at times of illness and great anxiety. Getting over the stutter was, in short, a significant victory for him – and a triumph for that prime encourager, his valiant wife.

George VI was a *good* king from the start. Through the years he came near to being a *great* one – by his own dedicated work and in his own right. But undoubtedly his steady rise in stature owed much to the inspiration and devoted partnership of Queen Elizabeth. Without her it would have been difficult for him to support the burdens of his office. At the beginning of the reign, had he been alone, his task might well have been utterly impossible.

But he was *not* alone. And the springtime of 1937 found the nation, with gloomy memories of the Abdication Crisis well out of mind, looking forward to the reassuring pageantry and ceremonial of the Coronation.

Wednesday, 12 May, the day on which King George VI and his Queen were crowned in Westminster Abbey, was dull and rainy, but London was thronged with cheering people. Inside the Abbey the ancient rite was carried out with unparalleled splendour. It was of course one of the most star-studded occasions of all time, an historic day for the Royal House of Windsor. By ancient tradition, a Dowager Queen does not attend the crowning of her husband's successor, but Queen Mary earnestly wished to see this son of hers consecrated and acclaimed as King of England; so, with his consent, she too was present at the service and in the long procession through the city streets.

Thus there was demonstrated in the early days of the new Georgian reign the solidity of the First Family. Queen Mary's grandchildren, the two small Princesses, were in the Abbey beside her. Elizabeth watched it all with glowing eyes. Margaret, only six at the time, had a little difficulty in keeping awake as she perched in the royal gallery during the long ceremony.

Towering above the two children, the old Queen – only a few weeks off her seventieth birthday – was wonderfully straight-backed and alert. No woman in the great church was more impressive that day. Her Majesty still had sixteen years of life ahead of her, and would almost live long enough to see the coronation of her granddaughter too – the Elizabeth who was an eleven-year-old Princess on this day of her father's crowning.

The Coronation service was, to most of those who were present in the Abbey to see it, a fine flawless spectacle of dignity and dedication. But to the new Monarch himself, a keen critic of ceremonial as well as a deeply religious man, there was more than one momentary contretemps in the progress of the ritual around him. He logged each small accident with a naval officer's punctiliousness in a crisp personal memorandum that very evening. The Dean at one point in the service tried to vest His Majesty in a surplice which he had turned inside out. At the altar, the Archbishop, holding the Form of Service book in front of the King, unknowingly covered with his thumb the words of the Oath which the monarch was required to speak (fortunately, the King had learned the words in his careful preparation). Then the Lord

LEFT *'Peace in our time.' Prime Minister Chamberlain returns from Munich in illusory triumph with the 'piece of paper' which in 1938 seemed to guarantee British immunity from German attack. He had agreed to the partition of Czechoslovakia at a meeting with Hitler, Mussolini and Daladier. Almost exactly a year later, on 3 September 1939, Germany had invaded Poland and Britain was at war.*

OPPOSITE *The King's wartime broadcasts to the nation – this one was on Christmas Day, 1944 – were a source of moral support as well as personal triumphs for a man worried by speech hesitations.*

Great Chamberlain fumbled so much when buckling the regalia sword round the royal waist that George VI had to discard patience and fix the belt himself. When it came to the supreme moment of putting the St Edward's Crown (which weighs seven pounds) on the royal brow, 'the Dean and the Primate had been juggling with it so much', the King wrote, 'that I never did know whether it was placed the right way round or not'. Finally, one of the bishops trod on His Majesty's robe when the King was leaving the Coronation Chair – 'and I was brought up all standing. I had to tell him to get off it pretty sharply as I nearly fell down.'

It was a symptom of the royal passion for perfection that the incidents were recorded at all. The general verdict was that the complicated rite had been carried out beautifully, and the King and Queen comported themselves with a knowledgeable sureness which profoundly impressed the clergy. They had given themselves heart and soul to the Abbey service and the life of duty which it consecrated. The King was already an infinitely more confident man than he had been six months before. There were signs already that, whilst adapting to the needs of the times, he was now following with a measure of cheerfulness the paths and patterns of valued service which had been those of his father. George V's ways were now George VI's.

Winston Churchill, who had supported and defended the defecting Edward VIII, looked at this new monarch enthroned in the Abbey and, turning to his wife who was sitting beside him in the congregation, whispered: 'I see now that "the other one" wouldn't have done.'

The subsequent public speaking was probably a greater trial to the new King than all the demands of archaic ceremonial in church had been. His voice was still uncertain at times in that Coronation evening when he broadcast from the Palace, but the content and the tone of the message had a firm ring. Never before had a newly crowned Sovereign been able to speak to his peoples in their own homes on the day of his Coronation, the King said. He had felt, moreover, that the whole Empire was with him in the Abbey. He was referring to the fact that the Coronation had been broadcast. In 1923 no radio coverage of his marriage service had been allowed, for the Westminster Chapter had vetoed the revolutionary and shocking idea that microphones should be put into the Abbey. Now, however, a world relay 'on the wireless', with commentary, was permitted, for the King was in favour of it – and so, rather at the last minute, was the Archbishop of Canterbury (the Dr Cosmo Gordon Lang who at the time of the Abdication had been popularly credited with the role of Uncharitable Expeller of Erring Monarchs). It was said that the Primate's conversion to a go-ahead, allowing full facilities to the British Broadcasting Corporation, was not unconnected with the discovery that he himself had an excellent broadcasting voice.

But the then infant television service was not allowed even a single peep inside the Abbey in 1937 – a situation worlds away from today's state of affairs in which the cameras are all-pervading, almost all-intrusive, and royal occasions at Westminster have become TV spectaculars.

At the close of a busy year the family gathered at Sandringham for Christmas, and this year the King did take up the practice of his father and broadcast from his home a Sovereign's Message on the afternoon of Christmas Day. Dutifully, he spoke 'live', from a special microphone placed on his study table, straight into the BBC's Home and Overseas Services – as he was to do each year until the very last December of his life, each year writing the script himself with the help of the Queen: 'We worked at it as a team job', he used to say. Like his father, he always hated the actual speaking of the broadcast, though the dislike never came through to the listeners for the simple reason that he was patently sincere in every word he said. Like his father too, he did not fully enjoy Christmas Day until the tension of the 3 p.m. appointment with the

LEFT *Neville Chamberlain resigned in May 1940, to be succeeded as Prime Minister by Winston Churchill, who, like his monarch, was an assiduous inspector of troops. Here they are Home Guards.*

OPPOSITE *When war came, King George scorned suggestions that he and his family should retreat to the safety of Canada. Instead he travelled great distances to visit the fighting forces. Here he inspects French troops during a visit to France in December 1939.*

microphone was over. He could have prerecorded his speech, even in the early days, but he always felt that there was an immediacy and intimacy about a direct transmission and that this was an essential feature of the annual link over the air between Sovereign and people; and he therefore chose to brave the worldwide 'live hook-up' each time.

Millions listened. For many, there was something reassuring in 1937 about the hopes and the faith which came over in the royal message, some comfort in the sound of a leader with a sense of honour and a badge of courage, a leader expressing Christian faith and praying for peace between nations.

For at the turn of the year and the arrival of 1938 the world outlook was more lowering than ever, and the grim prospect of war again occupied European minds. Adolf Hitler, with a flagrantly armed and indoctrinated Reich at his back, absorbed Austria into Germany, and an impotent Czechoslovakia was next on his list of 'last territorial claims'. Neville Chamberlain, who had succeeded Stanley Baldwin as the King's First Minister, shared his Sovereign's horror of war and had the King's sympathy and trust as he tried to stem the tide of aggression by, at first, conventional Foreign Office moves to reach *détente* with the Führer.

The monarchy did more than hope and pray. In July the King and Queen crossed the Channel on a State Visit to France which had become an urgent diplomatic act in view of the need to make firmer the ties with Britain's chief ally in Europe. The visit was a personal success for Their Majesties, who were rapturously received by Parisian crowds, Queen Elizabeth's elegant dresses and her spontaneous charm of manner making a special appeal. Edward VIII might have dazzled the French, but here were his successors delighting them with quieter but more gracious and lasting effect. Whether the visit itself significantly warmed the Gallic political heart was perhaps another matter. A vacillating Daladier was

Premier, yearnings for peace at any price and desires not to provoke Germany were strong, and indeed there were superstitious minds on the other side of the Channel which recalled that a similar visit to Paris had been paid twenty-four years before by King George V and Queen Mary and that Britain and France were at war with Germany less than four months after it.

Was history going to repeat itself? When the King and Queen returned to London it was to see air-raid precautions almost beneath the Palace windows, for lines were being marked for the digging of trenches in the royal parks. Plans for conscription, the mobilisation of the Fleet and the evacuation of children from cities left nobody in doubt now of the nearness of conflagration in 1938.

But Neville Chamberlain kept on trying, always believing that Hitler's ambitions would stop short of setting the world aflame. Acutely aware that his country was militarily ill-prepared and its people unwilling to face the full realities of war, especially when there seemed every possibility that one of our allies might be a Communist Russia, the Prime Minister pursued with unremitting personal initiative and desperate optimism his policy of appeasement. He made humiliating visits to Germany during September, but returned with little more than dispiriting reports of the arrogance and recalcritrance that had been his reception at the meetings with Hitler. Britain issued gas masks to its civilians and call-up papers to its reservist soldiers. The King, who corresponded very regularly with his mother, wrote to Queen Mary of 'this awful waiting for the worst to happen' and of his fear that Hitler was a madman.

Full-scale war was clearly imminent. Then, at the last moment, at a sudden signal from the Führer – it was called an invitation to a Four-Power Conference at Munich the next day, a meeting between Hitler and Mussolini, Daladier and Chamberlain – the Prime Minister leapt into the air once more, joyful at what sounded like a reprieve and a chance of peace, ready to attend the meeting

which became at the time famous and presently infamous. He returned from Germany triumphantly waving the so-called Pact, which seemed salvation then but was all too soon to be recognised as a document of shame and surrender. The document was the notorious 1938 Munich 'Agreement' which sold the Czechs and waved a flag of weakness before the Nazi leader.

Understandably enough, it was hailed with relief in Britain and the free world at that moment as a great deliverance. Chamberlain received King George's congratulations. But the pact was to prove only the provider of a brief breathing space, a postponement of war for twelve months. By 12 March 1939, the Germans were in Prague, Czechoslovakia had ceased to exist, and Hitler, the barefaced and contemptuous perjuror, had torn up Chamberlain's scrap of paper.

Thenceforward there was no more parleying. Aggression had to be met. During 1939 defence preparations were Britain's priority. Together with France we had guaranteed to go to the aid of Poland in the event of German attack, and negotiations with Russia were started for the military alliance without which the guarantee would be worth nothing. But then, in August, it was *Germany* which made the alliance. The news was a bombshell. Hitler's cynical pact with the Soviets made war a certainty.

There was need that summer for Britain to strengthen friend-ships, and in May and June the King and Queen, purposefully but with some misgivings about leaving the United Kingdom with the situation so tense, responded to long-standing invitations, crossed the Atlantic, and for seven weeks carried out a strenuous tour of North America, all across Canada and then into the United States. The tour was a fantastic success. Day after day the visitors left the royal train and plunged into crowds so huge and eager that often they were quite swallowed in the throng. Equerries, Mounties, bodyguards and attendant press corps were left floundering. Many of the welcomes were boisterous, but the royal couple usually

emerged from the cheering turmoil clearly exhausted but clearly having enjoyed those early 'walkabouts'. The Canadians were surprised and delighted with the informality of the British Sovereign and Consort. In Quebec, French-speaking Canadians talked as readily as did the English-speaking populations of the other Provinces of '*our* King and Queen'.

In both their official and informal meetings the royal travellers without doubt did much to make Canadian loyalties even firmer and rebuild Anglo-American understanding at a time when there had been an isolationist element in the United States trying to pretend that the evils of Hitler and his jackal Mussolini were of no concern 'to us over here'.

When Their Majesties crossed the border from Canada on the night of 9 June they were the first reigning Sovereign and Consort to set foot on American soil. They were the guests of Mr and Mrs Roosevelt in Washington and at the President's Hyde Park home, and were received with great personal warmth. Franklin Roosevelt was, even before the visit, an Anglophile President. From the start, 'F.D.R.' had wanted to make the visit a family affair as well as a formal mission: when plans were being made he had said he hoped that the two Princesses would be coming too – 'We'll try to have one or two Roosevelts of approximately the same age to play with them' – but the King, though attracted by the thought, had in reply regretted that 'the children are much too young for such a strenuous tour'.

Again there were enthusiastic crowds in a capital city. Queen Elizabeth 'mowed down' the Washington journalists covering the visit, some of whom, hard-bitten enough even without encourage-ment, had been briefed not to be afraid of 'debunking the Limeys'. The Queen was not putting on some public-relations act – she never did. It was, as always, the smile, the sparkle in the blue eyes, the natural way in which she talked to a person as though that person

was the only one in the world she had been wanting to meet, that was so engaging. The fairytale sight of her in crinoline ball-gown and tiara captivated both the public and the professional Queen-watchers. Columnists nominated her 'Woman of the Year'. Headlines announced: 'The British re-take Washington.'

Franklin and Eleanor Roosevelt had no doubts about the diplomatic importance of the British presence that fateful summer. They foresaw the involvement of the United States in what was to come in Europe. Mrs Roosevelt's diary was candid: 'My husband hoped that the visit would create a bond of friendship between the people of the two countries . . . We all might soon be engaged in a life and death struggle, in which Great Britain would be our first line of defence.'

Arriving back in the United Kingdom, Their Majesties were immediately made aware, by the affectionate greetings of the crowds and the grateful reactions of Cabinet ministers and officials, that their own country recognised that the tour had been a valuable international achievement. The personal triumph of it was seen too. For, in the event, the American journey of those two royal people, still young in years and experience of office, had been the antithesis of the bashful plod through lukewarm prairies which cynics had expected. Here were a King and Queen now proved to be self-possessed leaders and inspiring ambassadors. As Britain's hour of greatest trial approached, the Throne was already emerging as a looked-for focus of national identity and purpose.

The twentieth century's Restoration of the Monarchy was manifest beyond doubt.

The Second World War

The King had come back a changed man, still sensitive and sometimes irascible, but possessed now of a new confidence forged in the first-hand experiences of that American tour and forced by forebodings of the terror in Europe. He was fearful; he knew war

was coming; but he had been greatly moved and made firm in purpose by the clarity with which the issues were realised on both sides of the Atlantic. And personally it was never in his nature to react to danger with anything but courage and quiet determination.

Even his public speaking came with less difficulty. On one occasion, it had clearly improved almost out of recognition. When he and the Queen went to London's Guildhall in State to be welcomed home, both the matter and the manner of his speech showed him as a world leader of sincere beliefs, a man who would defend the democracy he headed. He spoke firmly of 'the institutions which have developed, century after century, beneath the aegis of the British Crown . . . grounded root and branch on British faith in liberty and justice and rights of free citizenship which are the heritage of every member of our great Commonwealth of Nations'. He went on to express his aim 'to show, if I could, that the Headship of that Commonwealth which I have been called upon to assume exists today as a potent force for promoting peace and goodwill'.

This was no weakling King. He was making a signal to the Dictators: Take note! We shall resist!

But in the sinister European quiet of the few weeks that followed there was a growing certainty that Hitler was beyond warnings. However, the King, like his subjects, hoped that sanity would somehow prevail; and, like them, he took a holiday in what was to prove the last summer of peace for six years. The happiest event of his time off was a visit, sailing in the old Royal Yacht *Victoria and Albert*, to the Royal Naval College at Dartmouth, to which he had never returned since leaving the place as a cadet. With him were the Queen and the two Princesses and Lord Louis Mountbatten, his cousin 'Dickie'. It was at Dartmouth on that occasion that Princess Elizabeth, who was thirteen, first met a cousin of *hers* – the eighteen-year-old Prince Philip of Greece, a good-looking, fair-haired and forthcoming senior cadet, nephew of Lord Louis. The encounter was to have prime consequence in British history (though

wrote: 'The country is calm, firm and united behind its leaders, resolved to fight until Liberty & Justice are once again safe in the World...'

He himself broadcast to the country at six in the evening: 'We have been forced into a conflict to meet the challenge of a principle which, if it were to prevail, would be fatal to any civilised order in the world.... Such a principle is the primitive doctrine that Might is Right ... It is unthinkable that we should refuse to meet the challenge ... To this high purpose I now call my people at home and my peoples across the seas. I ask them to stand calm and firm and united at this time of trial.' Prophetically he added: 'War can no longer be confined to the battlefield.'

So, from the first moment, Britain braced itself for onslaught. Many people feared that parts of London would be in ruins from cannonade out of the skies on that very Outbreak Sunday. But no bombs came. Not for a long time. Not for months. It was anticlimax. The worst hardships were the blacked-out streets and shuttered homes, the evacuation of children from the cities, and the nervy feeling that terrible things were certain to come but unaccountably were not starting. What was Hitler preparing? We had a British Expeditionary Force of properly equipped troops over in France, but it was waiting with its allies supinely behind the Maginot Line. Why wasn't Chamberlain prosecuting the war? Or somehow ending it? Inaction bred questioning. Quiet months went by, well into 1940, and there was still no real fighting on the Western Front. Only weird calm and sinister stalemate. We called it 'The Phoney War'.

Then suddenly – dramatically and all the more horrendously after seven stagnant months – the storm broke. Hitler had been waiting for the spring. In April 1940 Germany launched a lightning invasion of Denmark and Norway. The countries were soon overrun and occupied. Then, a month later, it was shattering full-scale war. Long and massively prepared by the German forces, the *Blitzkrieg* broke upon France and Holland and Belgium. The Netherlands was forced to capitulate. British and French troops moved into Belgium, but that country, under King Leopold III, was compelled to surrender.

The Allies faced utter disaster, and so did Neville Chamberlain. The King had sympathised with his First Minister's abhorrence of war, but the country's confidence in the man and his Government was shattered. Chamberlain had to go; and, to the relief of nation and Parliament, Winston Churchill – the man who had been for so long in the political wilderness, a Cassandra of the thirties, preaching the German menace into deaf ears – was called upon to be Prime Minister at the head of a national coalition government. It was the beginning of Churchill's own 'finest hours', the epic five years of wartime leadership which, whatever else he achieved in that long life, were to make him an immortal.

In the first week or two of the new regime, during which every day brought news of retreat and rout from across the Channel, King George was at times a little formal and cool in his contacts with Chamberlain's successor, perhaps even startled by his new firecracking Premier who had been something of a suspect maverick politician in past years and past warfare. But only for a short time. For Winston plainly meant business, knew exactly what he wanted, was a demon for work – and for making everybody else work – and provided the tonic the nation needed in what were now becoming its direst hours. Speedily, then, His Majesty gave to the new leader his firm support and complete collaboration. Confidence in Churchill grew; and in 1940 there developed between the two men, Monarch and Chief Minister, a deep and warm

the meeting was characteristically played down by Prince Philip when asked about it in later years, for his answer was: 'Significant? It was a very amusing experience. Hardly just casual acquaintance. There was, after all, a family relationship'). It was the meeting which began the royal romance.

The most important event of the holiday in the King's recollections, however, was probably his final Boys' Camp. Eighteen years before, he had founded an annual Duke of York's Camp for four hundred boys, half of them from public schools and the rest of them young workers from industrial areas. The gatherings had been highly successful, and the Duke had always given them his enthusiasm and personal participation. The 1939 camp was held in the grounds of Abergeldie Castle near Balmoral. Although its founder was King now, he chose to be more involved than ever and for a few days found happy relaxation, with the cares of State momentarily lifted from him, in taking part in the running of the event and leading parties of lads on long hikes over the Deeside hills he loved so well. He took the whole lot of them over to have tea at the Castle, after which the Queen and the young Princesses went with him to the camp for a supper and final singsong.

It was a lull before the storm. A few weeks later, many of those young men were in khaki.

On 1 September 1939, Germany invaded Poland. British and French ultimatums to the attacker expired at 11 a.m. on Sunday, 3 September, and Britain was at war with Germany again for the second time in twenty-five years. In his personal diary the King reflected that at the outbreak of the First World War he had been a midshipman, eighteen years of age, keeping the middle watch on the bridge of a battleship in the North Sea. Now he was monarch, symbolic leader of a nation which had been forced to resort to arms and to appease no more. The declaration of a state of war was almost a relief, he felt, after the strain of inaction in the face of Hitler's bloodless victories in the European countries around him. Now that the breakdown of negotiations had resulted in war, His Majesty

friendship which was to last all the wartime years and the rest of the Sovereign's lifetime. The hour of peril had produced the man to lead and to voice the defiance of a Britain in mortal danger.

As to the feelings of Winston Churchill himself, it is no exaggeration to say that he entered Number 10 Downing Street on 10 May 1940 an indestructible fighter, a warrior with no illusions whatever but glorying in the challenge of the desperate war situation. 'At last I had authority', he wrote, 'and I felt as though I were walking with destiny.'

By 22 May the Germans had smashed through the French lines and the spearheads of their armies had reached the Channel at Boulogne. Allied troops were pinned down in a shrinking patch of coastal land. Only the miracle of the Dunkirk beaches saved the British Army from annihilation. The Royal Navy assembled an unprecedented fleet for the rescue: two hundred naval craft of all sizes, ninety passenger ships and merchant vessels, and over four hundred little boats of every kind, from pleasure steamers to sailing dinghies, manned by yachtsmen and fishermen from the coasts and rivers. Those vessels, under constant enemy attack, evacuated more than 335,000 Allied troops, one third of them Frenchmen, and brought them to Britain.

The dramatic snatching of those forces from what had seemed a doom of surrender or destruction was hailed at the time as a marvellous deliverance, a feat that was almost a victory. And from that moment British morale soared. The fact that the Army, although it had escaped, had been defeated and almost all its equipment lost, seemed hardly to register in a sudden optimism in British minds; and the soldiers themselves, who had fought heroic rearguard actions, were convinced that, given modern equipment, they were man for man at least as good as the victorious enemy. A confidence was born with Dunkirk which was never lost, even in all the hideous experiences still to come.

To foreign observers this spirit was beyond belief. Here was a country alone and with its back to the wall (France had virtually given up the fight) and almost defenceless and weaponless save for a small airforce, prone to an invasion which now must surely and by all the odds victoriously come. Yet in the Britain of 1940 there was now no talk of defeat. The Churchill spirit and the presence of a steadfast King kindled a last-ditch defiance and determination which today, looking back, seems astonishing except to those of us who were in London in 1940 and experienced it.

This was the Britain which had gripped its pikestaffs and confronted the threat of the Spanish Armada, this the land which had soberly prepared to face the assault forces of Bonaparte assembling above his launching harbours less than thirty miles across the water.

Now, in 1940, a volunteer force of Home Guards was grasping its pickaxe handles and drilling with broomsticks and a few old shotguns as Hitler massed his invasion barges on the same Channel coast to fall upon his last enemy.

For our ally had fallen. The Germans, striking south through a demoralised France which had not heeded Churchill's rallying call and was deaf to King George's appeals to President Lebrun, had entered Paris early in June. Marshal Pétain and his government sued

OPPOSITE *Princess Margaret watches as her sister broadcasts a speech during a 'Children's Hour' programme in October 1940.*

TOP *Windsor Great Park provided plenty of room for the Princesses to pursue an enduring interest, horse-riding.*

ABOVE *Whenever duties allowed, the Royal Family would gather round the piano at Royal Lodge, Windsor.*

for terms, ordered their soldiers to stop fighting, and completed an armistice with the Germans on 22 June. A vengeful Führer, now that the tables were turned, arranged that the French surrender should be signed in the same railway coach on the same spot in the Forest of Compiègne where Marshal Foch had received the abject German emissaries who signed *their* instrument of defeat in 1918.

Meanwhile there had gathered in Britain, last redoubt of freedom, not only the combatants who had escaped the Nazi enslavement of their countries and the hell of the Dunkirk beaches but also all manner of fiercely patriotic men and women who had managed to slip out of a Europe in jackboot thrall because they were determined to regroup and one day return to fight again. Poles and Dutch, Norwegians and Danes, they formed their governments-in-exile and trained anew for battle. London was sanctuary and rallying point.

To London also came Heads of State who, after last efforts on their own soil and refusing to give themselves into captivity, had been snatched from German encirclement and venomous pursuit. The hospitality of Buckingham Palace was given to Norway's tall King Haakon, to Greece's King George, and to the intrepid Queen Wilhelmina of the Netherlands, who had left Rotterdam under fire in a destroyer, intending to join a remnant of her troops still resisting in Zeeland. But it was too late. She therefore landed at Harwich and telephoned to Buckingham Palace in order to make a personal plea to the King for British aircraft to defend her country. On being with difficulty convinced by His Majesty during that call that reports now showed that all of Holland had been overrun, the Queen was persuaded in spite of her reluctance to take the train and travel on to London. The King was on the platform at Liverpool Street station to meet her. She was wearing a tin hat and only the torn clothes she stood up in.

Her host King George, though not tin-hatted at that moment, was in Service dress with gas-mask haversack. He always wore uniform during the war. He was always at pains during official and not-so-official duties, on his visits to Forces' camps and civilian factories, in his counsels with Government ministers and his broadcasts to the nation, to be – and to be seen to be – a resolute leader at the head of his people, a focus of determination and an antidote for any faint-hearts. He had the sincerest faith in Britain's cause – and great intolerance of the jeremiads of occasional croakers either at home or overseas.

And the Royal Family were mobilised. The Duke of Gloucester, a professional soldier, was with the Army; the Duke of Kent, after his naval career, was now an Air Force officer; and the King's sister Mary, the Princess Royal, Countess of Harewood, who had been a Red Cross nurse in the Kaiser's War, was now in Auxiliary Territorial Service khaki. She was *mother* of a soldier too. Her elder son George – Earl of Harewood now but Viscount Lascelles then – was the first grandchild of George V and the eldest of a new royal generation. In Hitler's War he was not only old enough to be in National Service but democratic enough to work at first in a munitions factory and then enlist as a private in the Grenadier Guards. He was captured, wounded, in the fighting in Italy later in the war and, by then an officer, was imprisoned in the celebrated Colditz Castle. There is a nice story that when he was being interrogated he gave little information about his relatives but allowed that he had an uncle who lived near Victoria station.

His royal cousins were younger than he. Princess Elizabeth and Princess Margaret were aged thirteen and nine when war broke out. Prince Eddy, today's Duke of Kent, was almost four, and his sister Princess Alexandra two and a half (the younger Kent prince,

LEFT *Tragedy struck royal homes like any others. Three weeks after this photograph of the Duke and Duchess of Kent and their children was taken, in August 1942, the Duke, brother of the King, was killed on active service when his plane crashed in Scotland. (The picture was taken on the christening day of the infant Prince Michael.)*

BELOW *The King and Queen inspect the damage caused by a delayed-action bomb at Buckingham Palace, which was hit altogether nine times in the war, mostly during the heavy bombing of 1940–41.*

RIGHT *Another member of the Royal Family to see active service during the war was Viscount Lascelles (today's Lord Harewood), son of the King's sister. He served in the Grenadier Guards, was captured in Italy and then imprisoned in the notorious Colditz Castle. Here (left) he is on a map-reading exercise.*

BELOW *Having had her own home bombed, the Queen felt she could 'look the blitzed East End in the face', and with the King she made several visits to this most heavily assaulted part of London. Here they inspect a boarded-up bomb-crater.*

Michael, did not arrive until 1942). Prince William of Gloucester was also a wartime baby, born at the end of 1941. He was three years old – and Prince Richard, today's Duke, only a matter of weeks old – when their father, the then Duke, went to Australia as Governor-General in December 1944. His tenure of that office gave his small sons the advantage of two years in the Canberra sunshine at the beginning of their lives.

Their uncle, the Duke of Windsor who had been King Edward VIII, had no children (else those young Royals might have had some half-American cousins). From obscurity, the Duke of Windsor emerged briefly at the outbreak of war and as a soldier at once offered his services to his native country (he still held the rank of Field Marshal in the Army and its equivalents in the other armed forces). He was assigned as a member of the British Military Mission in Paris. But the French débâcle of 1940 was the end of any British presence there. The Duke, after an adventurous journey out of a country part German-occupied and part under the repressive Fascist-style Vichy Government of the aged collaborator Pétain, was appointed Governor of the peripheral Bahama Islands, a post he held until the end of the war. Little was heard of him. In a thunderously preoccupied world he was hardly even an echo in the past.

One royal echo which did sound faintly in the early years of the war came with the death of an old and in most minds long-forgotten foe, Demon King though he had once been. But for the passage of the years and the all-absorbing tempest of a new war, the tiny news item from Nazi-occupied Holland in the spring of 1941 would have been large in the headlines and the history books. For the item reported the death in his eighty-second year of the ex-Kaiser William II, the arch-enemy in the First World War. It was news to most people that he had been still alive, for he, like Edward VIII, had disappeared after bulking so large on the world stage.

The former German Emperor had in fact spent the past quarter of a century as a subdued civilian in circumstances which in 1918 had been officially described as internment. 'House arrest' perhaps, but it was a not uncomfortable life on a remote Dutch estate. After the storms of his earlier days, for twenty-three years he had led a gentle country existence of complete retirement at the Castle of Doorn. Grandeur was gone, ambition spent. He was old. The only reported activity, in his last years, of the 'Kaiser Bill' who had aimed to chop cousin England down to size seems to have been chopping logs. The one real change in his circumstances in the final phase had come in 1922, when he was sixty-three. Then, after the death of the Empress Augusta Victoria, he had made a second marriage with a widowed German princess. Now that he was dead, there came a surprising salute from the Netherlands' oppressor-in-chief, Adolf Hitler, who ordered a military funeral for the erstwhile Kaiser.

Hitler, the German Dictator, must have felt in 1940 and 1941 that he could order anything he wished, and be obeyed. Except the conquering of the United Kingdom. In that ambition, which had seemed to him and to most of the world an easy thing to achieve after the Wehrmacht's overwhelming of the continent of Europe, he signally failed. And that sealed his fate.

It is a matter of imperishable history that in the Battle of Britain in 1940, at the time when these islands faced the Axis powers of Hitler and Mussolini alone, the fighter pilots of the Royal Air Force, shooting down superior numbers of Luftwaffe bombers by the hundred, and the commanding vigilance of the Royal Navy thwarted the German plans. Hitler could not send his boatloads of troops across even the narrow waters to invade Britain unless he controlled the skies above the Channel and southern England,

unless he immobilised the airfields and broke the resistance of the civilian population by bombing. None of those objects was he able to attain. He was forced to turn his assault forces elsewhere, and he was never again to come so near to final victory.

The heroism of the young flyers in the Spitfires and Hurricanes was hailed by Winston Churchill in the most famous of the many memorable sentences he uttered in a long life of oratory: 'Never in the field of human conflict was so much owed by so many to so few.' Less remembered though even more succinct was his challenge to the enemy's massed assault boats: 'We are waiting for the long-promised invasion. So are the fishes.'

Invasion of the British Isles never came. But the Blitz of 1940 and 1941 did. Defeated overhead in the blue skies of south-east England in the summer of '40, the Germans switched from large-scale bombing in daylight to their huge air raids by night, which brought widespread devastation and death, but not defeatism. Even in the battered cities the country stood firm.

Then in June 1941 Germany turned on its 'ally' and attacked the Soviet Union. Churchill immediately promised wholehearted aid to the Russian people. Communism was an anathema to him but, as he said, 'If Hitler invaded Hell I would make at least a favourable reference to the Devil in the House of Commons.' Stalin thenceforward became a combatant on the British side. Next, less than six months later, Japanese aggression, beginning with the attack on the Pacific naval base of Pearl Harbor, brought the United States of America into the war, another and in the end an overwhelmingly powerful and decisive factor in the liberation of the world from the German and the Japanese yoke.

King George gave all the support of his office and his personal example to a Prime Minister and War Cabinet working ceaselessly to unite the strategy of the three nations in the Grand Alliance which was eventually to win the war. It was in the Middle East, at El Alamein, that the turn of the tide began with the defeat of the German–Italian forces by the British Eighth Army on the northern sands of Egypt in 1942. Before that Desert Victory, terrible losses had been suffered, the Japanese and the Germans triumphing on land and at sea. The King rarely gave way to despondency, but shocking reverses such as the surrender of the Malayan bastion of Singapore and its garrison of seventy thousand men sent him into black depression when first the evil tidings came. To Churchill the fall of Singapore was 'the greatest disaster to British arms which our history records'.

The balance of war was slow to alter, even after Montgomery's rout of Rommel and the beginning of the telling fight back by Britain's warships and bomber squadrons. Only after the Russians' epic defence of Stalingrad in 1942–43 and the subsequent advances of the British and American forces in the Mediterranean zone was the enemy's fate spelt out. In early June 1944, though the hardest fighting was yet to come, ultimate victory could be discerned. By then the tide of liberation had surged painfully north from Africa into the 'Axis underbelly' of the South European mainland, and Rome had been reached. Two days after the day on which the Italian capital had been freed, the long-awaited Allied landings on the beaches of Normandy began the campaign which finally crushed the German divisions in the North-West. In May 1945 the fighting in Europe was over, and in August that year, after atom bombs had been dropped on Japan, Emperor Hirohito also surrendered. Peace had come at last.

*   *   *

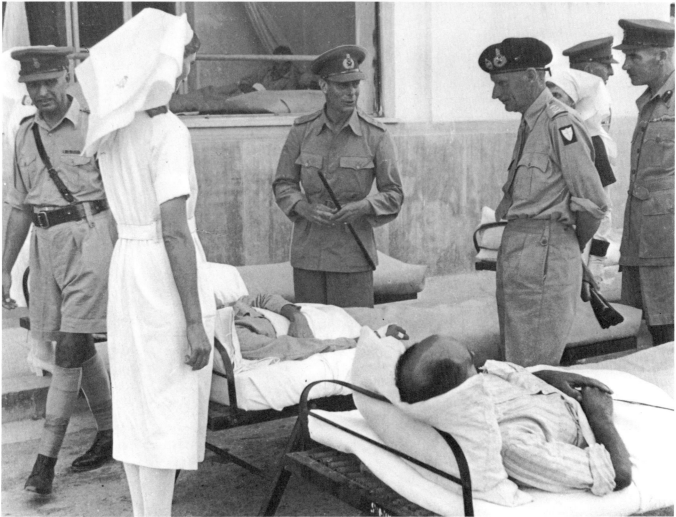

TOP *The Queen and Queen Mary were no less enthusiastic than the King in visiting troops and attended some of his inspections. Here they are seen with General Sir Oliver Leese on a visit to the Guards Second Division at Warminster in 1942.*

ABOVE *In June 1943 King George VI was in Tripoli meeting some of the heroes of the Desert War. He chatted with patients at a hospital for British troops under the eye of their commander, General Montgomery.*

ABOVE *War or no, the education of the Princesses had to continue. This picture shows them in the schoolroom at Windsor Castle in 1940.*

OPPOSITE, TOP *The Waterloo Chamber of Windsor Castle. Built to commemorate victory over Napoleon, it was the scene of the Princesses' wartime Christmas pantomimes.*

OPPOSITE, BOTTOM *The grand paintings of the Waterloo Chamber were removed to the Castle vaults during the war for fear of bomb damage. At the instigation of the King and Queen the empty picture-frames were filled with such characters as Red Riding Hood and Aladdin. (The story is told on pages 114–15.)*

It had been the most widespread and desperate war in world history and many nations had been involved. Shrinking though the British Empire and Commonwealth was, even then, overseas armies had come to fight alongside the forces of the United Kingdom – splendid divisions from Canada, Australia, New Zealand, the Union of South Africa and Rhodesia, from India too, and contingents from colonial lands of the south. The King, flying out insistently and often in hazard, paid visits to British and Allied troops and naval and air bases on the North African, Italian and other fronts in the Mediterranean area of operations; and later, in North-West Europe, he was an early arrival on the D-Day beaches and the fighting zones beyond. He was never a stay-behind – except when he refused to desert his homeland in those perilous early days of the war when England was besieged.

King George and Queen Elizabeth had remained with their people throughout the war. Britain was where they belonged, bombed and battered London was their headquarters under fire. More than once, when Goering's sky fleets were creating havoc in their bid to wipe out London and make British cities uninhabitable, and especially at the time when German army landings on the south coast of England from sea and air were a real possibility, some advisers felt strongly that the Royal Family should, at least temporarily, transfer to a safer country. Would it not be best to allow themselves to be evacuated to a base in Canada? Would it not be prudent for at any rate the Queen and the two daughters to go? But no such ideas were ever entertained by the King or by Queen Elizabeth. 'We stay put with our people' was the order of the day.

When Her Majesty was asked about the possibility of retreating overseas, she gave her answer with a smile – and not merely echoing the King's view (which may not improperly be summed up as 'Not Pygmalion likely!'). The Queen's reply was quite short and final: 'The Princesses cannot go without me. I cannot go without the King. The King will never go.'

They stayed put – and were bombed like everybody else. Their home, Buckingham Palace, was directly hit or blast-damaged by bombs, flying bombs or rocket missiles nine times in all. The Palace Chapel – where the Queen's Gallery of pictures shown to the public now stands – was completely destroyed by a direct hit. On one occasion, when an unheralded low-flying raider dropped a stick of bombs right across the Palace, the King and Queen had a narrow escape (the story was disclosed only years later, and not by them). They were at work in a room overlooking the quadrangle when – although there had been no air-raid warning – a German plane came out of low clouds and streaked along the line of the Mall just above the plane trees. Whistles of bombs and loud explosions sounded, and windows and doors crashed in on the royal occupants of that room. Their Majesties were unhurt. Sometimes their staffs had experienced difficulty in getting their employers to go down to an air-raid shelter during raids. On this occasion there had been no time even to get away from the windows. The Queen said: 'I'm almost comforted that the Palace has been hit. I feel I can look the blitzed East End in the face.'

Her Majesty believed that not all the bombs or craters of that raid were found, and that one bomb from the stick of six was missing. Is there, to this day, an unexploded German missile buried somewhere in the forty acres of Palace garden? The thought has been no worry to myriads of garden party guests in the subsequent forty years!

The King and Queen, when they were not away on visits to blitzed cities and towns, coastal defence sites and camps, ordnance factories and airfields, travelling long distances and sleeping for many a gunfire- and siren-ridden night in the royal train, would normally do their work in London and then, if there were a succession of exceptionally noisy nights, go to Windsor Castle to get a few hours of – if they were lucky – relatively quiet sleep.

The two Princesses, Elizabeth and Margaret, lived at Windsor for much of the time during the war, and the Queen was near enough to them to continue personally the supervision of their education by governess and specially chosen teachers. There was no question, in King George's reign, of royal children going away to school as they do now: their classrooms were in palace and castle, and regular and concentrated periods of study were part of the Windsor routine in the nineteen-forties. The Vice-Provost of Eton and two or three of the College's most talented masters went up the road and across the river to the Castle several times each week to give lessons to the Princesses.

The two girls worked hard – and, within the restrictions of wartime, played hard too. Particularly enjoyed were the holiday breaks when Christmas pantomimes were put on at Windsor, beginning in 1941. These entertainments were staged in the huge and famous Waterloo Chamber of the Castle. The performers were local schoolchildren from royal estates' families, a few young evacuees from London, child friends of the Princesses, and Their Royal Highnesses themselves. Both Elizabeth and Margaret delighted in dressing up and wearing the variety of pantomime costumes and wigs, and they soon proved that they possessed acting talent and a pretty wit too. Princess Margaret's singing, very young though she was, came to be a hit of the shows (which were written and produced and acted in by the very versatile Headmaster who presided at that time over the School in the 'royal village' in Windsor Great Park, a Mr Hubert Tanner).

It was not simply because they *were* the Princesses that the two young ladies who lived in the Castle had leading roles in *Cinderella*, *Aladdin* and *Old Mother Red Riding Boots*. They took to the stage with outstanding gusto and grace. The Queen had a particular interest in the productions, especially the first of the royal pantomimes, *Cinderella*, in which her daughters starred as a dashing Prince Charming and a very lively little Cinders. Her Majesty, whenever she was at Windsor during the early stages of the rehearsals, used to make a point of going through the scripts with the girls, prompting them and making sure that they knew their word-

cues. The schoolmaster, Mr Tanner, played the Baron, and Buttons was the brother of one of the Queen's maids.

As to the local audiences at the performances, they packed the Waterloo Chamber and always included a good number of uniformed soldiers from the troops stationed in the Windsor district and on guard duty at the Castle. Each member of the audiences was required to pay for admission and the money went to the Royal Household knitting-wool funds.

In normal times the walls of that Waterloo Chamber – as visitors to the Castle's State Apartments know – are hung with large and very grand paintings of the monarchs, generals and other leading figures of the Europe which shared in the defeat of Napoleon. But during the last World War, and therefore at the times when the great chamber was a Christmastime theatre, the portraits were taken out of their handsome gilt frames for fear of bomb damage (they had safe storage in the Castle vaults together with many other treasures, including Crown Jewels wrapped in newspapers and crammed into leather hatboxes).

So the walls were bare, but only for a time. The King and Queen were jointly inspired to get someone to paint pantomime figures along the newly austere surfaces all round the great room, in order to brighten the Chamber. Local art students were brought in to depict, for the time being, a whole series of large fairytale and pantomime characters on the walls themselves, one figure in each of the spaces within the picture-frames.

When the war ended and the precious canvases – most of them the work of Sir Thomas Lawrence – were about to be replaced in their frames on the walls, the King decided that the jolly panto pictures should not be erased, but that the splendid portraits of great men should be put back *over them*, thus preserving in secret the pictorial souvenirs of his daughters' happier wartime moments. So the wall drawings are still there, hidden.

It is a diverting thought that today, were the painting of the Emperor of Russia to slip down from the Chamber's wall, Dick Whittington would leap incongruously into view; that George IV himself is masking Mother Goose; and that his father George III has Aladdin in hiding behind *his* portrait.

The King and Queen saw the pantomimes whenever they could (sitting in the front row of the audiences at the Castle and taking pride in their daughters' duets); but for most of the time during the war years it was London rather than Windsor which remained the scene of a great many of Their Majesties' days, and of their nights too. At times, through shattered streets strewn with brick debris and firemen's hoses, they travelled about the city even during 'alerts' and raids, and their frequent visits were not only to newly wrecked roads but to communal air-raid shelters, sandbagged and subterranean.

They went down also to a number of the deep Tube stations of the London Underground railway system where thousands of citizens took refuge every night, sleeping on the platforms with the trains roaring by their mattresses. An extraordinary community night life sprouted in those London Tubes. For many people, a few feet of blanket-covered platform was their home as they lay or sat, crowded – almost cosily, they began to feel – with scores of others on those underground platforms night after night. Vacuum-flask cocoa, sandwiches and buns were enjoyed; card parties, singsongs and impromptu concerts were bedtime preludes. Underground life even had its discernible social patterns. Far below the streets, there developed a touch of class-distinction and snobbery. The people who 'lived' at Oxford Circus and Piccadilly felt themselves superior to the Tube-dwellers of the stations of the East End.

But the spirits of both up-town and down-town were for much of the time astonishingly perky. It was the same all over the country, even amongst numbers of people who had lost their homes and were camping out with relatives or in community shelters and furnished bunkers. Laughter – laughter through the tragedies and the tears – was sustained as a point of honour.

The standards and the humour of the times found expression in the radio output of the BBC, which experienced its own 'finest hours' during the war years when the Corporation was both unrivalled entertainer and upholder of morale with its uncom-promisingly honest and truthful News Bulletins (given in clear, well-spoken English, civilised, grammatical and immediately understood – unlike the sloppy journalese, the windy American-isms and gross mispronunciations which have slouched in during more recent years). Everyone tuned in to the radio variety shows, 'Band Waggon' and 'ITMA' especially. With those programmes, making fun of Hitler and the traitor German broadcaster called Lord Haw-Haw was relief and ritual. Hearing and imitating the funny phrases of the fictitious Fünf the Spy and other grotesques was a national pastime. Arthur Askey 'on the air' became as well known as Winston Churchill. Tommy Handley's matchless frivolity and the catchphrases of the characters in his weekly show were essential listening from Wapping to Windsor Castle. The King and Queen were such devotees of the programme that the whole cast went by invitation to Windsor and did a special show which was broadcast from the Castle itself on Princess Elizabeth's sixteenth birthday in 1942.

We used to say that if the war were to end between 8.30 and 9 on a Thursday evening nobody would dare to tell the King until 'ITMA' was over.

Sovereign's Guard

But the Germans did not joke. Not noticeably. Their wartime radio was almost entirely devoted to doctored news and drummed propaganda. No funny business. No 'ITMA'.

In Britain, on the other hand, it was characteristic – of the Royal Family as well as everybody else – that grave purpose should frequently wear for a few minutes a mask of levity, token of the country's defiance and resolve. It was not to gainsay the grimness of the situation, which in all conscience was terrifying in the early years of the war. The threat to Britain's whole existence was real and near, and we were braced for instant invasion, a people on stand-by.

The emergency was such that precautions had to be made for the security of the Sovereign and the Royal Family. From Intelligence sources it was known that one of Hitler's plans in 1940 envisaged the capture of the King and Queen, possibly by a strong force of airborne storm-troopers dropped by parachute, in order to hold them hostage for the subservience of their people once the English south-east coastal regions had been invaded and subdued.

His own army's schemes to whisk him away if invasion came aroused no enthusiasm in King George. He was not going to run away, and anyone connected with the Family knew that. Though they were neither imprudent nor reckless, the King and Queen were never happy to be 'fussed over' by soldiers or civil servants anxious to safeguard them from the hazards which hostilities had brought. They were not 'dugout-minded' and were never known to run for shelter when the sirens wailed and the bombs fell. They disliked, in wartime just as much as in peacetime, moving about in anything that looked like a ring of steel. They were sensible enough to co-operate with the security experts, but their desire was that a low profile should be kept – not by themselves but by the people who

LEFT *Tommy Handley (right) at the microphone with Clarence Wright during a broadcast of 'ITMA' in 1942. It was one of the King's favourite wartime programmes and the whole cast was invited to do a special show at Windsor Castle to celebrate Princess Elizabeth's sixteenth birthday in that year.*

OPPOSITE *When the Sovereign visits Scotland the ceremonial bodyguard is the Royal Company of Archers, whose Captain General of 1953 is here presenting Elizabeth II with an arrow-shaped brooch during her Coronation visit to the Palace of Holyroodhouse.*

were looking after them. They themselves, as we have seen, 'stayed put' with their people through all the risks and raids; and the anxiety of the Government for their lives had to be sharpened into practical but secret designs for their safety in Britain in all foreseeable eventualities.

There is a security net round royal persons even in peacetime, unobtrusive though it normally is. The Royal Family has always been, always is, guarded. Naturally, little is disclosed on the subject, but it has a fascinating history; and it is perhaps not malapropos at this point in our story to take stock of Royal Guards. Some of these guards are very much on view in peacetime, for there exist a number of remarkable *ceremonial* guardians, who are splendidly noticeable on great occasions – and who of course are in contrast to the essential guards, the ever-vigilant and self-effacing protectors, whose aim is *not* to be noticed.

King George VI and Queen Elizabeth – whatever soldiery might be near them in wartime – always had, war or peace, a police officer in plain clothes who travelled with them everywhere, just as today the Queen and the Duke of Edinburgh have each a police officer of senior rank specially assigned to them. In the same way, Queen Elizabeth (the Queen Mother as she now is), the Prince of Wales, Princess Anne, Princess Margaret, the Duke and Duchess of Gloucester, the Duke and Duchess of Kent and Princess Alexandra each have a police officer. These men are popularly called 'the detectives'. The Queen's Police Officer – and it is a very special position demanding much responsibility and the closest attendance – is in fact from the Metropolitan Force. So are the guardians permanently attached to the entourages of the other members of the Royal Family.

So much for the professionally subfusc. The ceremonial guards are the antithesis of them. In normal times, when the country is not at war, there enter the royal picture those Guardians of the Sovereign who, far from secret, are a glad and glittering decoration of traditional occasions, part of the panoply of State, features of our national pageantry, highly decorative personal troops. Defenders nonetheless.

First, the Household Troops, the Household Cavalry and the Foot Guards, fighting men, but also charged with carrying out

formal duties of attendance in full fig – which is when their plumes and breastplates are the targets of a million tourists' cameras. The mounted soldiers are the Life Guards and the Blues and Royals; the foot soldiers, in scarlet tunics and tall black bearskin caps, are the Grenadier, Coldstream, Scots, Irish and Welsh Guards. They are regular fighting soldiers, but units of them parade in full dress uniform on State occasions and when on guard duty at the palaces.

Then there are the other military bodies whose members are *former* serving officers and men, and who when on duty come even more strikingly into the public eye. These are the Yeomen of the Guard, the Gentlemen-at-Arms, and the Royal Company of Archers.

The Gentlemen are an Honourable Corps who, by royal decree, are 'The Nearest Guard', nearest to the person of the Sovereign on the most important occasions. They number some thirty only, and membership is an honour. The officers of the Guard are made members of the Royal Household. Each Gentleman has reached senior rank in the Army or Royal Marines (colonels are the least of them). The full title of this select band is Her Majesty's Body Guard of the Honourable Corps of Gentlemen-at-Arms. They were founded, possibly out of jealousy of the French King's bodyguard, by that lover of military splendour, Henry VIII, in 1509, a band of young gentlemen of noble families whose privilege it was to attend the King in battle and serve him at Court. Henry would have approved of the Corps's present-day dress. With their tailed coatees of scarlet and sashes of gold, helmets of burnished gilt adorned with long plumes of swan's feathers, their swords and their spurs, they look like dragoons of the 1840s, except for the long decorative poleaxe which each Gentleman carries. Life-size toy soldiers of the most magnificent kind, they seem, and a majestic sight on any day. A pageant in themselves.

More ancient in history, however, more numerous and more unusually resplendent, more sought by the visitors who focus their camera lenses on traditional London, are the Yeomen, the senior Guard. They are the men who will proudly tell you: 'We are the oldest military corps in the world, and the only time we go anywhere it is with the Queen.' Together they rejoice in the sonorous title of 'The Queen's Bodyguard of Yeomen of the Guard' (not to be

confused with the Yeomen Warders who are custodians of the Tower of London and whose Tudor-style uniforms are similar to the Yeomen Bodyguards' though lacking the distinctive shoulder-strap which was originally an arquebus support). Henry VII founded the Yeomen of the Guard in 1485, when there was no regular army. He, when he was Henry Tudor, Earl of Richmond, who through the House of Lancaster was claimant to the Throne, had a band of faithful followers round him when he came over from Brittany to fight and defeat Richard III at the battle of Bosworth Field. King Richard wore his crown at that fight, and when he was killed it rolled into a hawthorn bush. One of that first Tudor's 'private guard' retrieved it and, when it was there and then placed on the head of his victorious master, Henry was hailed as King Henry VII of England. Three weeks later the new monarch formally instituted his faithful friends who had fought at his side at Bosworth Field as the Bodyguard of Yeomen.

To this day, the uniform of the Yeomen is a reminder that they were established almost five hundred years ago: long-skirted doublets of scarlet and gold, scarlet knee breeches and hose, hard low-crowned hats of blue velvet, with red, white and blue flowers and rosettes on head, garters and shoe buckles. The Yeomen carry eight-foot-long spears called partisans. The half-dozen officers of this Guard, however – and these are distinguished Army officers – dress in plumed helmets and military tailcoats as in the year of Waterloo.

Sir Walter Raleigh was one of the early Captains of the Yeomen. Half a century after his time, the Guard soldiered abroad, for they went into exile with Charles II. The last occasion on which the Yeomen actually fought in the field was at Dettingen under George II in 1743; and the last time they saved a monarch's life was in 1800 when a shot was fired at George III as he entered the royal box at Drury Lane Theatre. A Yeoman caught the would-be assassin before he could fire a second shot.

Four of the Yeomen of the Guard rejoice in the title of Yeoman Bed-goer. The name – not the duty! – has been retained from Tudor days when a Bed-goer used to bounce up and down each evening on the King's bed to make sure that no poisoned dagger, point uppermost, was hidden there.

Today the Yeomen number eighty. Their establishment is kept at that mark, and there is a long waiting-list for the honour of serving in what is essentially a very proud brotherhood. Candidates have to wait for six or seven years before vacancies in the ranks bring their turn to be considered for membership of the Guard. The recruiting nowadays is only from fighting-fit ex-war service men who have completed at least twenty-one years in the Army or the Royal Marines or the Royal Air Force and have attained the rank of warrant officer or sergeant. They must possess an unblemished record.

Neither the Gentlemen-at-Arms nor the Yeomen of the Guard form the ceremonial escort when the Sovereign goes north of the Border, however. In Scotland, in particular at the Palace of Holyroodhouse in Edinburgh, the attendants are the Royal Company of Archers, the official royal Bodyguard in the Northern Realm. The Archers are a society whose membership is a much sought-after privilege. Many famous names and ancient titles in the nobility are on the roll of this large and élite Guard. Prominent professional and business men and gentlemen who have distinguished themselves in the Forces are also in these ranks.

The Archers have a history going back to 1676, when a bowmen's club was formed in Edinburgh. Their uniform includes a long tunic of dark green and a Balmoral bonnet decorated with tall eagle feathers. At their side, the Archers carry each a longbow such as was employed so devastatingly by the English archers at Crécy, and each man when on duty has arrows ready in his belt. Though a number of this Royal Company are gentlemen of mature years – and perhaps when standing on parade for a long time are glad of the longbow as surreptitious support! – many Archers are men in their prime, formidable practising toxophiles who, in ordained competitions, regularly shoot with both power and skill. Indeed, in their hands, the modern hickory bow and its goose-feathered arrows are as fearsome as, and undoubtedly more accurate than, the shafts which were discharged from pliant yews in the wars of the fourteenth century to bring their 'whispering death' to the enemies of the Crown.

So much for the ceremonial protectors – of yesterday and today.

In the year 1940 and throughout all the years of the Second World War no token, picturesque bodyguards were on the scene. The guarding of George VI and his Queen and family was a matter of stern reality and quiet performance, the business of small but special units of men, some of them in Service battledress and some in civilian clothes. They were administered in strict secrecy by Royal Security planners.

As to the Monarch himself, far from making appeals to them to take care of him, King George was evidently more interested in the wartime welfare of the remaining staff at Buckingham Palace than in looking after himself. The air-raid precautions for the staff were perfected long before he paid attention to the constructing of a reinforced gas-proof shelter in his part of the Palace – this in fact was not built until 1941, after the peak of the Blitz. No special treatment was asked for. The rations and the food served to the Queen and himself were the same as those of the servants, and in several ways the King set examples of economy and frugal life. The rooms of Household officials had more electric lights burning, behind the blackout shutters, than ever the royal apartments had; their bathwater levels were probably more generous than the Sovereign's. Scarlet liveries of pages and footmen were carefully put away, and throughout the war staff wore a plain dark-blue battledress of a neat style personally designed by the King, who was an essentially practical man and always interested in matters of dress, civil or military.

Austerity reigned also at Windsor, where the Castle was once more a fortress as well as a residence as it had been after William the Conqueror founded it nine centuries before. The massive stone walls presented an aspect of reassuring security; and, against the bombs, there was built below ground a strongroom, well equipped with bunks, washroom, chairs, plenty of reading matter and boxes of card-table games. Princess Elizabeth and Princess Margaret and their governess repaired to this refuge once or twice during particularly heavy night raids. Windsor was an armed camp. Troops, police, Civil Defence wardens and the Windsor Home Guard formed a watchful and knowledgeable ring of protectors. The royal Librarian of the Castle, the distinguished Sir Owen Morshead, who had served gallantly in the First World War, was now the Officer Commanding the 9th Berkshire Battalion of the Home Guard.

Centred in London, a picked unit of soldiers from Foot Guards regiments and the Household Cavalry had the specific task of protecting Their Majesties. Plans were made ready to evacuate them and others of the Royal Family if invasion really came. Armoured cars stood ready night and day.

The King, though admitting the circumspection of such preparations, said he would not go off in any such vehicle himself except in direst emergency; and in fact he never made armour-plated journeys by road. However, the royal train – much used and several times in various parts of the country narrowly missed by bombs – did have a bullet-proof boxcar, blacked-out windows and khaki and drab-green camouflage plastered over the carriages' shining paintwork.

On one occasion, during an air raid in London, Queen Elizabeth did travel to an engagement in an armoured car, but only after being persuaded that the choice was either to make the short journey that way or stay at home and disappoint the meeting which was expecting her.

There had to be certain exercises for if the worst came. Mock emergencies involving cars and trains were staged in 1940, and aircraft flights were rehearsed too. The King and Queen and the two Princesses drove more than once in secret to Farnborough in Hampshire to board a black-painted, utility-furnished bomber and make a thirty-minute circuit of the airfield. King George complied with these routines but habitually complained about the exercises. He declared flatly that he had 'no intention of doing a bolt'. If Hitler had succeeded in invading, His Majesty told a questioner later, it was his intention to offer his services 'in any capacity' to the leader of the British Resistance Movement. Meanwhile, from the beginning of the war, he made certain personal defence preparations and, not without relish, joined his equerries, the Queen and others of his family in regular shooting practice with rifles, revolvers and automatic Tommy guns under the expert instructors at ranges in the royal gardens, sometimes at Buckingham Palace and sometimes at Windsor.

So it was with buoyancy and defiance that King George VI traversed the war years. Outwardly, his optimism and confidence did not waver. But he worried constantly about the setbacks and the casualties, and the prickly paths of Allied co-operation. Memoranda flowed from his desk as he studied the minutiae of munitions and supplies, Atlantic convoy planning, tank turret problems and slowness of aircraft production. Fears and sorrows, as well as experienced counsel, studded the letters to his Ministers. Privately, as his diary showed, he went through periods of deep anxiety and days which brought black depression. Bad news hit him hard.

And bad news of a very personal kind came with sudden shock one night in August 1942 when he was called from dinner to take an urgent personal message from the Secretary of State for Air. It was to tell him that his youngest brother, the Duke of Kent – the good-looking Prince George, a great favourite in the family, whom hostilities had toughened to fine stature – had died in a tragic accident whilst on active service. Airborne from Invergordon, his Sunderland flying boat, *en route* for Iceland for an inspection of RAF establishments, encountered vile weather – low cloud, rain, and storm from the east – and crashed into a mountainside in north-west Scotland. The Duke was killed instantaneously.

This bereavement was a lasting sadness to all the Royal Family. Though comparatively little known to the public until his popular marriage to Princess Marina, Prince George was to those who had savoured his company a charmer and a man of taste, both socially smooth and happily domesticated. The war, which had sent him on tours of duty overseas as an Air Commodore in the RAF, had brought out the steel in him. The Kents were – as the new

generation today are – a close-knit and attractive family, and the nation's sympathy went out to the graceful, talented and cosmopolitan Princess Marina, who was the mother of the present Duke. He, Prince Eddy, the elder son, succeeded to the title at the age of seven on his father's death. Princess Alexandra was a lively five-year-old at the time. Prince Michael of Kent, the second son and youngest of the three children, had been born on 4 July, less than two months before the accident – and, the date being American Independence Day, the baby had been given Franklin as one of his names in salute to President Roosevelt.

It was perhaps a mercy that the children were then too young to comprehend their loss. But the fact was that the Royal House of Windsor was once more in the casualty lists of war and had at its heart one of the countless families made fatherless in the year of 1942.

A Court in Exile

At no one did grief after the Duke of Kent's death strike more cruelly than at his mother, Queen Mary, now seventy-five years old – and an evacuee. The prince who had gone was her youngest surviving son, the one who used to talk with her more entertainingly than the others, who had inherited her passion for collecting works of art, who shared many of her enthusiasms and was best able to make her relax and laugh. She loved George. Only three weeks before the tragedy she had gone over to Windsor for the day to be present at the christening of his infant son Prince Michael. Only three days before, Prince George himself had come to visit *her* in her country retreat.

Not that the Dowager Queen *betrayed* her sorrow, even in the

LEFT *George V had cast a critical eye over Queen Mary's potato-digging efforts at Windsor in 1917. There was more Digging for Victory in another war twenty-five years later.*

OPPOSITE, TOP *Badminton House, Gloucestershire, where Queen Mary spent the war years as the guest of her niece, the Duchess of Beaufort.*

OPPOSITE, BOTTOM *Queen Mary renews her acquaintance with agricultural implements at Badminton in 1940. The Duchess of Beaufort is on the left.*

moments after an abrupt telephone message had told her the news of the fatal crash. As always, her stoicism and self-control was amazing. In the code which ruled her life, emotion was never to be displayed to onlookers. All her thoughts went to the widowed Princess Marina and the children; her immediate action was to drive over to Coppins, their house in the Buckinghamshire village of Iver, to give what comfort she could to the daughter-in-law whom she had liked and helped ever since the time when she had come to Britain to be married. Queen Mary had then, in 1934, spent agreeable hours, in a high-backed chair at Balmoral, explaining to the elegant twenty-eight-year-old Greek princess the duties expected of the *English* Royal Family. In the eight years since then, the bond of appreciation between the older woman and the newcomer had grown to close and affectionate *rapport*.

In 1942, the year the tragedy came, Queen Mary, Londoner of Londoners, for three years had been living what was for her an utterly unaccustomed rural life in the West of England. Badminton House, Gloucestershire, residence of her niece, the Duchess of Beaufort, was her wartime home for six years. The period of royal residence deep in the country was a revelation to her – and she was a revelation to her relatives and friends and neighbours too.

Because of security restrictions which governed press and radio during hostilities, the reporting of the whereabouts and activities of members of the Royal Family was very limited, and therefore the story of those particular years of Queen Mary's is little known. It is a fascinating tale, however, not only because the period was totally different from the rest of her long life but because it brought to the

surface the real character of Her Majesty, the fun and the lively spirits that lay behind those composed features, that stately carriage and unchanging costume which the world had known for decades and had taken to indicate an inflexible and humourless life. It is true that Queen Mary was outwardly stiff and dated, a Victorian lady of old-fashioned dignity and rectitude. But the not-very-human image of her which has been left in many people's minds is a distorted one: that sojourn in the country disclosed something of the other side of the coin. The Palladian mansion of the Beauforts, one of the spacious treasure-houses of England, was not exactly a tumble-down Little Grey Home in the West, but it was there that the old Queen did find 'hands that would welcome her in', contentment and rest, and also education and action such as she had never known before. At Badminton, without shedding for a moment her famous shell, she became another person.

At the outbreak of war Queen Mary, reluctantly but on the advice of her son the King, had left Sandringham and her home at Marlborough House in London and travelled – with a train of sixty-three servants and their dependants, seventy pieces of personal luggage, and loads of furniture – to accept the hospitality in Badminton of her niece and her husband, the tenth Duke of

Beaufort. He himself was absent, having joined his Regiment, the Blues, and it was the Duchess who, with pleasure but also some dismay at the sight of the massive convoy, received the aunt for whom she had always entertained fondness and respect. The Duchess was, before her marriage in 1923, Lady Mary Cambridge, daughter of the first Marquess of Cambridge, Queen Mary's eldest brother, who before those name changes in the First World War had been His Serene Highness Adolphus, Duke of Teck, his sister's favourite 'Prince Dolly'.

The Duchess of Beaufort therefore was a member of the old Royal Family. There was royal blood, too, in the Duke's ancestry and he, Henry Somerset, Knight of the Garter, was even then an eminent sporting nobleman and landowner. Today he is well known to anybody in Britain who has taken interest, if only by way of television and newspaper picture, in equestrian occasions. He held for an unprecedented forty-two years, until he retired from the post in 1978, the historic office of the Sovereign's Master of the Horse, the third of the three 'Great Officers' of the Royal Household. His is a name to conjure with amongst riders. By family and friends he is simply called 'Master' because that has been an affectionate nickname since babyhood, because as titular head he was for so long the master of the Royal Mews and officer in personal horseback attendance on the Queen as she rode out on many important ceremonial occasions, because he is the great landowning master of the estate of Badminton where the horse world's famous competitive Three-Day Event takes place each year, and especially because he has such an unparalleled record as a Master of Hounds,

lord of the Beaufort Hunt. He has remained, disregarding injuries and his own years, an inveterate and apparently indestructible foxhunter, a natural and enthusiastic horseman who, had Surtees not invented the sentiment for Mr Jorrocks, might well have vowed that 'all time is lost wot is not spent in 'unting'.

There was no hunting for His Grace during the war, and he was away from Badminton House for much of the Royal Dowager's residence there. At the times when he was able to go to his ancestral home he found it specially guarded by soldiers. For Britain's Queen Mother had made Gloucestershire her kingdom for the duration and was firmly established in command of the great house (which was, however, considerably less great then as regards the number of its inhabitants and visitors: the State rooms were all shut up and so were the huge bedrooms, banishing the memories they used to conjure of a very different era during which, in 1905 for instance, the ninth Duke entertained six thousand guests and their servants). Queen Mary's take-over of the relatively small part of the house which was in wartime use presented no problem. The Duchess of Beaufort, who in any case was never a person to be bullied, was happy and honoured that her aunt should have Badminton as her home, glad that the Queen should be playing a major part in the house's domestic activities. Her Grace, indeed, now had little time for what in normal years were the niceties of ordering menus, organising guests and the social and culinary details of gracious living. She was too busy outside with other things. If the Queen ruled the roost, the Duchess ruled the cowshed. The cowmen, like most of the men on the estate, had been called up, and the Duchess

OPPOSITE *General Eisenhower expounds a theory to the King during His Majesty's visit to Supreme Headquarters in October 1944.*

RIGHT *Having reached the age of eighteen, Princess Elizabeth was allowed by her parents to join the ATS, where she became a junior officer in a transport section. Here, in 1945, she tackles the intricacies of changing a wheel.*

ABOVE *A family-album picture from 21 April 1944 – Princess Elizabeth's eighteenth birthday. The King was seldom out of uniform during the war.*

took over byre and dairy herself. Seven days a week, she was up at 5 a.m. and off to milk every cow. Each evening too Her Grace was the milkmaid, and sometimes at night she was called out to assist at a calving.

Her royal aunt lived in some of the most agreeable rooms of the house. She took over a large first-floor bedroom, which was handsomely equipped with a huge four-poster and had an adjoining private bathroom and sitting room. She often received guests in the large former dining room downstairs, and dined with the Beauforts in homely fashion in the impressive and historic Oak Room which is lined from floor to ceiling with heavy black Jacobean panelling.

At first, Queen Mary was inclined to be restless and ill at ease at being away from London and isolated in the rustic West. It was all very strange to her. She was, after all, in her nature and experience and interests, essentially a town person, and remarkably innocent of country life. Being a little bothered by flying insects in her bedroom one night, and deciding that the flies were coming in from 'the tiresome tree outside my windows, which also spoils the view over the park', she calmly asked her niece if she would see to having the tree cut down. Whereupon she had to be gently dissuaded from any such impiety as the destruction of a magnificent centuries-old cedar!

On one of her first excursions round the estate and its farmlands she confessed that she had never actually seen hay before, remarking: 'So *that's* what it looks like!' She had no idea that fields of wheat and barley were different in appearance. Conversation about crops and livestock was double-dutch to her. But she learned; and she worked. She was a briskly adaptable woman when faced with a new situation, and in any case idleness was sheer immorality in her eyes. She had to be busy, and she was determined to play some part in the war effort, however much of a small gesture it might be, whilst 'down on the farm'.

And she turned – though not with cedars as victims – to the axe and the saw. Discovering that it was in the national interest to keep the land in trim, and that almost all the Badminton foresters and gardeners had vanished into the Forces, leaving tracts of trees and coppices neglected and overgrown, she organised and led daily posses to blitz the trees. These became famous locally as Her Majesty's 'Wooding Squads' – her own name. Their object was lopping and pruning, stacking and clearing, cleaning up and clearing out the woods and thickets, and preparing plantations. She became what her entourage termed 'exhaustingly keen' on this novel exercise which, saw in hand, she set about with great cheer and chatter, roping into her teams every available human being around her – equerry, private secretary, lady-in-waiting, chauffeur, footman, visitors, detective and duty dispatch riders.

With these press-ganged amateurs she would slash for hours in overgrown areas of ducal acres, allowing only short breaks in each shift (during which she would hand round cigarettes and smoke one herself).

No twisted sapling or gnarled branch was safe from septuagenarian attack. Ivy was a target of special enmity as Her Majesty and her squads hacked away day after day. She was now embracing rural life with evident enthusiasm. Parasol, petit point and porcelain were, for the time being, giving way as interests to a new dedication to the Great Outdoors, though in appearance and style of dress there was no essential change in the Queen: she wore her high-collared coats, ankle-length skirts and the famous toques even whilst wielding handsaw and chopper.

Anxious to save rationed petrol, she would sometimes ride to the more remote plantations in a horse-drawn farm cart in which she sat in a basketwork armchair. When her niece remarked that it looked as though she were in a tumbril, the new fresh-air-and-forestry 'Aunt May' replied with a laughing 'It may come to that yet!'

Queen Mary was also an avid collector of salvage, concentrating

on old bottles and tins and scrap metal for the 'Saucepans into Spitfires' campaign. There were no metal railings at Badminton to be uprooted but she formed a habit of gathering up and bringing back to the house any items of 'old iron' which she came across when marching round the fields. Sometimes she was carried away by a combination of collecting mania and ignorance of farm habits: she had not learned that some agricultural implements are left out in all weathers, and therefore her activities as patriotic rag-and-bone man had whimsical sequels. Badminton's back door would sometimes be opened of an evening to disclose a farmer asking for his field-harrow back!

But there was no acrimony. The estate tenants and the villagers were tickled to have a Queen in their midst; and in her excursions she got to know and to like the country people she met. She remembered the children's names, talked to them without shyness, held hands and danced, found out just which ones were having birthdays, leaving school or recovering from whooping cough.

As time went on, she began to make more distant excursions, using her old green Daimler limousine, an unmistakable high and square motor vehicle. Denied visits to London shops and art galleries and theatres, she drove off from time to time to shop in Bristol, visit the BBC's West Regional studios, and discover with delight the eighteenth-century architecture of Bath and such of that city's antique dealers as were available for her acquisitive raiding. She toured local industries and camps – and on her journeys along the country roads gave a great deal of attention to what she had found to be the useful and patriotic practice of giving lifts to men and women in uniform. So whenever she saw one or more of her country's defenders tramping along the highway to or from duty the old car would pull up, the door would open, a smiling, straight-backed lady in a swathed hat would incline her head and beckon and, with the car's Court of ladies and gentlemen-in-attendance squeezing up painfully to make room, soldiers, airmen and land girls would crowd in. As they rode, they would be questioned animatedly by the gracious traveller about their Service life and camp conditions. When the hitchhikers got out a little medallion bearing the letters 'M.R.' would be pressed into their hands.

Recipients of such rare souvenirs in their astonishment sometimes were on the point of refusing the token of a royal ride, thinking for a moment that they were being given a piece of money. But realisation of what the object was, and the manner of its bestowal, brought delight. 'Like an investiture', one of them said. Queen Mary might have become informal, but the imperial gesture still came naturally.

Her beckoning smile was commanding. A certain RAF station lived for years on the story of a young aircraftman in uniform who on one damp evening had been waiting for his girl at a country crossroads when an old-fashioned motor car pulled up and swept him in. He was not in fact wanting a lift at all but was so awed by the invitation to step in that he had travelled four miles from his trysting place before he summoned courage to ask to get out. When he had foot-slogged back to his starting-point his irate young woman, a WAAF corporal, was in no mood to regard a royal medallion as entirely suitable compensation for an hour's wait in the rain.

In Badminton House no doubts were possible as to who was in charge, but Her Majesty's reign there was cosy rather than grandiose. She accepted and soon liked and joined in the country-house talk of horses and crops; she became accustomed to such habits as imprecise time-keeping, relaxed manners and (by others) casual clothes-wearing. Although for most of her life she had discouraged house dogs, she now seemed to enjoy having families of small animals under her feet when she was downstairs with her hosts and visitors. But in any situation she was, without any effort at all, a redoubtable and compelling figure; and her word was law. One day an ageing bishop, invited to lunch and placed at table next to the Queen, attracted the hopeful attention of one of the Duchess's

OPPOSITE *On his return from a visit to the Italian battlefields in August 1944, His Majesty received the War Cabinet at Buckingham Palace. Mr Churchill and Mr Attlee are on either side of the King. Future Prime Minister Anthony Eden is next to Mr Churchill.*

RIGHT *The King photographed with his Prime Minister, Winston Churchill, on VE Day, 1945. The deep and warm friendship which had developed between them during the war years was to last for the rest of the King's life.*

small dogs which sat up patiently begging beside his chair during the meal. His Lordship ignored the pet, but Her Majesty handed to him a tough and discarded piece of meat from her plate, saying 'Give it to the little chap'. The bishop, who was deaf, took the meat, looked at Queen Mary's face, popped the scrap into his own mouth and chewed valiantly. He imagined that the Royal Personage had given him an order. Her Majesty was amused.

Royal decrees ran the house. The Queen made it her business to see that no food was wasted in the kitchen, that individual ration scales were strictly adhered to, and that nobody ate too much butter. She was herself naturally frugal. By long habit, she would unknot parcel string, save buttons from old garments, thriftily re-cork a wine bottle if there were a couple of inches of liquid left.

Contrary to general belief, in the right environment she could and did laugh a great deal and a sense of fun was never far from the surface. In her country retreat of those war years the ambience was right for the sunny side of her nature, nourishing an appetite for new experience. She twinkled, she 'unwound', she would tell diverting and sometimes irreverent stories. She got on well with the soldiers who guarded her – a hundred men of the Gloucesters were billeted in the Badminton stables and they became familiar friends. The Queen used to wear one of their regimental cap badges in her hat. She sat with the troops at the concerts and film shows which were

put on in the house's front hall (the place where the battledore-and-shuttlecock game got its name, for it was in that hall that it was first played in England). Though rather scared at first, the soldiers became devoted to her. For her part, she encouraged them to pour out frank descriptions of military life in the ranks. It was all part of an opening of new worlds for the widow from Marlborough House.

Work did not end with daytime. During the evenings she continued to be busy, her fine needlework now alternating with rougher sewing and knitting as she helped to provide khaki socks and scarves and balaclava helmets as 'comforts for the boys'. Often too she would spend fastidious hours, whilst a lady-in-waiting read to her, in cataloguing family papers and arranging photographs from frames and albums which she had brought with her to Gloucestershire. She pasted, and herself captioned, hundreds of snapshots in giant leather-bound albums, a library in themselves.

Her Sundays were usually quiet. Each Sunday morning, with best clothes on, and accompanied by her niece and any visitors and members of the household, she would attend morning service at Badminton's eighteenth-century parish church. This was no distant or uncomfortable exercise, for the church is part of the ancestral home, being attached to a wing of the house. So all the little royal party had to do was to walk along a passage and through a series of rooms, arriving straight into the church and the Beaufort family

pew. They used to call this pew 'The Tribune' – and no wonder, for it is no ordinary pew. It hangs over the back of the church like a box in a theatre and its occupants are mostly out of congregational sight. Within the 'pew' the scene is not unlike a comfortable living room, complete with its own fireplace and a sofa.

During the cold winter Sundays of Queen Mary's stay at Badminton a log fire blazed in the Tribune. With her back to it, Her Majesty would sit in the middle of the pew in an armchair, as though enthroned – but during prayers unfailingly knelt on a ledge of hardest wood.

Life was not peaceful existence all the time, however. The war came to Badminton when the Luftwaffe raided nearby Bristol and the big Admiralty establishment at Bath. Bombs were dropped on Badminton village, near the Big House, and in the surrounding flat parkland on which large poles had been erected to prevent enemy planes from landing.

Often, in the years of air raids, the Queen would stay upstairs in her private rooms and ignore the night alarms, but during some of the severest blitzes of 1940, when nights were very noisy and the windows shaking, she would descend and join the others in one of Badminton's handsome ground-floor rooms which had been specially reinforced in order to be used as a shelter. Even then there was nothing *déshabillé* about her. One recollection from those times is of the Duchess of Beaufort arriving at about 3 a.m. in the refuge, 'half asleep and wrapped in a torn old dressing-gown', to find Queen Mary sitting 'quite composed but rather cross, bolt upright in her chair, immaculately dressed in pale grey, hair carefully done with the usual well-arranged curls at the forehead, wearing diamonds and huge sapphires, and those ropes of magnificent pearls round her neck'. Another memory from a similar disturbed night leaves a picture of the same fully dressed, unperturbed but angry lady pausing occasionally to look up from her crossword as a loud explosion shook the air – in order to call Hitler a number of very unparliamentary names in German.

In English, in a letter about that time, Queen Mary wrote of the arch-enemy as 'that vile, that hateful fiend'. She added: 'I've never liked the Germans, but never realised I could really *hate* them.'

Life in the country took Her Majesty into the most 'different' world of her life, out beyond the walls of royal routine and protocol. She was able to see and to know something of the everyday ways of ordinary people. As the war years went on she became very settled and very much part of the Badminton village and vast estate, almost inordinately fond of the life there, especially when, in the later years, she was able to receive at the house some of her own kin. The many visits which members of the Royal Family paid were joy days, and it was a particular pleasure when the grandchildren came: the

ABOVE *Princess Elizabeth in her sitting room at Buckingham Palace in 1946.*

LEFT *Princess Elizabeth shares a joke with her father in the grounds of Royal Lodge, Windsor.*

OPPOSITE *The Duke and Duchess of Gloucester photographed at York House, St James's Palace, then their London residence. With them are their two children, Prince William (who was to die in an air crash in 1972) and Prince Richard (the present Duke). The children were seven and four at the time.*

LEFT *Young Philip Mountbatten (left) in costume for his part in Shakespeare's* Macbeth, *a production mounted in August 1935 at Gordonstoun, the Scottish school to which his sons were later to follow him.*

OPPOSITE, TOP *An historic meeting. Thirteen-year-old Princess Elizabeth visits Dartmouth College with her parents and sister on 22 July 1939 and is photographed for probably the first time with the young naval cadet destined to become her husband. Standing next to the uniformed Philip is his uncle and mentor, Lord Mountbatten. (See story on pages 104–5.)*

OPPOSITE, BOTTOM *Princess Elizabeth's engagement was announced on 9 July 1947 and Lieutenant Mountbatten was soon swept into the round of royal duties, making appearances at several Buckingham Palace garden parties with his fiancée and her family.*

Gloucesters and Kents (a young Princess Alexandra was often staying) and above all the two Princesses from Windsor. When Princess Elizabeth went over to see Grannie in 1944 she had become a young woman in uniform, proud that on reaching the age of eighteen she had been allowed by her parents to join the ATS, the Auxiliary Territorial Service, in which she became a junior officer in a transport section. After taking a special training course, she was passed as qualified 'to drive and maintain all classes of military vehicles'.

When peace came at last to Europe with the Allied victory in 1945 it soon brought to the old Queen the time to which in theory she had been looking forward for six years: the day of return to London and her Marlborough House home (where bomb and blast damage had been temporarily repaired). But in fact when the day arrived, leaving the West Country was a wrench, and there were tears in Her Majesty's eyes as she said good-bye to her own Cotswold scene. She told one of the Duke's estate staff: 'Here, I've been anybody to everybody. Back in London, I must now begin to be Queen Mary all over again.'

Joys and Sorrows

Back then to the post-war world.

Life in patched-up London in the early years of the peace was austere and uneasy. The fruits of victory were tasting a morsel sour. It was the same in all the battered towns. Food shortages, strict rationing, economic crises – they would not go away, and were all the harder to bear now that there were no compelling bombs, no whipcracks of war as excuses and stimulants. A sense of unreality and anticlimax pervaded Britain. It was a mercy of course that the killing had stopped, but we just were not used to peace, and it was difficult to relax and rejoice. We had time now to look round and see all the squalor and ugliness we had been too busy to take in. It was almost a let-down.

The Royal Family felt the same reaction as almost everybody else. For King George VI it was hardly a Brave New World: battles for survival remained, new ones and under a New Order: no working with Churchill and Roosevelt now, but a Labour Government and Mr Attlee's welfare state, a President Truman and the atomic age.

ABOVE *One of the official photographs taken outside Buckingham Palace to mark the engagement of Princess Elizabeth to 'Lieutenant Philip Mountbatten, RN'.*

OPPOSITE *After their wedding in Westminster Abbey on 20 November 1947 Princess Elizabeth and the Duke of Edinburgh acknowledge the cheers of the crowds from the balcony of Buckingham Palace.*

True, the easing of pressure was a blessing for the King. The cease-fires of 1945 brought to a spirit always conscientious and a body never robust a great wave of relief and thankfulness. He had almost worn himself out in the performance of duties which the Abdication and then the war had thrust upon him. He had, within a decade, become a wise and experienced Head of State, and elder statesman to Ministers; and he and Queen Elizabeth in unfaltering partnership had attracted a nation's deep loyalty and high regard. Yet, as Her Majesty especially knew, the war had been for the King a six years of Calvary. He was mentally jaded and physically frail.

However, the day-to-day strain was gone, and the family were able to be together again. Restorative happiness gradually came back with the reunions at Windsor and Sandringham and Balmoral.

What was more, romance was in the air. Princess Elizabeth and that tall Prince Philip of Greece, who after a prize-winning cadetship had become a naval officer and had served with distinction during the war in the Mediterranean and the Far East, had 'kept in touch' since the meeting at Dartmouth College in 1939. Letters and photographs had been exchanged. Occasionally they had seen each other when the Royal Navy allowed the young man a spell of home leave, which whenever possible he spent at

Windsor. For England was home. He was still a Greek prince by name but there was in fact no Greek blood in him, though several European national strains were in his ancestry. He was the youngest child of that Prince Andrew who was nominally of Greece but in fact of Danish descent. His mother was Princess Alice of Battenberg, a great-grandchild of Queen Victoria and a sister of Louis Mountbatten. Most of his schooling and his upbringing had been in Great Britain, and in looks and manners and speech he was very much the confident, clipped-voiced, sporting public-school Englishman. He had renounced all rights to the Greek throne, and his care and training since the very early years had been in the hands of the English branch of his mother's family. At first, his guide and guardian was the second Lord Milford Haven. After that, Philip's great formative influence was the Battenberg-Milford Haven *younger* brother, the famous uncle, Lord Louis Mountbatten, who in 1947 was made Earl Mountbatten of Burma. This was the Royal Family's 'Uncle Dickie', the man who after years of brilliant leadership in war and peace was shockingly to meet his death by murdering terrorists' bomb in Ireland in the summer of 1979.

In 1946 his nephew Philip, a dashing twenty-five-year-old Lieutenant Mountbatten – who had taken his mother's family name on receiving British nationality – was visiting Buckingham Palace

frequently and spending all the time he possibly could with the Sovereign's elder daughter. The attraction was mutual: Elizabeth and Philip were in love. For the Princess there was no one else, and it had been so ever since that first meeting of a girl of thirteen and a young cadet of eighteen at Dartmouth.

An engagement might have been announced during the Christmas holidays at the end of 1946, but the King and Queen were about to go on an extensive full-scale tour through South Africa and Southern Rhodesia. This was scheduled for early in 1947, and they were taking the two Princesses with them. Their Majesties persuaded Elizabeth that no announcement should be made until the tour had been completed. It would be Her Royal Highness's first official visit overseas, and that suggested the wisdom of postponement; but in the minds of the King and Queen, anxious for their daughter's happiness, a more precise reason for deferring was the thought that four months of separation would give the

young couple a pause in which they could be fully sure of their feelings towards one another.

During the South African tour – which, though fatiguing, was much enjoyed by the King – Princess Elizabeth, Heir to the Throne, celebrated her twenty-first birthday, on which she made a world broadcast dedicating herself to the service of the Common-wealth.

Neither Elizabeth nor Philip relished the months they had to spend apart; and on the return of the Royal Family to London they were 'quite sure' about their love. A betrothal was soon announced, and they were married in Westminster Abbey on 20 November 1947. Lieutenant Mountbatten, RN, was twenty-six years old and no longer a foreign prince, for he had relinquished his Greek title and become a British citizen in February. But on the day before the wedding the bride's father created him Duke of Edinburgh, with authority to use the prefix 'His Royal Highness'. So from then

onwards he was really a British prince, though the titular dignity was not granted for another ten years.

The wedding and its pageantry received a popular welcome, not only because of the romantic appeal of the union of the King's daughter and her Viking sailor (who in the Abbey wore the sword of his Battenberg grandfather) but also because the occasion brought to the still drab streets of London a splash of the old full-dress splendour of carriages and cavalry escorts such as we had not seen for more than eight chill and khaki years. Brilliance flooded the Abbey too. No such gathering of Royalty had been seen since the Coronation ten years before. Young members of the new generation were in the centre of the stage: two five-year-olds, Prince William of Gloucester and Prince Michael of Kent, in fine white shirt and tartan kilt, bore their cousin's bridal train. Altogether, that wedding day was a glimpse of fairytale in a forlorn world and was felt, by a large number of weary people who watched it, to be a tonic break in the clouds, something wholesome and cheerful, a token of assurance that life would not always be oppressed by clothing coupons and bread queues but would get back to a more joyful normality one day. At any rate, looking at this brave white wedding gave the feeling that we were another step on the road away from bombs and Belsen.

But there was of course the Morning After, the return to the harsh realities of the post-war world – including a vanishing Empire and a squabbling Dominion. India was a headache. The waves of violent nationalism which were sweeping the country under the leadership of Gandhi were not to be assuaged by piecemeal concessions. Independence, a handing-over from British rule to self-government, had been promised, but the deterioration of Hindu–Muslim relations within the subcontinent was making it difficult to find a clear authority to whom power could be transferred. Commissions of inquiry did no good. All sections of Indian opinion were intransigent. It had therefore become imperative that someone of stature should be sent out from Britain with untrammelled authority to break the deadlock and, arbitrarily if necessary, create the form of independence. So in March 1947 the Labour Government had taken the surprising and controversial step of asking, of all people, the King's cousin, Earl Mountbatten, to go out and wind up the British Raj. Mountbatten again – the last Viceroy.

The appointment brought into the centre of world events the talented, much-decorated sailor who had scintillated with the utmost gallantry in the war, holding high commands in the Royal Navy and Combined Operations and finishing up as Supreme Commander in South-East Asia. Lord Mountbatten had known and loved India for a quarter of a century, but he accepted Clement Attlee's offer only after anxious thought and a consultation with King George. On reaching Delhi he soon realised that dismemberment of the country, whatever pain might ensue, was the only way to independence: Partition would have to be forced through. At midnight on 14–15 August power was formally transferred to two new Dominions within the British Commonwealth: predominantly Hindu India and a huge Muslim country now called Pakistan. India's first Prime Minister, Pandit Nehru, asked Mountbatten to be his country's first Governor-General, representing the Crown (Mohammed Ali Jinnah took similar office in Pakistan); and he thus became, after being the last Viceroy, the last symbol in India of Britain's continuing concern for her relinquished Asian Realm. Ironically, he presided over the dismantling of a great country over which his great-grandmother had ruled as Queen Empress.

Partition, some form of which had doubtless been inevitable, was no magic formula for peace. Massacres and great hardships followed it. The Punjab was a battleground. India was still in a state of crisis when Lord Mountbatten and his dauntless wife Edwina (who was tragically to die, of sheer overwork, in Borneo in 1960 when she was Superintendent-in-Chief of the St John Ambulance Brigade) took a quick home leave to attend that wedding of their nephew and Princess Elizabeth. But it was a short break indeed. Even while the young couple were honeymooning at Broadlands, the Mountbattens' home, their uncle and aunt were on their way back to face an India which was a cauldron of communal violence. A long time was to pass before the worst horrors were over. Before that happened, Lord Mountbatten had to hand over the Governor-Generalship to an Indian civilian and leave the country. He came home to a greeting from Mr Attlee but hostility from some people who blamed him for the tragic repercussions which his Independence Operation was bringing.

Making little comment, Louis Mountbatten went back to the Navy. His outstanding abilities soon had him climbing the promotion ladder again, and by 1952 he was Commander-in-Chief Mediterranean and Commander-in-Chief of the North Atlantic Treaty Organization forces – the outstanding naval officer of his generation. Four years later he was promoted to Admiral of the Fleet, and the posts of Chief of the United Kingdom Defence Staff and Chairman of the Chiefs of Staff Committee were to

LEFT *Queen Mary's 83rd-birthday mail, 26 May 1950.*

OPPOSITE *Buckingham Palace, later in 1950. Two queens and a future queen concentrate on a newly christened Princess Anne, Princess Elizabeth's second child, who was born at Clarence House.*

follow. But the crown was his appointment – by Winston Churchill, in one of his last acts as Prime Minister – as First Sea Lord, the supreme position his father had held in the First War. The wheel had turned full circle.

But to return to the early post-war period: In 1948, the year after the royal wedding, the new peace looked precarious as in the month of June the Russians squared up to their so-called allies and made a bid to grab the whole of the city of Berlin, which was deep within that part of Germany over which they gained control when frontiers were drawn after the war. Berlin itself was in four-Power Allied occupation, its western part an exclave of non-Communist West Germany. With flimsiest excuses, the Russians put barriers across all land routes to Berlin and stopped food and fuel supplies to the city's western zone. But by a massive and quite unparalleled airlift the beleaguered city of three million people was kept fed and functioning, the Soviet blockade was broken, and Anglo-American co-operation and efficiency was demonstrated as never before. Day and night for 323 days, until the spring of 1949, British and American aircraft kept that sole and unique lifeline in operation. It was in constant hazard and was a wonder to the world. Every few minutes, all round the clock, planes landed at Tempelhof and Gatow with food and with materials to help rebuild the civilised sectors of the war-devastated capital. Royal Air Force Transport Command alone carried out fifty thousand flights.

The King took particular pride in the determined stand against Stalin's threat which the airlift so powerfully illustrated. The new defence of Europe, and the need for American help in the 'Cold War' which was already beginning, were major preoccupations to him. The powder keg of the Korean war and the strain which that Asian fighting brought to his country's relations with Mr Truman's

United States and to the peace of the world clouded the Sovereign's closing years. He worried unceasingly – more about Europe and the Far East in danger than about the decline of Britain's status from ruler of Empire to regulator of Commonwealth. He was no imperialist; he did not disapprove of bestowing distinct identity and freedom upon colonies remaining within his Family of Nations.

His personal family life, close and affectionate, was, as always, a refuge, a solace and a sustaining joy when he was depressed by a world atmosphere of menace and maelstrom. Anniversaries were observed agreeably. In April 1948 he and the Queen celebrated their Silver Wedding with thanksgiving both private and public. Enthusiastic crowds lined the streets for the drives to and from St Paul's Cathedral where a memorable service was held. Then, in November, came the day when the King and Queen were grandparents: at Buckingham Palace a son, Prince Charles, was born to Princess Elizabeth and Prince Philip, assuring the succession to a second generation (Princess Anne was born two years later at Clarence House, along the Mall, which had become her father and mother's home).

But Princess Elizabeth was not able fully to enjoy a carefree life as wife of a serving naval officer and mother of lively children. She was needed by her parents, and soon she found herself at times having to act on public occasions as Sovereign Surrogate, for the King was not only an emotionally worried man but a tired and ailing one too. Concern over his health clouded the domestic scene. By his wish, the extent of her father's suffering was not told to the Princess during her first pregnancy in 1948, but the fact was that as a new life entered the family the tide of the King's life began to ebb. When Prince Charles was born, his grandfather lay ill under the same roof. The cramp in his right foot about which he had complained was

diagnosed as a dangerous hardening of the arteries, and eventually he had to undergo an operation to improve the blood supply. From then onwards it was necessary for His Majesty to take things gently, to rest often and severely cut down the numbers of official engagements he undertook. Overseas tours were out of the question. The Queen carried out many public duties for him, giving to them the same care and infectious enthusiasm as she brought to the work of nursing a husband infirm in body and impatient to be 'on the mend'. Princess Elizabeth and her husband were also drawn more and more into official work: Her Royal Highness, an apprentice in kingship but an accomplished horsewoman, serenely and very impressively took her first salute on uniformed horseback at the annual Trooping the Colour parade in place of her father in 1949. Later, Prince Philip, who had held ships' commands and seemed set to steer as brilliant a sailor's course as his Mountbatten uncle had done, relinquished active service in the Navy for increasingly active service as a member of the Royal Family.

King George recovered sufficiently to play his part, in the spring of 1951, at the opening of the Festival of Britain, for which a collection of architecturally fantastic buildings was put up on the South Bank of the Thames. The futuristic pylons and pavilions caught the eye, if not the approval, of all who saw them. The connoisseur Queen Mary, nearly 84 now, was taken by wheel-chair to inspect them, and made one comment: 'Simply frightful!' The Festival sought to signal the country's emergence from post-war doldrums, though ostensibly it was organised to mark the centenary of Prince Albert's Great Exhibition, splendidly staged in the Crystal Palace built in Hyde Park in 1851. The King's opinion of the new buildings was similar to his mother's, but he willingly consented to be the official starter of the celebrations. The Festival Committee had asked him if he would perform the ceremony from Tower Hill and then sail up river in the State Barge, but His Majesty spiritedly squashed any such fancies with the retort that the Tower had too many bloody associations and that the old barge was so full of holes that it would sink. He inaugurated the Festival at St Paul's Cathedral.

But illness, with all the dangers of thrombosis, came back soon afterwards; and in the autumn, following more unpleasant treatment and more suffering, he faced with exemplary courage a risky but imperative major operation – his fifth – for the removal of a malignant growth. It meant the removal of the left lung. There was the utmost concern for his life, and the Queen hardly left his bedside for a week. But the operation was successful and, little by little, the King began yet again to improve in body and in spirit. The second of December, 1951, was a day of National Thanksgiving for his recovery.

By then, his daughter and her husband were back from a mission whose manifest success gave him great pride. This was a tour which to an older couple would have been a punishing, unrelenting programme; but the six weeks in North America, across Canada coast to coast twice and into the United States, proved to be an odyssey during which, representing the King and Queen, a vigorous Elizabeth and Philip scored a popular triumph whose impact, even after the scores of big royal tours which have followed in modern times, is still remembered with pleasure and excitement by those who had a hand in it.

The King went down to Sandringham for the customary family Christmas in surprisingly buoyant form, happy that he had come through his illnesses, and relieved that he did not have to make his broadcast on Christmas Day. The royal message went out all the same, for, of necessity, it had been put on records in advance. In the

surgical operation of the previous September, the nerves of the King's larynx suffered and this, together with the increased difficulty with breathing, had accentuated speech hesitations and hoarseness. So the BBC had sent engineers to the Palace earlier in December to record the message, tiny phrase by tiny phrase, in a long series of 'takes', using the King's room as a studio, and afterwards piecing recorded bits together to make a passable whole. It was the first time His Majesty had failed to speak 'live' before the microphone at Christmas. Millions who heard that broadcast were moved alike by the evident courage with which the speaker was battling for life and the choice of words which with simple faith he used as he counted his blessings and gave his thanks.

Early in the New Year, 1952, hope rose again as the doctors expressed satisfaction with the progress of their patient. And meanwhile on the Sandringham estate the King had started again, with a light gun, the shooting which he loved. He was back to his normal high standard of getting on to the bird fast and accurately. His general behaviour was quietly cheerful and confident. He spoke optimistically of the days to come when, with the Queen and Princess Margaret, he went to London Airport on 31 January to wish godspeed to Princess Elizabeth and Prince Philip, who flew off on what was to have been a five months' tour, in his stead, through Australia and New Zealand, by way of East Africa. But he looked pinched and old as, obstinately hatless in the bitter wind of a Heathrow morning, he waved good-bye and stood out on the tarmac for a long time, refusing to leave until his daughter's airliner diminished to a speck and vanished into the leaden sky.

It was a last farewell.

Next day he returned to Sandringham. On 5 February he was out and about in fine sharp weather and enjoyed Keepers' Day, several hours of rough shooting. At dinner he was happy and relaxed, planning the next day's sport. He retired to his bedroom on the ground floor in good time, and at about midnight a watchman in the garden saw him fastening the latch of his window before going to bed. When a valet took in a cup of tea next morning the King did not move. He had died in his sleep in the early hours. He was fifty-six years old.

On that sixth day of February his daughter, the Heir to the Throne, was four thousand miles away. She and Prince Philip had got as far as Kenya, their tour scarcely begun. Nobody will know precisely at what hour she ceased to be Princess and became Queen Elizabeth II, inexorably succeeding her father in the hereditary monarchy and becoming the sixth Queen Regnant in the history of the realm, for the time at which the King's tired heart had stopped beating as he slept in faraway Norfolk could only be guessed. What we do know is that the young Princess became Sovereign Lady whilst up a tree in the middle of Africa – and did not know it until half a day later.

She and Prince Philip had spent most of the night on the balcony of Treetops Hotel, a wooden observation lodge built high up in a giant fig tree in the Aberdare Forest. By artificial moonlight, they watched and photographed big game at the water-hole below. Next morning they returned to the house beside the Sagana stream where they were staying whilst at the game reserve. And not until lunchtime did news get through to that house that the King had died. Elizabeth flew home at once.

One week after leaving London Airport, a princess, she was back on the same spot, reigning Queen at twenty-five.

Britain was in mourning for the brave, quiet King who in war and peace had constantly strained to do the utmost of his duty in the high station he had never sought. He had come to the Throne as a

RIGHT *Accompanied by her grandchildren, William of Gloucester and Michael of Kent, Queen Mary is wheeled round the 1951 Festival of Britain site on London's South Bank. Her verdict on the exhibition's architecture was: 'Simply frightful.'*

hesitant and untrained Duke of York; he had grown in stature to become a recognised leader of the nation, a respected statesman in his own right. No Demosthenes, and yet men held on to his words when he spoke, and followed his example. An irascible man at times, but a loving head of a family whose members knew the great tenderness of him, the enormous sense of infectious fun that he had. Even the outside world was aware that he had become physically fragile, but few people beyond the inner circle knew that his life had hung by a thread for two years. Winston Churchill put it, as only he could, in a broadcast tribute: 'During these last months the King walked with death as if death were a companion, an acquaintance whom he recognised and did not fear. In the end, death came as a friend.'

London, in grief, went into paralysis on the day George VI died. Lights were dimmed, theatres closed, Parliament adjourned, shops took bright-coloured goods from their windows and put in black crepe, newspapers came out with black-edged columns, and the BBC became silent save for occasional bulletins and solemn music.

Most tragically bereft of all, Consort no longer, a widow and Queen Mother now, was Queen Elizabeth who with shining faith and devotion had been at her husband's side in all the days of joys and sorrows for almost three decades.

There was comfort in the glow of memories ... That Sunday morning in the Strathmores' Hertfordshire garden at St Paul's Walden Bury when a shy Prince proposed to her; the early happiness of the marriage; Bertie all laughter when she danced with him; Bertie playing (left-handed) in an all-England lawn tennis championship at Wimbledon; the pair of them, in old clothes caked with soil, making the garden at Royal Lodge, Windsor; the long duty tours of the world when they were beautifully gowned and uniformed; the births of the babies and the romping holidays with them as they grew up; the sharing of grim times too, soldiering on together through the war; walking the Deeside hills at Balmoral when peace had come; and all the different things that had lifted her

husband's heart – being out watching birds on the clean, windswept heaths and marshlands of Sandringham, his birthplace; then home for fireside tea with his own family about him, and a new generation too for him to smile at as he lately had done with special pride – grandparent's pride.

To the bereaved Queen, the cherished memories, and the family's love in her hour of loss, were sustaining. But the fact was that now another was *The Queen*; and, inevitably, not only had a husband gone but a whole world and a pattern of life had collapsed round the elder Queen Elizabeth.

To the much older Dowager, the octogenarian Queen Mary, the death of her son was an almost mortal shock, one from which she never really recovered. When the bleak news came, she seemed – in the eyes of her lady-in-waiting – to have aged even more in a few moments. Nevertheless, true to rule, the straight back did not bend and no tears came. First, the continuity of the Crown had to be acknowledged yet again: within half an hour of her grand-daughter's arrival at her London home from Kenya, Queen Mary was driving out from Marlborough House and along the two hundred yards to Clarence House, where the Royal Standard flew for the first time, to do homage to a new Sovereign. In her own words, 'Her old Grannie and subject must be the first to kiss Her hand.'

Next day, with fanfares, Elizabeth II was proclaimed from St James's Palace. The body of her father lay in State in Westminster Hall before burial at Windsor. At the funeral, four royal Dukes followed the coffin on foot: Edinburgh, Gloucester, Windsor (over from France, briefly), and a sixteen-year-old Edward of Kent. The new Queen and her widowed mother, pallid and poignant and veiled in black, stood beside the bier in St George's Chapel as the body was lowered to the vault and George VI's Lord Chamberlain stepped forward and broke his wand of office to symbolise the ending of his master's days.

The Second Elizabethan Reign had begun.

PART SIX

Elizabeth II – The Royal House

New Reign, New Styles

A SCHOOLBOY of the future, assaying the long perspective of British history, may discover with understandable surprise that in his textbook the same heading covers two outstanding eras, four centuries apart. Each period may carry the docket 'Elizabeth and Philip'. However, the boy would not be puzzled for long. The first label would mean a Tudor queen and her Spanish adversary, the second a Windsor queen and her consort and adjutant – the present reign, in fact.

When the student had absorbed the first Elizabeth and the glittering excitements of the Armada, when he had traversed the four hundred years and reached our own days, he would find that the second chapter title was the more apt – though its story no less tempestuous than the first one. Perhaps, too, it would emerge that the Elizabeth-and-Philip reign was, in its own very different fashion, as great as Gloriana's.

The start of the age of Elizabeth II and her husband, Prince Philip, was a watershed, a Great Divide. This was not of course at any conscious behest of the new Queen; but it could be said that Modern Times as we know them did start when we had once more a Queen Regnant. Arguably, 1952 was New World Year, not only because it was then that royalty, with the circle of the House of Windsor widening, began to move into everyman's orbit, but because the life of the people was in many ways changing its shape and style – not always for the better. Go-as-you-please informality was the noisy keynote. Gone was Britain's dying but decent traditionalism, to be replaced by shambling trendiness. We no longer stood round the piano of an evening, nicely dressed and singing tender patriotic songs; pop-star caterwaulings on disc were sweeping in instead, and the evenings were more likely to be spent slumped in armchairs being stultified by television soap operas. It seemed that there were increasing numbers of people to whom hard work was becoming a dirty word, for a free cushion called Social Security had arrived. We were on the road to government by trade unions and egalitarian excesses. And meanwhile Old Empire was out and New Europe was in. Surprising times.

Society indeed was on the move, and the new Sovereign, herself altering and adapting, was to be not only an emblem of tradition but an instrument of change. When she was so, it was change for the better, streamlining the ways of palace and people.

Not that there was much New World *discernible* at first. There was too much dazzle to see the progress and the pragmatism and the parting of the ways. The new Queen might have been something made of fairytale candy floss to judge by the manner in which she was popularly treated in the early days of the reign. Newspapers were busy presenting to us a storybook monarch. It did not matter that what the nation had acquired, in truth, was a quiet and very diligent young woman, reserved and reflective, notably down to earth and sensible, and innately camera-shy. Though never behaving like one, she was more photographed than a film star.

In short, a gilding limelight of publicity blazed upon her and upon Prince Philip and their family during her first years as Queen. To Fleet Street the picture was irresistible: two great-great-grandchildren of Great Victoria: a young and attractive female Sovereign and a handsome husband buzzing with all sorts of innovation and enterprise and the old Mountbatten flair for leadership – plus two nice young children. Newspaper and magazine columns were awash with euphoria and adulation. Calm appraisal of the new regime was impossible (it would come later) in the surges of saccharin reporting about the 'Golden Age' that had

OPPOSITE *One of the first Royal Tours of the reign, through Nigeria in 1956, began with the splendour of chiefs' welcomes in Lagos.*

RIGHT *In Tonga, on their world tour, the visitors call on Queen Salote and admire the islands' oldest inhabitant, the royal tortoise.*

dawned. 'Romantic Royalty' was a temporary blindfold and emollient for a nation's disillusion and continuing hard times; and the treatment was widely enjoyed. The slightest gestures and chance remarks of Her Majesty and His Royal Highness when they appeared in public were recorded and flashed round the world. The Queen's subjects, it is true to say, appreciated the hoo-ha more than the Queen did. But there was no denying the prevailing mood: anyone who at that time had ventured to criticise Britain's Head of State would have been stoned in the streets.

So the first – and the biggest ever – Royal Tour of the present reign, in 1953 and 1954, was ecstatically 'covered' in length and in detail. This was basically the round-the-globe Commonwealth journey which Her Majesty, as Princess Elizabeth, was about to accomplish when her father died, but now the itinerary was greatly extended and the programme stuffed with engagements beyond counting (the endless, tight-packed schedules strike horror and incredulity in the breasts of tour-planners of the nineteen-eighties). The travellers were away from the United Kingdom for six months and logged fifty thousand miles, visiting Bermuda, Jamaica, Fiji, Tonga, New Zealand (for six weeks), Australia (for two months), Ceylon, Aden, Uganda, Libya, Malta and Gibraltar.

Even the over-lavishly bestowed paeans of reporting, which presented the Queen almost as a sugarplum fairy rather than a real person, could not gainsay the solid success of the journey from start to finish. Triumph was the word. It was the first of innumerable tours and State visits overseas all over the world throughout the ensuing years, and its impact has never been surpassed. It had all the more glamour because it immediately followed the vast pageant of the 1953 Coronation which – all genuflexion and grandees apart – was an event never to be forgotten.

The story of the Crowning on 2 June 1953 has now been told and retold for over a quarter of a century. The weather was cold and wet but two million people were in the processional streets and many had camped on the pavements for two days and nights. In the Abbey, where seven thousand spectacularly robed guests formed a congregation that scintillated in tier upon tier of ornamental galleries reaching from floor to lofty roof, we saw that the whole church had been transformed into a magnificent theatre by the armies of workmen under the supreme direction of the sixteenth Duke of Norfolk, Earl Marshal of England and for many years the impresario-in-chief of State ceremonial. Preparations for the great event by Bernard Norfolk and all his committees and teams had been thorough and long – the Queen had reigned for almost a year and a half before she was crowned.

Excitement on the morning of The Day was heightened by the arrival of news that, for the first time, the peak of Mount Everest in the Himalayas had been climbed and conquered, four days earlier, by a British expedition led by Colonel John Hunt – a superbly timed Coronation salute from the roof of the world.

Memories of the Abbey service – which television brought to millions of people miles away as no occasion had ever been brought before – are indelible to those of us who were present on the spot that day. Above all is memory of how a twenty-seven-year-old Queen went through the three-hour complicated ritual, its form a thousand years old, quite flawlessly, her bearing, to all who saw its indefinable air of faith and dedication, a reminder of standards of duty and conduct which, in the years since 1953, it has become fashionable to deride. Then there was Winston Churchill, a septuagenarian in his

TOP *The Royal Family at Ascot in the late 1950s. With the Queen are the Queen Mother, Princess Margaret, the Duchess of Gloucester, the Dukes of Edinburgh, Gloucester and (far right) Norfolk.*

LEFT AND ABOVE *Two charming photographs of a three-year-old Prince Charles at Clarence House on his birthday. He marches with his own pipe and drum on hearing the band march past the garden.*

LEFT *The Duke and Duchess of Kent with their firstborn, George, Earl of St Andrews – today a tall and talented teenager.*

BELOW *The Queen with (from left to right) Prince Edward, Lady Sarah Armstrong-Jones, Princess Anne and Prince Andrew. A summer-holidays picture from 1970.*

OPPOSITE *During the world tour of 1953–54 the Queen visited Fiji and is here presented with a ceremonial whale's tooth on board the royal Gothic.*

last innings as her Prime Minister, coming into church like a galleon in full sail and almost airborne with pride: he was wearing the dress uniform of Lord Warden of the Cinque Ports and full Garter robes on top of that. As the service unfolded, the soaring sound of trumpets and choirs and the 'Vivat!' shouts of acclamation shook us in our places; but you could have heard a pin drop as the Archbishop held the Crown of St Edward high in the air and slowly lowered it to the youthful brow of 'Your Undoubted Queen'.

And the little human touches. Half way through, I remember, a little boy in cream silk blouse and trousers and with his hair slicked down was popped into the Royal Gallery for a while to see all the things that were going on around his mother. It was the Prince of Wales (he was at that time the four-year-old Charles, Duke of Cornwall) who stood on a stool, his elbows on the gilded balustrade, pointing and gesticulating and shooting questions at his relatives on either side of him – his aunt, Princess Margaret, and his grandmother, Queen Elizabeth The Queen Mother. He was sustained by periodical burrowings into Grannie's handbag for a sweet.

Princess Anne was not yet three and, not without protest, had been left behind at the Palace. She was one of those who looked at the Crowning by means of what was still in those days something of a novelty: a television set. There were seven hours of special pictures-by-radio that day, and the coverage was rivetingly successful. The Coronation was The Day That Television Came of Age. Afterwards, people who had not previously contemplated the marvel of The Box rushed off to buy sets. Mass TV had arrived.

'Viewing' was second best to being there in the Abbey and then out in the streets of course, but at least those who stayed at home did not get wet. It rained for a good deal of the time when the two-mile-long procession of carriages and troops was winding slowly along the decorated six-mile route through the middle of London to get back to Buckingham Palace (arriving six and a half hours after it had left for the service!). There were fourteen thousand troops and thirty bands on the march, a marvellous sight: field marshals on horseback, every kind and nation of private soldier on foot, earls and emirs in carriages – they were all drenched. Boots squelched, plumes drooped, peers' ermine was sopping and smelled like wet weasel. But it did not matter: it was the occasion of a lifetime. To the public purse it cost less than a million pounds, one thirtieth of the price of inaugurating an American President.

During that historic day, and especially on the processional drive after the service, one unusual person is remembered as endearing herself to everybody: Queen Salote of Tonga, all six feet four and nineteen stones of her, sitting bolt upright in an open landau, waving and blowing kisses, beaming fit to burst, scorning umbrella or carriage hood as the London downpour tried, but failed, to extinguish the smile from the Commonwealth kingdom in the islands of the South Pacific.

Sadly, Britain's own Senior Lady of many years was not at the Coronation: she did not quite live to see it. Queen Mary died, at almost eighty-six years of age, ten weeks before, on 24 March 1953. For eight years after the war she had lived her old busy life at Marlborough House in London again; and, one day early in Coronation Year, she had driven out to have a look at the stands being erected along the route that her granddaughter's coach would take. But she had told Buckingham Palace that, should she no longer be alive when the day of Crowning came, the solemn rite and the joyful celebrations must on no account be postponed or pruned. It was a characteristic final gesture: to the end, Queen Mary put service to the British Throne before every other consideration. So

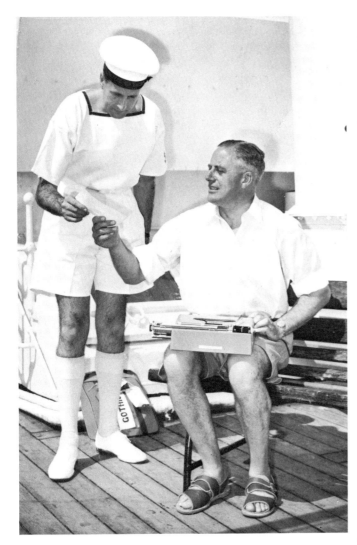

London and the world which had known her for so long had already mourned the steadfast and outwardly unchanging Lady in the Toque. She had finally been recognised and revered as much more than a stiff Victorian person, and had become loved indeed as a spirited figure of the contemporary scene who would mutter 'Tiresome bore, this getting old!' as she accepted assistance in getting out of her car to see – not only an art gallery or antiques display but the latest film or musical comedy. She belonged to the past but was fascinated by the present. Grief and tragedy had been heaped upon her but she never bowed to fell circumstance or clung to the insubstantial shadows of what had been.

Now two British Queens remained, two Elizabeths – the reigning daughter and also the widowed mother, the fifty-two-year-old former Consort to whom the creaking title of 'Dowager' would never be given, such was her enduring radiance. Queen Elizabeth The Queen Mother had become a legend in her long lifetime. Her record in four reigns – as daughter-in-law of George V, sister-in-law of Edward VIII, wife of George VI, and mother of the present Queen – is without compare.

For her, the nineteen-fifties were a Beginning Again. It was not until two months after Queen Mary's death and shortly before the Coronation that she and her daughter, the new Queen Regnant, changed houses, for Buckingham Palace now belonged to the daughter, and the Queen Mother took up residence in Clarence House. By then, she had been back in public life for almost a year after the brief retreat which followed the shock of the King's death.

In the first weeks of her widowhood in 1952 she gave the fullest and fondest support to her daughter, but for a time stepped back so decisively from the light which beat upon the *new* Queen that we wondered whether she might be about to retire into seclusion. Fear that this might be so, and that a vital figure would be lost to the public scene, was increased when it was known that she had bought (for herself and from her own funds) an astonishingly remote house,

OPPOSITE, TOP *The author on board* Gothic *when covering the Royal Tour of 1953–54 for the BBC.*

OPPOSITE, BOTTOM Britannia *(taking over from* Gothic*) is cheered by the crew of the battleship* Vanguard.

RIGHT *An investiture at Enugu, eastern Nigeria.*

a small and dilapidated sixteenth-century castle on the windswept coast of Caithness – the forlorn Castle of Mey near the road to John o' Groats on the most distant coast of the Scottish mainland. Happily, however, Her Majesty had simply fallen in love with the old place and its situation on the wild shores of the Pentland Firth from the first glimpse; she saw it as part of Scotland's artistic heritage in danger, declared that it must be saved from ruin, and became determined to restore it with the utmost care and to live in it whenever she could. Restore it and furnish it she did, over the years, so that today it is a gem preserved and a unique habitation, Queen Elizabeth's own haven beside the sea, the last royal castle.

So the Queen Mother certainly did not retire. She was, in any case, too firmly established in the affections of the British people, too involved in the life of the country and busy and happy to be so, to be allowed to fade into the background. And the Castle of Mey, though she adores being up there and out in the invigorating air, is not a hiding place but a holiday house – for just three or four weeks each year.

Clarence House, which was built by Nash for William IV and adjoins St James's Palace, is Her Majesty's home and headquarters. She – and Princess Margaret then – moved there from Buckingham Palace in 1953. It was, as we have seen, an exchange of dwellings, for the house had been the home of Princess Elizabeth and the Duke of Edinburgh since their marriage. Now, as Sovereign and Consort, new brooms, they began their occupation of the Palace.

As to Queen Elizabeth The Queen Mother, she began her already long 'third life', during which she has become even better known and loved than before, a royal great-grandmother and a national institution. She is, and has been in these last three decades of widowhood, a unique and effervescent adornment of the public scene, extraordinarily active and in demand, presiding patron of three hundred organisations. When people talk about her they call her simply 'The Queen Mum'. The title is a world salute.

When she went into occupation of Clarence House, leaving the Palace, she retained Royal Lodge, Windsor, which remains to this day Her Majesty's week-end country home. It is delightfully set with lovely gardens in a private corner of the Great Park, and is specially dear to its occupant.

In the fifties, Princess Margaret was still living with her mother; and it was about that time that the high-spirited younger daughter began to present problems. She was in her early twenties. She had fallen in love with a very personable courtier named Group Captain Peter Townsend and wished to marry him. He was fifteen years older then her – and was a divorced man. That was the main, though not the only difficulty. It was a near impossibility for a divorced man to be taken in marriage by a sister of the Sovereign who was Head of the Church of England and Defender of the Faith. Townsend was posted abroad but he and the Princess continued their friendship, and Margaret was left to make her own decision. That came in 1955 when she issued a statement that, 'mindful of the Church's teaching that Christian marriage is indissoluble, and conscious of my duty to the Commonwealth', she would not marry the Group Captain.

Less than five years later Her Royal Highness married the noted

OPPOSITE *The Queen's six-month world journey formally ends in London with a procession to Buckingham Palace.*

ABOVE *During the 1956 tour of Nigeria splendidly decorated gigs passed before the Royal Pavilion at Port Harcourt.*

photographer, Antony Armstrong-Jones, later created Earl of Snowdon. They produced two delightful children, Lord Linley, who was born in 1961, and Lady Sarah Armstrong-Jones, born in 1964. But the marriage was dissolved in 1978. At the end of that year Lord Snowdon married again, this time a lady with whom he had often worked on film-making and photographic assignments, Mrs Lucy Lindsay-Hogg, a professional television researcher. She, like Princess Margaret, enjoys the title of Countess of Snowdon.

It was in the year of Princess Margaret's marriage, 1960, that her sister the Queen gave birth to her third child, a second son, Prince Andrew – named after Prince Philip's father and destined to be the tallest and most smilingly extrovert of his generation of royal children. Andrew was born on 19 February 1960; and Prince Edward, the Queen's youngest child, came four years later. There is a space of almost ten years between Her Majesty's two elder children and the two younger ones.

The eldest of the royal children, Prince Charles, the Heir to the Throne, who is now in his thirties, became 'Wales' whilst he was still a small boy at his preparatory school. His mother had chosen 26 July 1958, when she was due to attend the ending of the Commonwealth and Empire Games at Cardiff, for the declaration of her decision to create him the twenty-first Prince of Wales. It was a special day in the Principality's history and was during the year of the Festival of Wales. When the day arrived, however, the Queen was not present at the ceremony, but the news was given by her all

the same. Temporarily indisposed because of sinus trouble, she realised a few days before the closing ceremony that she was not going to be able to make the date. A BBC engineer was called to the Palace where, in her sitting room, she recorded her speech on disc. The recording was taken down to Cardiff, secretly and under guard, and when the announcement was played unheralded to the crowd over the stadium's public address system, the royal voice was received as a happy surprise as the opening sentiments about the Games came through to the ears of a silently listening crowd. But that surprise was nothing compared to the reaction of the people in the famous Arms Park Rugby ground a few minutes later: the whole place exploded with Celtic joy at the words 'I intend to create my son, Charles, Prince of Wales today'.

The boy himself was a hundred miles away. Nine years old, he watched the scene and listened to his mother's voice at a television set in his headmaster's study at Cheam School, on the Hampshire-Berkshire border. Years later, Prince Charles confessed that it was the moment when his 'awful, inexorable fate' really began to dawn upon him. Eleven years were to elapse before *Creation* was succeeded by the *Investiture* of the Prince of Wales at the grand ceremony in Caernarvon Castle on 1 July 1969.

The Queen gave attention to the naming of her whole dynasty, making several pronouncements about it, during the first decade of her reign. Her statements called to memory the historic declarations made by her grandfather King George V in 1917, which not only established a family surname but also regulated the titles of the royal line, confining 'Royal Highness', for instance, to the children of the Sovereign and the children of the Sovereign's sons. What Queen Elizabeth II announced in Council in 1952, first, was her 'will and

pleasure' that she and her children should *continue* to be known as 'The House and Family of Windsor'.

It may be wondered why she found it necessary to say that, for her grandfather had done the naming quite clearly. The nice point is that the Queen had come to the Throne under her old name, Windsor, and yet, like any other woman, she had received her husband's name on marriage – though the additional name she then acquired was Duchess of Edinburgh, not Mountbatten. But she might have been regarded as the last Sovereign of the purely Windsor line and the first of the Family of Mountbatten. So the early declaration of 1952 – perhaps made under both constitutional and public pressure at the time – contained no mention of the husband's name.

But Prince Philip was soon placed well in the picture and in the pedigree, for his position as husband and father, and as First Gentleman of the Realm, was established when the Queen, later in 1952, said by Royal Warrant that he would 'enjoy Place, Pre-eminence and Precedence next to Her Majesty'. Then, in 1960, the Queen was pleased to make a further and fundamental declaration. She had been giving the matter further consideration, she said, and now she varied the earlier words.

The new announcement made clear her wish that, without changing the name of the Royal House established by George V, the name of her husband should be associated with her own and his descendants. It proclaimed unequivocally that such descendants as needed to bear a surname would have 'Mountbatten' in that name. The royal word was that 'While I and my children shall continue to be styled and known as the House and Family of Windsor, my descendants – other than descendants enjoying the style, title or attribute of Royal Highness and the titular dignity of Prince or Princess, and female descendants who marry, and their descendants – shall bear the name of Mountbatten-Windsor'.

All the children of the Queen and the Duke of Edinburgh, three princes and a princess, do have the surname of Mountbatten-Windsor but it is for use only on any particular occasion when there may be a requirement or a wish for it. The name was used for the first time on an official document – by the Queen's explicit decision

– at the wedding of her daughter Princess Anne and Captain Mark Phillips in 1973. The entry in the marriage register is 'Anne Elizabeth Alice Louise Mountbatten-Windsor'.

Perhaps the requited shade of one Prince Louis of Battenberg looked down on that day and bowed to honour done!

Titles, as we have noted, descend in the *male* line. Princess Anne's son is no Royal Highness, but *Master* Peter Phillips, just as Princess Alexandra's children are plain James and Marina Ogilvy (whereas the children of her brother, the Duke of Kent, for instance, are by courtesy titled the Earl of St Andrews, Lady Helen Windsor and Lord Nicholas Windsor).

The naming of one of the newest arrivals, little Lord Frederick Windsor, son of Prince and Princess Michael of Kent (Prince Michael being the younger son of the Kent branch of the Royal Family) raised an interesting echo of 1917 as recently as 1979. In fact the baby at once had a secure place in the history of styles and titles. The style of 'Lord', followed by a Christian name and a surname, is commonly held by the younger son of a duke or marquess – and Prince Michael is *not* a peer. And princely sons of a King or Queen are customarily made Royal Dukes in adult life, and eldest sons succeed to the ducal titles (thus we have the present Dukes of Gloucester and Kent) – but only eldest sons in the next generation assume such titles, not other sons, and therefore not Prince Michael.

This is where Lord Frederick (born on 6 April 1979) made history. He was christened Frederick Michael George David Louis; but the noteworthy point was that he had 'Lord' at the beginning of his style and the surname 'Windsor' at the end – precisely because the great-grandfather of the child had made that foreseeing ordinance of 1917, over sixty years before. Though deliberately planning to restrict the number of princes in future times, George V evidently did not want the Royal Family to plunge too suddenly into mere Misters and Misses, so he laid it down that the third generation through younger sons should take the new family surname he had adopted, and should have rank and precedence as the younger sons of Dukes.

The children of the present Duke of Gloucester and the Duke of Kent are lords and ladies because their fathers were dukes when they

ABOVE *Her Majesty and His Royal Highness at their Highland home,*
Balmoral: a relaxing moment during Silver Jubilee Year, 1977.

OPPOSITE, TOP *At Badminton in 1977, the Queen and Princess Margaret with Lady Sarah Armstrong-Jones, Prince Edward, Lord Linley – and Beaufort hounds.*

OPPOSITE, BOTTOM *Again at Badminton – the Queen with Princess Margaret's children, Lady Sarah Armstrong-Jones and Viscount Linley.*

RIGHT *A recent picture of Prince Charles at Balmoral. His kilt is of Hunting Stewart tartan and once belonged to his grandfather, King George VI.*

ABOVE *The Queen keeps an eye on her two youngest sons – Prince Andrew (with his back to the camera) and Prince Edward.*

OPPOSITE *Prince Philip, with his friend the late Uffa Fox, racing in Coweslip at Cowes in 1968.*

were born. To have 'a handle to their names' they did not need the edict of Great-grandfather. But Lord Freddie did.

So the name of the Royal House goes on. Windsor it remains. And because the Queen's own family is Prince Philip's family too, 'Mountbatten-Windsor' is there also, the surname-in-waiting for any descendants who may have no other style or title and therefore may need it. It will be for generations still distant, and is unlikely to come into use during this century.

Meanwhile, it is pertinent and illuminating to take stock of the *present* House and the wider Royal Kin. For the family has become a large and freshly interesting group of people.

The Royal Kin

Queen Elizabeth II and Prince Philip are still in the prime of their early middle age, but already three of their four children have entered the adult world. Already some of the workload of the Monarchy can be shared with them. It will not be many years before Prince Edward too emerges from the schoolboy stage and will be seen engagingly assisting as well as accompanying his parents on official travels and public duties. Sovereign and Consort are well supported from their own home. And from their kindred.

The fact that the British Queen, though linchpin of our system of government, reigns but does not personally rule is incontrovertible; but it is also true that she is widely regarded as the nation's supreme representative, a leader and an example of leadership. A respected chief of a group of related working people too. There is constant public interest in the Head of State and the Royal House, and one of the reasons for this is that there is 'a family on the Throne'. Whatever republicans may say or do, a situation exists in which millions look up to the Queen and her relatives, not with some sort of blind loyalty to puppets or bloodless symbols of something old fashioned, but to a particular section of the modern human race they can comprehend and like – and on the whole admire. A good family, in fact. Fortunately, an exemplary one in its happiness.

In what is still the classic essay on the Monarchy, *The English Constitution*, the Victorian economist Bagehot wrote in his curt way that a Royal Family 'brings down the pride of sovereignty to the level of petty life.' His point remains pertinent. A Family Monarchy establishes a common denominator, something that other families can identify themselves with in an age when – without any doubt whatever (ask any magazine editor) – royal engagements and marriages and babies, royal dwellings and gardens and the pastimes and public work of those who live in them, are unfailing magnets. A family and a family's homes, especially when they are projected to the public as they are now, form something immediately understandable and appetising.

The Queen is fortunate in having her immediate family near her – an indefatigable husband and their children, her agelessly sparkling mother, and her sister Princess Margaret – and also her many other relations, the wider and expanding family – the royal Gloucesters and Kents, active not only in the limelight of official duty but in less publicised fields of chosen welfare work and in regular jobs that are part of the fabric of the country's life. These royal people are far busier, their lives far fuller, than any previous generations of related satellites orbiting round a Sovereign.

Simply to enumerate the spread of the First Family today is to point to the fact that prolificness did not cease with Victorian times. Tracing modern relationships is not the trek through a European maze that it used to be, but the long journey is attractive. As we make it, and see where members of the Royal Family live, we discover that, apart from Buckingham Palace, there are two 'royal villages' in London, two historic sites and collections of buildings in which are concentrated State Apartments, the homes and offices of royal persons, official dwellings of senior servants of the Crown, and headquarters of departments which are part of the machinery of the Monarchy.

One of these focal points is Kensington Palace, west of Hyde Park, embowered in its gardens and an oasis of quietness in the roaring maelstrom of London. As a royal residence the Palace dates

ABOVE *A delightful photograph of the Royal Family at Balmoral in 1960. The baby is Prince Andrew, then less than a year old. Prince Edward was born four years later.*

LEFT *Helping a young Princess Anne adjust a bridle while on holiday at Balmoral in 1955.*

OPPOSITE *The Royal Family in 1957 in the grounds of Buckingham Palace.*

from the reign of William and Mary, and much of the original building is Christopher Wren's work. Queen Anne died there; so did George II. He was the last monarch to live there; but Kensington has a long and unbroken record of royal occupation. Princess Victoria of Kent, Queen-to-be, was born in the Palace in 1819. It was also the birthplace of Princess May of Teck, who became Queen Mary – she was born in the very room where, thirty years before, an Archbishop had knelt in the dawn at the feet of the eighteen-year-old Victoria to tell her that she had become Queen.

Here in the mass of buildings that is Kensington Palace today, in courts and apartments and houses adjoining the State Rooms, live Princess Alice, the dowager Duchess of Gloucester and aunt of the Queen, the Duke and Duchess of Gloucester and their small children, Princess Alice, Countess of Athlone – doyenne of the royal circle, for she was born in 1883 and is the last surviving granddaughter of Queen Victoria – Princess Margaret, the Queen's sister, and Prince and Princess Michael of Kent. Several important members of the royal Households also have homes in Kensington's royal reserve.

The other 'royal village' – this one in the heart of Westminster, with Marlborough House and the Queen Mother's Clarence House as immediate neighbours – is St James's Palace. This was a Tudor palace, built in red brick by King Henry VIII for himself and Anne Boleyn. It spread impressively round four courts, three of which remain. But the buildings have been much damaged and restored through the centuries, and little is left of Henry's palace except the clocktower gatehouse, which makes a massive and much-photographed sight for tourists at the foot of St James's Street. This great house was for long the birthplace and the home of kings, and was made the official residence of the reigning monarch in 1698, in the later Stuart years. It remained so until Queen Victoria made Buckingham Palace her home and the centre of Court activities. Foreign ambassadors to Great Britain, however, are still accredited 'to the Court of St James's', although it is at Buckingham Palace that the Queen receives them at the beginning and end of their missions.

St James's has two chapels: the Chapel Royal within the Palace, which has a ceiling of 1540 panelled in octagons and crosses with painted decorations attributed to Holbein, and the Queen's Chapel

on the opposite side of Marlborough Road, built by Inigo Jones in 1626-27 for Henrietta Maria, Roman Catholic consort of Charles I.

There exists also, forming part of the northern and western side of the Palace, a suite of apartments called York House. George V lived in this house before he became King; it was refurbished for the Prince of Wales who lived there (as did his younger brother, Prince George, the late Duke of Kent, before he was married) before his brief reign as Edward VIII; and later it became the London house of the third son of George V, the late Duke of Gloucester and his Duchess (today's Princess Alice, his widow).

Nowadays York House is the London home of the Duke and Duchess of Kent – though they have only a relatively small part of this wing of the Palace, for York House's grander apartments are now the offices of the Lord Chamberlain's Department. The offices of the Central Chancery of the Orders of Knighthood are next door. There is also an Ascot Office at St James's. The Lord Chamberlain has not only his offices but his London residence there, and so have a number of other senior officers of royal Households. In the Friary Court of the Palace are the headquarters of the Gentlemen at Arms and the Yeomen of the Guard.

In short, Kensington Palace and St James's Palace are two great concentration points on the map of monarchy, each a focus of domestic and official activity; they are second only to Buckingham Palace and Windsor Castle as centres of royal life and work.

It is worth taking a closer look at the residents, those of Kensington Palace first. Princess Margaret's house, the London home of Her Royal Highness and her children at times when the two are not away at school, is in the Clock Court of the Kensington complex. Neighbour to Her Royal Highness is the Royal Family's oldest member, a wonderful repository of lively memories of days gone by – the nonagenarian Princess Alice, Countess of Athlone, who was a seventeen-year-old girl when her grandmother Queen Victoria died at Osborne in the arms of the Kaiser. The Queen is her great-niece. She is related to Her Majesty through her father, who was the youngest of Queen Victoria's four sons, and through marriage: her husband was the Prince Alexander of Teck, Queen Mary's younger brother, who was created Earl of Athlone. Until 1971, Princess Alice was for over twenty years Chancellor of the University of the West Indies; and, delighting rather than being

LEFT *Kensington Palace. Queen Victoria was born here and grew up here, and Princess May of Teck, later Queen Mary, was born in the very room where Queen Victoria had learned of her accession. The Palace is still a royal residence.*

OPPOSITE *The Queen in 1959, wearing her Parliamentary robes, the collar of the Garter and a diamond diadem. This photograph was released before a Canadian tour during which, with President Eisenhower, she opened the St Lawrence Seaway.*

daunted by the far location of that seat of learning, she used to take the greatest pleasure in sailing out to the Caribbean each year by banana boat. She has through the years been one of the most zestful of world travellers.

After Princess Margaret, the best-known and most important members of the Royal Family who inhabit Kensington Palace are 'The Gloucesters'. Their family country home is Barnwell Manor, a few miles south-west of Peterborough in Northamptonshire, standing in a well-run agricultural estate of some two thousand acres which was bought by the late Duke in 1938. Barnwell is a Tudor manor house with the remains of thirteenth-century Barnwell Castle standing in its grounds. The house and its farms are much prized by the family and they go there whenever they can. The young Duke has become keenly involved in country life and the management of the estate, and visitors may find that his activities range from driving tractors to tackling the paperwork of the farm offices. But the Gloucesters' London home, where most of their days are spent, is at Kensington Palace.

There are three generations of them now, headed by the unobtrusive dowager Duchess, Princess Alice, widow of the Prince Henry who was the third son of King George V. Daughter of the seventh Duke of Buccleuch, Her Royal Highness – like Queen Elizabeth The Queen Mother – brought good Scots blood into the Royal Family on her marriage and has the characteristic hard-

working devotion to public service which marks her ancestry. Quiet Princess Alice is one of the best loved and most modest, one of the most conscientiously active members of the Royal Family. And, incidentally, Her Royal Highness not only comes from an ancient and distinguished Scottish ducal house, but is descended in the male line from the royal Stuarts through the famous Duke of Monmouth, Charles II's illegitimate son, who became the first Duke of Buccleuch in the seventeenth century on marrying Anne Scott who was Countess in her own right.

She was born in 1901 on a Christmas Day, as was Princess Alexandra, though her niece's arrival was thirty-five years later. Princess Alice is patron of a great many organisations and particularly concerned with a variety of women's services, both civilian and military. She is Colonel-in-Chief of the King's Own Scottish Borderers and of the Royal Hussars, the Royal Corps of Transport and the Royal Australian Corps of Transport. Hospitals and the world of nursing are one of her special interests: she herself trained as a nurse before her marriage. With her husband, the late Duke, who followed a military career before he left regular army service to devote himself to public duties, she has travelled extensively and at times excitingly, though has always shunned publicity to a remarkable degree. In earlier years and in many countries, Her Royal Highness found time between official engagements to exercise her artistic talent; and there are landscapes in her own and her relatives' homes which testify to her skill as a painter in watercolours. Flowers and outdoor scenes are her favourite subjects: she is a countrywoman by nature, and never happier than when at her home among the fields of Northamptonshire.

The Duchess suffered a tragic loss in the summer of 1972 when her elder son Prince William, who was the heir to the royal Dukedom and a most promising member of the family's younger generation, was killed at the age of thirty whilst adventurously piloting his own small aircraft in a race. William, a darkly good-looking and sociable young man, had been a professional diplomat overseas in the Foreign Service for several years but was about to assume responsibilities at home when he met his death.

So when the late Duke died, after a long illness, in 1974, the younger son, Prince Richard, became Duke of Gloucester. He had inherited his mother's artistic bent, and even as a boy at Eton was exhibiting admirable paintings and pottery. He read architecture at Cambridge and later became a professional architect, practising with a London firm. This full-time career had to be abandoned when he came into the royal Dukedom and the demanding Barnwell property. He has developed fast and is now one of the busiest members of the family: the list of the offices he holds and the patronages he has undertaken is very long already, and he has officially represented his cousin the Queen at a number of independence ceremonies and on other engagements overseas.

As Prince Richard, he married in February 1972 an accomplished Danish girl, Miss Birgitte van Deurs, daughter of an Odense lawyer. The two first met when she was attending language schools in Cambridge. Later she was a secretary at the Danish Embassy in London. The first child of the Duke and Duchess, Alexander, who has the title of Earl of Ulster, was born in 1974, and a daughter, Lady Davina Windsor, followed in 1977. The third child, another girl, was born on the first day of March 1980 and was given the names Rose Victoria Birgitte Louise. She is known as Lady Rose Windsor.

The children, like their cousins, grow rapidly. Alexander has for some time attended a day school not far from his London home – and, more often than not, is taken there in the morning by his father. There is no 'standing on ceremony' about this or any other of the Duke of Gloucester's activities. He frequently rides about London unrecognised on a motor cycle. Informality rules in the Kensington family home, where the small staff of the Gloucester household are accustomed to transacting office business amid a nursery hubbub, with the young Duchess or her mother-in-law acting as nanny.

Another inhabitant of Kensington Palace is Prince Michael of Kent, younger brother of the Duke of Kent and Princess Alexandra. He and his wife and their infant son now have an apartment there. Michael is a professional soldier and for a number of years he has followed the career of an officer in the mechanised cavalry. Formerly of the 11th Hussars – which like many famous regiments has been subjected to merger – he is today a major in the Royal Hussars and, in the Ministry of Defence, an Intelligence officer and a specialist Russian interpreter. He is also, like his brother, a sports-car and motor-racing enthusiast – 'mad keen on rallies and driving in them', his friends will say. He is also an aviator, a very expert skier, and a bobsleigh champion – 'no slouch', as the Americans say. Sporting interests apart, he applies himself very seriously to his position as President of the Institute of the Motor Industry, an examining body concerned with the industry's standards and programmes and personnel.

Until he was thirty-five, Prince Michael was a bachelor, but in June 1978 he married thirty-three-year-old Baroness Marie-Christine von Reibnitz; and their son, Lord Frederick Windsor – whom we have discussed – was born in April 1979.

The circumstances under which Prince and Princess Michael became man and wife were not easy. The laws of England and Wales and the tenets of the Roman Catholic Church were obstacles. The Baroness, an Austrian-born interior decorator, was a Catholic and a divorcee. This meant that the Queen's special permission for the marriage had to be sought. It was given after consultations with the Archbishop of Canterbury, a special meeting of the Privy Council, and a petition to the Vatican – all

OPPOSITE *The wedding of Princess Alexandra, the Queen's cousin, to the Hon. Angus Ogilvy on 24 April 1963. Princess Anne, chief bridesmaid, was beginning to look grown-up.*

RIGHT *Prince Charles (centre) was twenty when he appeared in several sketches in a revue at Trinity College, Cambridge, in 1969.*

that being needed because eighteenth-century Acts still in force in England forbid marriages between members of the Royal Family and Roman Catholics, and because a Vatican annulment of the bride's first marriage was required. Permission to marry in a church – something which the Prince and Princess dearly wished – was not given, so the wedding ceremony was a civil one in Vienna's Town Hall. Princess Michael has not renounced her faith, and her husband remains an Anglican, but he has renounced his position in the succession to the Throne (an academic point: he was sixteenth in line). Children of the marriage, who will be brought up in the Church of England, by the Prince's wish, will not however forfeit their Succession rights.

The Prince's marriage has pleased his family, the new Princess is well liked, and the 'youngest Kents' are a happy family at Kensington Palace.

The 'senior Kents' – for their mother Princess Marina died in 1968 – are the present Duke and Duchess, Michael's brother and sister-in-law, and their London home is three miles away to the east: for they are tucked into York House, St James's Palace.

The Duke of Kent – Prince Edward George Nicholas Paul Patrick – is now in his middle forties and, quite apart from his royal duties, is industriously following a second successful career – as a spokesman and sales stimulator for British trade and technology. His first career was in the Army: he has twenty-one years of professional soldiering behind him. After Sandhurst, he was gazetted to the Royal Scots Greys. He passed out from the Staff College in the top ten, and served with his regiment in Hong Kong, Germany and Cyprus. He had advanced to the rank of Lieutenant-

Colonel by the time he left the Army in 1976.

The Duke became a centre of publicity and controversy early in 1971 when the squadron of armoured cars he commanded was suddenly ordered to Northern Ireland as part of emergency reinforcements to deal with mounting violence by IRA gunmen and street rioters. The news that he was among those sent to Ulster roused protesting voices in England. Critics said that the Queen's cousin was too tempting a target for terrorists and that it was a mistake to involve him in a sensitive political situation and what was almost civil war. There was no excuse in precedents, the objectors declared. It was true that Prince Philip served 'in battle conditions' in the Royal Navy in the Second World War, but that was before he married into the inner circle of the Family. The fact was that the Duke of Kent was the first modern Royal Highness to be in the army 'firing line', certainly the first since that Duke of Kent who was Queen Victoria's father faced the French in the West Indies in 1794 and served in North America.

The War Office move of 1971 was of course simply the posting of serving officers and men, not the dispatching of a VIP. The

Duke was an able and popular officer. Some of his troopers, when they heard the first rumblings of the fuss and the possibility of their commander being stopped from crossing to Northern Ireland, declared that they were not going to move 'without our Prince Eddie'. The Duke himself resented the press agitation and was reported as saying: 'The fact that I am a member of the Royal Family makes no difference whatever. I have a job to do, like anyone else in the Army.' He took it badly when an order to withdraw from Ulster came after only three weeks of service there.

Since leaving the Army, His Royal Highness has been a busy civilian, no mere royal figurehead though he has represented the Queen on numerous missions. His work in the United Kingdom and his extensive travels overseas, including a pioneer visit to China in 1979, have been chiefly in promoting British technological skills and exports in his capacity as Vice-Chairman of the British Overseas Trade Board. He has proved very professional and hard-

working in this post. He is an expert linguist and, like the late Lord Mountbatten and his nephew Prince Philip, has practical interest and personal experience in electronics. The chairmanship of the National Electronics Council is one of the offices he holds. Fast motor cars have long been one of his loves. Another love, surprisingly only to some single-minded automobile fanatics, is opera, of which he is a devoted patron. True to Royal Family style in generation after generation, shooting is one of his favourite sports. Snow sports engage him too: he skis well, as many of his relations do. Wimbledon knows him as a tennis enthusiast, as his mother was. He is President of the All England Lawn Tennis and Croquet Club, and of the Football Association too.

His wife the Duchess of Kent, formerly Miss Katharine Worsley, daughter of a landowning family in North Yorkshire, accompanied the Duke on a number of his tours of duty overseas during his military career. They have now been married almost

twenty years: their wedding in York Minster on 8 June 1961 was one of the events of the year. Their first child, George Philip Nicholas, who has the title of Earl of St Andrews, was born in the following year. This son, now a tall, fair-haired young man, is the outstanding 'academic' of the Royal Family: he won a foundation scholarship to become a King's Scholar of Eton. The daughter of the Duke and Duchess comes next in age: Lady Helen Windsor was born in 1964, and is one of the happy extroverts of the youngest generation. The younger boy, Lord Nicholas Windsor, born in 1970, also shows signs that there are brains in the family.

It is a natural and uninhibited family, as indeed the Duke and his brother and sister also were as children, for Princess Marina's children were attractively unsegregated, 'mixing' as royal youngsters never had done before. Probably some of their happiest memories are of cycling round the village shops in Iver and of spending gregarious bucket-and-spade holidays on South Country beaches.

The present Duchess of Kent is one of the most likeable royal ladies of the modern scene and is always in demand for social, ceremonial and charitable occasions. She is happiest in country life, but enjoys the busy days in town. Felicitous in all she does, she has taken on a great number of patronages, of which the welfare of old people has become a very special concern. She is musical, a pianist and an organist too, and sings in a choir.

Happily, because accommodation in York House in London is limited and there is no garden at all, the Duke and Duchess now have a country house in Norfolk, Anmer Hall near Sandringham, a family home with a long history, most of which has been lost in the mists of antiquity. Parts of the present house were built in Elizabethan times but the main structure is Georgian. Anmer became part of the Sandringham estate in 1898 – when the Prince of Wales, the future Edward VII, had been for many years the royal 'squire' – and was bought by the present Duke of Kent in 1973. It is

not a huge mansion ('four bedrooms and a nursery wing') but stands in ten acres of pleasant parkland and gardens. It is an agreeable retreat for the Duke and Duchess and their children.

Of all the Kent family – to return to the children of the late Prince George and Princess Marina, the Duke and Duchess of a generation ago – Princess Alexandra (now Princess Alexandra, the Hon. Mrs Angus Ogilvy) is best known, extremely popular and charming. Both to the public and to those who know her personally, this cousin of the Queen, ten years younger than Her Majesty, is unaffectedly attractive, possessor of spontaneous zests and infectious enthusiasms. She has a strong look of her father and the tall grace of her mother. Hard-working and full of fun, deliciously natural, she will light up any scene. In these days of cool and sometimes critical assessments of the Royal Family, search and scrutinise as you will, no adverse word against this lady is found. She commands the sort of respect that the Queen herself receives, and is a shining example of the integrity and loyal service which members of the Family bring to the assistance of the Sovereign in the representational duties of royalty.

After being brought up with her two brothers in their Buckinghamshire home, Princess Alexandra was a pupil at a girls' boarding school at Ascot – the first British princess to be given a normal school career. She went to a finishing school in Paris, took a nursing course in London, and soon afterwards – at first with her mother – she began to undertake official engagements and to go on tours abroad, making a delightful impact by her youthful spontaneity wherever she appeared. Today she holds a great variety of offices, and a study of her patronages and engagements shows especially her interest in music. She herself plays the piano well, for the sheer pleasure of it. She adores her private family life, revelling, as they all do, in the times which crowded programmes of official engagements allow for it.

OPPOSITE *In 1970, in Pacific warmth, the Queen and Prince Philip, accompanied by Princess Anne, visited Tonga. King Taufa'ahau Tupou IV, son of Salote, was their host.*

RIGHT *In cool England, Viscount Linley and his sister Sarah enjoy ice lollies at the Badminton Horse Trials of 1970.*

BELOW *In August 1971 the Aga Khan (right) picked up the Armstrong-Jones family in his private jet at London Airport. They holidayed at his Costa Smeralda development in Sardinia.*

OPPOSITE, TOP LEFT *Jackstay transfer at sea. Prince Charles being hauled from HMS* Minerva *to* Ark Royal *during his naval training in 1973.*

OPPOSITE, TOP RIGHT *'Cameraman' Viscount Linley follows in his father's footsteps at the Badminton Horse Trials – but needs some strap-disentangling help from the Queen.*

OPPOSITE, BOTTOM *In February 1973 the Queen flew to Norfolk for a family weekend at Sandringham. The transfer of five royal corgis into the plane provided amusement.*

ABOVE *As his father has been, the Prince of Wales is a keen polo player. Here he is playing for the Royal Navy against the Army.*

ABOVE *The annual Garter procession at Windsor. The Order of the Garter is our premier order of chivalry, founded in 1348.*

LEFT *Acting as the nation's host to visiting Heads of State is one of the Sovereign's duties and privileges. Here the visitor, from Malaysia, is being driven from Victoria Station in London.*

The Princess has represented the Queen and her country at national ceremonies all over the world, and possibly has more experience of overseas trade fairs than any woman in the land. Often she has been accompanied by her husband.

Her Royal Highness married, in the spring of 1963, the Hon. Angus Ogilvy, second son of the twelfth Earl of Airlie. The Airlies are one of the great patrician families of Scotland, and with the entry of the Honourable Angus into the Queen's family a valued link with the Royal House was strengthened: his family has a distinguished record of service to and friendship with royalty. The Earl, his father, was for many years Lord Chamberlain to Queen Elizabeth The Queen Mother, and his grandmother, Mabell, Countess of Airlie, with whom he had a strong bond of affection, was Lady of the Bedchamber and a close friend of Queen Mary for half a century.

The 1963 royal wedding – 'Alex and Angus Day', they called it – gave enormous public pleasure and London was *en fête* for the event. The Princess had already won the hearts even of persistent and pernickety pressmen, and newspaper reports of the service in Westminster Abbey on that twenty-fourth day of April described the ceremony as 'sheer fairy-tale, bride and groom smiling their joy and looking at each other as though no one else was there'.

Their son, James Ogilvy (James Robert Bruce), was born in 1964, and their daughter, Marina (Marina Victoria Alexandra), in 1966. These two royal children are 'Mr' and 'Miss'; and doubtless their ancestry is honour enough without other titles. To say that the Ogilvys are a close and happy family is a barely adequate statement. They live life to the full and love being together in a home that rings with fortunate laughter.

The house into which the Princess and her husband moved when they married, and which is still their home, is one of the most interesting but lesser known – the Ogilvys cherish their privacy – of all royal dwellings. It is Thatched House Lodge, which stands on a knoll in the southern corner of Richmond Park, a country house within Greater London. And a piece of Crown property with a history. It started life as one of the keepers' houses and was later a hunting lodge in the royal deer park of the seventeenth century. In Stuart times it had a much used ice well for the venison. The house takes its name from an unusual little gazebo, thatched and beehive-roofed, which still stands in the grounds. As to the house itself, it has been altered and added to many times, but the Lodge retains the appearance of a good-sized, comfortable eighteenth-century residence. Sir Robert Walpole, George II's chief minister, who had been given the park Rangership by the King, had the place built, and Sir John Soane was its architect. Its occupants through the years make an impressive list: military and political leaders and administrators holding prominent positions at Court. Artists and professional men too. Sir Joshua Reynolds once lived there, and not unnaturally supervised some of the interior decorations. One resident was Sir Frederick Treves, the eminent surgeon who performed the emergency appendicectomy on King Edward VII on the eve of his long-prepared Crowning Day – the operation which unfortunately postponed the Coronation but unquestionably saved the Monarch's life.

Thatched House Lodge has become a home of which Princess Alexandra's husband has become as fond as she and the children are, and no doubt it has come to vie with his ancestral homes, Cortachy and Airlie Castle, in his affections. The Lodge has the advantages of quiet and privacy and country setting, and yet it is only a few miles from the heart of London – a combination which has served Mr Ogilvy well, for he has had an extraordinarily busy

TOP *The Queen and the Queen Mother, expert owners, discuss the points of the race with jockey Joe Mercer, who had just ridden the Queen's colt, Carlton House, to victory in the Fenwolf Stakes at Ascot in June 1974.*

ABOVE *The Queen enters the coalface at Silverwood Colliery near Rotherham, Yorkshire, singularly attired in white overalls and helmet.*

commercial life and at one time held fifty City directorships. This load is now greatly reduced, though he still has a few seats on boards, and a main occupation for him these days is his work as an adviser-director at Sotheby's, the world's best-known firm of fine-art auctioneers.

Such are the people who form, and who have formed, the wider circle of the Royal Family – with one omission. This survey of the branches of the House of Windsor and their spread in the twentieth century has to include the famous man – his life already part of our story – who, although never in the order of Succession to the Throne, always had considerable influence in the family's affairs, Admiral of the Fleet Earl Mountbatten of Burma, the gifted, liberal-minded and forward-looking 'Uncle Dickie' whose years ran like a golden thread of distinguished service through decade after decade. He was always close to the Throne and the centres of military and political power.

Lord Mountbatten's life came tragically to an end, in its eightieth

year, when on Bank Holiday Monday, 27 August 1979, he was killed by an Irish terrorists' bomb in his boat in the harbour of Mullaghmore, County Sligo, in the Republic of Eire, where he was on holiday at his Irish house, Classiebawn Castle. Also murdered in the explosion aboard the boat were one of his grandsons, Nicholas, aged fourteen, the Dowager Lady Brabourne, and a young boatman, Paul Maxwell. The parents of that young Nicholas Knatchbull, Lord and Lady Brabourne – she the elder Mountbatten daughter, heiress to the earldom and therefore now Countess Mountbatten – and another son, Timothy, the twin brother of Nicholas, were seriously injured. On the same day, the so-called Irish Republican Army callously massacred eighteen British soldiers in a landmine explosion in County Down, Ulster.

The killings aroused horror and grief throughout the civilised world, and the funeral of Lord Mountbatten in London nine days later was an occasion not only of royal family mourning at the ecumenical service in Westminster Abbey but was also, in its

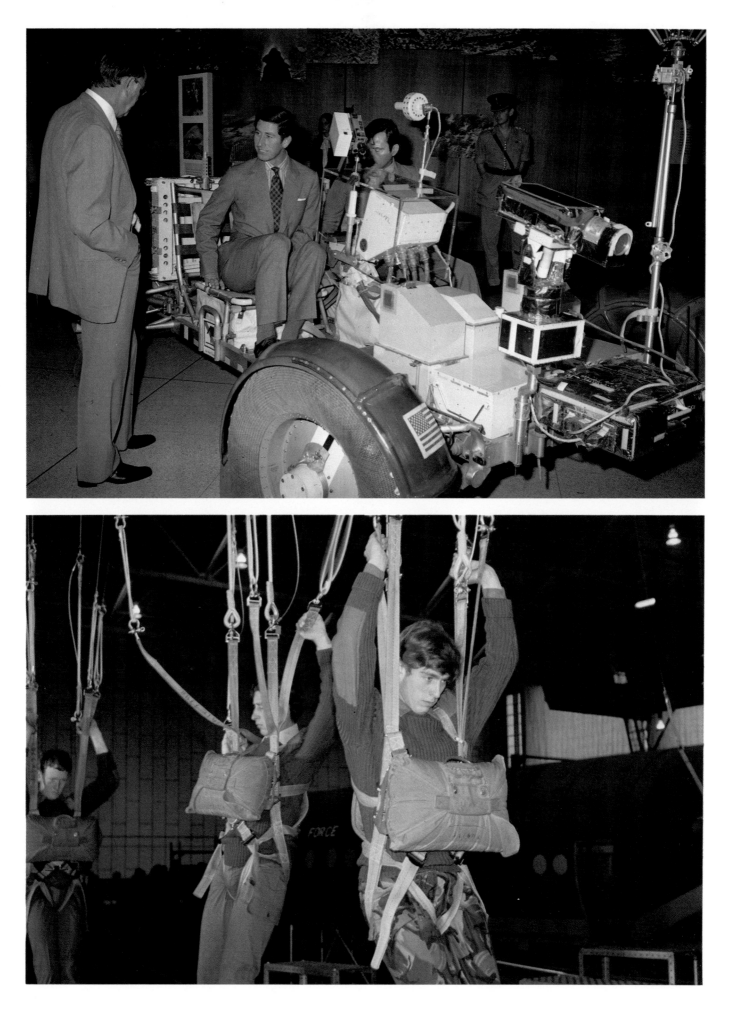

LEFT *The Queen and her family by the lakeshore of Bromont, Canada, at the end of the Royal Visit of 1976, during which she opened the Montreal Olympics in which her daughter was a competitor.*

TOP *Prince Edward, the Queen's youngest son.*

ABOVE *Prince Andrew, a studio portrait of the vigorous second son, who is now, following tradition, in the Royal Navy.*

ABOVE *Queen Elizabeth The Queen Mother. A photograph taken specially at Clarence House, her London home. Born in 1900, the 'Queen Mum' is as old as the century, but retains a zest for life equalled by few.*

OPPOSITE *The Queen Mother with her two eldest grandsons on her seventy-fifth birthday. Prince Andrew (right) has just presented her with a gift of two pottery dishes he had made himself.*

processions and all their ceremonial of marching men and military bands, a tribute of public and international magnitude comparable to the State obsequies for Winston Churchill fourteen years before.

The passing of Louis Mountbatten, the shock of the evil deed which killed him, was a blow which fell cruelly and personally on the Queen and Prince Philip and the whole House of Windsor. There seemed never to have been a time when he was not a towering figure in the gatherings and councils of the family. There was no parallel to his stature and influence in the service of kin and Crown.

Servants of the Crown

Any muster-roll of Servants of the Crown must be headed by the Queen herself. And, after her, her own family. For the Queen is 'in service', just as her ministers and staffs are. She is 'one of the workers' not only when at her desk but when in historic pageantry too. An incident concerning a Labour politician, the late Richard Crossman, illustrates this.

Crossman was a cabinet minister, Lord President of the Council, a functionary of importance – and, in his case, of arrogance – and one of his duties was to attend the Queen when she opened Parliament in State. He wanted, however, to dodge his part in what he regarded as outworn and irksome ceremony; and, asking leave to be absent from the dignified occasion, he approached the Palace. Her Majesty's Private Secretary – it was the then Sir Michael Adeane – told him that all he needed to do was to write a letter asking to be excused. But Sir Michael at the same time made the point – the *whole* point, and beautifully made – that 'it will certainly occur to Her Majesty to ask herself if you should be excused when she herself has to go, since you are both officials'.

Crossman went to Westminster and played his part.

Whole books have been written about Crown servants, running the Palace gamut from courtiers to coachmen. More will no doubt be written, for the simple reason that royalty and 'those about the Throne' fascinate even hard-eyed egalitarians in a Britain beginning the nineteen-eighties. It is interesting to go backstage in order to see the people in the wings and to disclose some of the figures whose work it is to support the Royal Family in their duties.

But not all the Crown servants are in the wings. The principals are on stage. So it is proper to begin with the Royal Family themselves, because they are not only employers but are employed too – in working for the State. First is the Queen, the chief, the most responsible and hard-working Servant of all, foremost in sustaining the Crown she has inherited. It is she who is the Number One Public Servant. For her position is People's Representative rather than Ruler.

The sweepingly popular – and, to some who at first doubted about the celebrations, surprisingly popular – events of 1977, the Queen's Silver Jubilee Year, proved to be nothing less than a great freewill national thanksgiving, not for mere pageantry or a passage of time but for this very work of representation and for the qualities which Her Majesty gives to her office. We were saluting a human being.

Since Accession and Crowning, since 1952 and 1953, the aspect of the monarchy has changed, and the nature of public interest in the reign has changed too. But regard for the Queen, far from fading, has increased and turned from liking to love. The Sovereign Lady has taken the years smoothly in her stride and now is the most experienced and most travelled Head of State in the world, serene

and sensible, quite unflappable, combining dignity and friendliness as few people can, in an age when dignity and selflessness are at a discount. In public and in her family, she keeps up standards and traditions but is no slave of outworn precedents. Her monarchy has moved with the times and she is at pains to see that it keeps its adaptability – that is why it has survived and strengthened. Successive Prime Ministers have emerged from audiences testifying to her grasp of affairs. She spends two or three hours a day reading State Papers. Hers is a non-stop job. It is not only at Buckingham Palace that she 'lives over the shop': the shop pursues her with streams of official documents wherever she goes. Out on tour, in all settings and temperatures, she is under unremitting examination by vast numbers of people, for hours at a time the cynosure of all eyes. A sense of fun as well as a sense of fitness buoy her. She is strong and resilient, else she would not emerge poised and fresh – more so, often, than her entourages – from programmes of work that would exhaust a dray-horse.

In her service to the Throne, the help of her husband, Prince Philip, Duke of Edinburgh, has been immense. A male Consort has no defined position, but this indefatigable man has made a name and a place for himself both as Her Majesty's right hand and as a sharp-minded leader in the public life of the nation. With his many talents, his restless drive, impatience and keen intelligence, he could never have been merely an ornamental one-step-behind figure around the Court. He is known throughout the world for his outspoken spurring of youth, industry, technology, conservation and sport. He is both a stimulus and a challenge; and his reported intolerance is streaked with great kindness. He speaks in public very well indeed and often controversially (which the Queen, officially impartial, may not do). Sometimes, with an excess of Mountbatten brio, and tiring of suffering fools gladly, he has acted the oratorical freebooter, has thrown sound advice to trades not his own, and has cut down platitudes and pomposity with a tongue like a cutlass, thus becoming to some small critics a crackerbarrel philosopher, and not everybody's darling.

It is at first glance tempting, but dangerous and on the whole deluding, to seek a parallel in his forebear, Victoria's admirable Albert, for he was a reforming eager beaver too. But *that* Prince Consort was a horse of a different colour, a pedant and a foreigner, whereas Prince Philip is neither. He is one of Britain's public men of first quality – but not because he is of the Royal Family. What he has done, however, is help to give the Monarchy much of its bright modern image; and always his first consideration has been, and remains, the care of the Queen, laying all his gifts at her service to maintain her position as an esteemed focus of national ideals and endeavour.

The children of the Queen and Prince Philip, too, have entered into public view and the orbit of public duty in their own right, though the younger two, the mettlesome Prince Andrew – following tradition by training now for the Royal Navy – and Prince Edward – lively but shyer and more studious and still at school – are as yet out of the day-to-day news.

OPPOSITE *The Queen, Prince Philip beside her, at the State Opening of Parliament in 1970. Prince Charles and Princess Anne are present. Earl Mountbatten holds the Sword of State.*

ABOVE *Six Canadian Indian chiefs and their wives visited the Queen in 1976, on the centenary of treaties made with Queen Victoria.*

Prince Charles, twenty-first Prince of Wales (of whom we shall take stock presently in this story), and Princess Anne for several years have been active in royal service. However much she may wish to step backwards from royal floodlighting, the Princess *is* news. Even her distinct private life tempts attention. Whilst taking her share of official duties, she now concentrates on her farming and family life in the country. To those who know her best, the riding-stable side of her life and the role of Cotswold wife and mother come first, the 'princess part' second.

Even as a small girl, Princess Anne was adventurous and unconventional: Charles watched whilst Anne climbed the trees, an open-air tomboy with a will of her own. Not long cocooned in private tutoring, she went away to a boarding school in Kent. She is today best known as a competitive equestrienne of world class. It was mutual love of horses and the ambitions and skills of expert riding which began the friendship with Captain Mark Phillips, of Great Somerford in Wiltshire and the Queen's Dragoon Guards, a brilliant horseman and Olympic gold-medallist, the man she married in 1973.

The ceremony in Westminster Abbey was a splendid but not a State occasion. For once, the congregation at a royal gathering of this kind lacked the routine ranks of diplomats and officials: all the people present in the Abbey had been invited personally and most were friends of bride or groom, of high and of low degree. The occasion had all the relaxed and joyful atmosphere of a village wedding translated into London's most famous church – and by 'live' television was watched and enjoyed by 500 million people round the world.

The birth of a son of the marriage in November 1977 – Master Peter Mark Andrew Phillips, first of the newest generation – made Queen Elizabeth II a grandmother at fifty-one in her Silver Jubilee Year.

At the end of 1977 Captain Phillips left the Army to concentrate on farming; and now he and the Princess live at Gatcombe Park near Stroud in Gloucestershire, an imposing Georgian house and estate, now with a big stable complex, which the Queen bought for them. With Gatcombe and an adjacent farm also bought, a little later, by the Queen, Her Royal Highness the Princess, Mrs Mark Phillips, and her husband are able to lead a working country life surrounded by horses, beef cattle and some good arable land on an estate of over 1,200 acres. This is their natural ambience; here they are truly at home.

Next, Princess Margaret, who is also still at times in the service of the Crown. Though readers of the gossip columns of certain newspapers may not know it, the Queen's sister does share the

ABOVE, LEFT *The former Duke and Duchess of Gloucester with their sons at Barnwell Manor, Northamptonshire, in 1950. Their elder son, Prince William, died tragically in 1972. Prince Richard (here on horseback) inherited the Dukedom in 1974.*

ABOVE, RIGHT *Prince and Princess Richard of Gloucester, now the Duke and Duchess of Gloucester, in 1973. They have undertaken many foreign visits on behalf of the Queen.*

LEFT *Barnwell, country home of the Gloucester family.*

OPPOSITE *From St Mary's Hospital, Paddington, emerges Lady Rose Windsor in the arms of a nurse. The baby, the third child of the Duke and Duchess of Gloucester, was born on 1 March 1980. Here the Duchess is holding her other daughter, Lady Davina, then aged two.*

work-load of the Family and has a considerable diary of official duties. In her tastes and much of her character – though aunt and niece are both extrovert, volatile individuals – Princess Margaret is as essentially urban as Princess Anne is rural. Parties for Margaret are sophisticated club nights rather than hunt balls; country life to her is the Caribbean, not the Cotswolds. There have been difficult times in recent years for Princess Margaret, whose friends know her as an artistic and entertaining companion, at times unpredictable, on her dignity one day, kicking up her heels the next, wilfulness and captivating charm doing battle. She is quick-humoured, amusing, one of the most musically talented and socially inclined of all the members of the Royal Family. The year 1978 was a particular twelvemonth of uncertainty, and of illness, for her. She completed public engagements with grace and dignity, but some of her companionships and not-so-private life made steady fodder for Fleet Street. She has suffered press hostility.

A problem Her Royal Highness may be, but she remains close within the Family. There is no ostracising; rather, a loving sympathy is held out to her. Nor does a rift exist between her former husband, Lord Snowdon, and the Royal Family. He, and his camera, are welcomed at their homes.

As to the Senior Lady of the Family, Her Majesty Queen Elizabeth The Queen Mother, perhaps the most respected and widely admired Queen in British history, there is scarcely need to dilate on the delight and duty which together she has given to the business of the Monarchy. It is hard to believe that she is now over her eightieth year: she can dance most people off their feet. The world knows her wit and sparkle and sterling qualities as a public figure. She is also an adored Great-Grannie and a marvellous matriarch. No one enjoys more the sort of life she leads. When she smiles – which is a great deal of the time – she means it and the blue eyes flash. She charms and disarms the people she meets, from dukes to dustmen. Her engagement diary is almost as full as her daughter's. She is a worker – and loves it. The very personification of royalty, she is almost incredible, yet very very real. It would have been impossible to invent her.

Such are the members of the Family who are Servants of the Crown. Behind them is the Permanent Service, the officials and their staffs who, whatever Sovereign may be upon the Throne, maintain their employers, keep the monarchy in continuous constitutional existence and form a highly professional and industrious unseen organisation, perfectionist and businesslike to a degree, second to none in untrumpeted efficiency.

To list 'royal' officials and offices would occupy many pages of this or any other book, and many people on the roll would be concerned with Parliament, State politics and the Government departments, for law and order and legislation are all 'in the Queen's name'. Our business in these pages, however, is with those whose work is within the Households of the Queen and others of her family, particularly at Buckingham Palace. We have already recalled the notable series of men, supremely dependable personal advisers, who have occupied the position of Private Secretary. With his Deputy and Assistant, the Secretary is in constant touch with the Queen, is the main link between Her Majesty and the Government of the day, the man who arranges her engagements and deals with her correspondence. Influential and important, the Private Secretary is the key Servant.

But the Lord Chamberlain is the senior officer and functioning head of the Household. There are other 'Great Officers of State' but for the most part they are not in continuous service and are political appointments: the Treasurer and Comptroller are examples. And

TOP *Thatched House Lodge, Richmond Park, home of Princess Alexandra and Mr Angus Ogilvy.*

ABOVE *The Princess and her husband with their children in 1971 – an airport picture at the start of a journey to New Zealand. Now tall teenagers, James Ogilvy was then seven and Marina four.*

OPPOSITE *A family group in Richmond Park, just before the Princess and her husband left home for the opening of a British industrial exhibition in Brazil in the autumn of 1974.*

TOP *The Kent wedding, 1961. The Duke and his bride, formerly Miss Katharine Worsley, emerge from York Minster. It was the first royal wedding there for over six hundred years.*

ABOVE, LEFT *An aerial view of the Norfolk home of 'the Kents': Anmer Hall, near Sandringham.*

ABOVE, RIGHT *The Duchess, a keen lawn-tennis follower, presents the Women's Singles Trophy to Martina Navratilova on the Centre Court at Wimbledon in 1979.*

OPPOSITE *The Duke and Duchess of Kent with their family in early childhood. Lord Nicholas Windsor is on the pony, with the Earl of St Andrews and Lady Helen Windsor beside him.*

the Vice-Chamberlain does not work at the Palace either; he is a Government Whip, but he does have one duty to do for the Sovereign: he has to see that the Queen receives a daily confidential report on Parliamentary proceedings.

The Lord Chamberlain's Office itself has a Comptroller, but in this case he is a full-time official and an all-important one, the chief executive of a very busy department. His responsibilities include almost all ceremonial, State visits to London, royal weddings, christenings, garden parties, and the overseeing of many Court appointments. Under his care also are such figures as the Queen's Bargemaster and the Watermen, the Keeper of the Royal Swans (echoes of the days when palaces were on the banks of the Thames and the quickest way to travel between them was by river), the College of Chaplains and its Clerk of the Closet (a bishop who heads the Ecclesiastical Household with its chaplains and Chapels Royal). But the Comptroller is no Poo-Bah. There are other authorities in other places. He is not, for instance, the master of the occasional Constables of Holyrood, and is absolved from the management of Her Majesty's racing pigeons at Sandringham.

The Lord Chamberlain himself is personally of the highest importance. Since 1971 the office has been held by Lord Maclean of Duart Castle on the Isle of Mull – the Scottish home from which his duties in London keep him for much of each year. He is twenty-seventh Chief of his Clan and a former Chief Scout of the Commonwealth, a charming man, patently happy and able in his work – all the happier no doubt because nowadays the Lord Chamberlain's duties no longer include the age-old task of censorship of plays. There used to be many storms over that part of the job. Dramatic waters may now be calmer, but plays are not cleaner.

The man who 'runs the Palace' domestically is the Master of the Household, Britain's most important major-domo. The interior arrangements of Windsor, Holyroodhouse, Sandringham and Balmoral are also in his charge. He controls the supply department – though it is the Lord Chamberlain who issues that prized royal cachet to shops and commercial firms, the Royal Warrant – and is lord of the stewards, the housekeepers, the butlers, the footmen, the housemaids, the table-layers, the cleaners and even the men who wind Buckingham Palace's two hundred fascinating clocks. His is a staff of many experienced perfectionists, some of them rejoicing in such archaic titles as Page of the Backstairs, Royal Pastry Chef, Sergeant Footman, Yeoman of the Gold and Silver Pantry and Yeoman of the Cellars. These belong to the 'Downstairs' of the Palace, a tight little Court itself, a world which still retains numbers of centuries-old job definitions, its status brackets clear and proud, its Servants' Hall hierarchy and class distinctions as sharp as anything Upstairs.

Another department, thoroughly modern in its business practices and headed by a very up-to-date businessman, is that of the Keeper of the Privy Purse. The Keeper is the Queen's treasurer, the man who administers the royal finances, both personal payments from Her Majesty's private resources and the salaries and wages of Household officers and servants, which are household running costs partly met by State funds voted by Parliament. These State allowances are called the Civil List, and three-quarters of the money is for salaries of Household officials and staff (the Queen receives no *pay*). Critics can juggle and jab sharply with the finance figures, but in fact the British people spend about thirty times as much on football pools and on bingo as on the monarchy. The Crown costs even less than the annual bill for National Health Service tranquillisers.

An important man who is in the top bracket of royal employees is the Crown Equerry, who is the day-to-day deputy of the Master of the Horse. In his charge is the Royal Mews and all its services of

LEFT *Earl Mountbatten, who was an outstanding 'Servant of the Crown', with Prince Philip at a Royal Marines ceremony.*

OPPOSITE *Prince Charles with his great-uncle, who was 'Lord Louis' to the world, 'Uncle Dickie' to the Royal Family.*

horses, carriages and motor cars. Again, terminology needs a little explaining, for the Royal Household includes aides-de-camp in working attendance on the Queen who are also called equerries. Like many of the Court titles, the word 'equerry' is of great antiquity and is an anglicised form of the French 'écurie', meaning 'a stable'. A glance at the history of the office shows that the commonly heard accenting of the first syllable of the word as '*EKK*werry' is a mispronunciation. In documents dating from the reign of Charles II the spelling is simply 'querry', and equerries were called 'Equerries of the Crown Stable'. They were in general attendance on the Sovereign, and in particular they accompanied him when he rode out on horseback.

One more survival from ages past is to be seen when the royal Heralds appear in public, as they do on important ceremonial occasions, their medieval tabards of most brilliant colours providing unrivalled pictures for any tourist who can tote a camera and tiptoe near. The English heralds (Scotland has its own Court of Chivalry, its own heralds) belong to the College of Arms, whose head is the Earl Marshal, the Duke of Norfolk. Genealogical research and the establishment of right to armorial bearings is their expert business. As fascinating as their dress when they attend the Sovereign are the ancient titles which they and their next in rank, the pursuivants, bear: Clarenceux, Portcullis, Bluemantle, Rouge Croix and Rouge Dragon are some of them.

So much for male servants of royalty. There are important female attendants too – and here we are in the intimate Palace world again. For these are the Ladies-in-Waiting, members of the Queen's Household. Their posts do not sport quite such resounding names as the heralds' do, but there are one or two old titles here also, and a hierarchical tradition. Some of the ladies' own names, moreover, are grand in themselves. The Mistress of the Robes, usually a duchess, is the senior lady, equivalent in rank to the Lord Chamberlain. She arranges the in-waiting rotas and herself accompanies the Queen on major occasions. Then there are two Ladies of the Bedchamber, who are the wives of peers. But the regular Ladies-in-Waiting, who work full-time in rotation, are four *Women* of the Bedchamber, who are not necessarily titled though some are daughters of peers. Their business is to attend Her Majesty on most of her public and semi-private engagements and also to make arrangements of a more personal kind, doing some shopping for their employer, for instance, and dealing with much of the Queen's personal correspondence. Their job is anything but a nominal one. They spend a fortnight at a time 'in waiting', but do not nowadays sleep in the Palace. All the Ladies are appointed by the Queen personally, and are her friends.

All these Servants of the Crown, employers and employed, may be said to have Buckingham Palace as their operational headquarters, but they are itinerant. Other work-places are of course Windsor, Sandringham, Balmoral and Holyroodhouse.

It may seem that Her Majesty has an abundance of abiding places (though not if one remembers that Elizabeth I had fourteen palaces and Henry VIII twenty!) and that she lives in an enclosed world of private treasure-houses of fine pictures and furniture, as the Tudors and Stuarts did. But in fact nowadays the State homes are increasingly seen by the public, their gardens and galleries and works of art put on view. Sandringham, for instance, has become a summertime Mecca of popular pilgrimage, and since the Queen first opened it to the public in 1977 it has given pleasure to many thousands of visitors. Besides the house and gardens, there is a museum and a nicely organised cafeteria run by royal estate employees.

And the public exhibitions in the Queen's Gallery at Buckingham Palace – a gallery created in 1962 in part of the private chapel which was wrecked by bombs in the last war – demonstrate

Her Majesty's awareness that works of art can never be purely private possessions, and that her palaces and her pictures are part of British history.

Since the Queen and her family travel overseas a great deal, the mobility of their staffs naturally means much more than commuting between castles and palaces within the United Kingdom. Indeed, never have royal Households been so accustomed to working from time to time in strange foreign climes as in the present reign. Where the Queen goes, a nucleus of staff must go too, for the Sovereign's daily business of State does not ever stop. That flow of telegrams and boxes of official papers is incessant, no matter what tour of Commonwealth or foreign country may be in progress. A house in some remote game reserve may temporarily be a royal headquarters, and certainly HM Yacht *Britannia* is a floating office.

It would be impressive to enumerate the overseas visits paid by the Queen in her first three decades of duty – or even to record the mileages of Household travel-planners on their reconnaissances before a royal tour takes place – but too many pages would be needed for such a log. To recite the countries of the world to which the Queen has *not* been would be a briefer exercise.

Countries of the overseas Commonwealth, of course, frequently receive her, Australia and New Zealand and Canada especially. She has visited North and Central and South America, India, Pakistan, almost every Continental European and Scandinavian country, most parts of Africa, the Caribbean, the Far East, the South Seas. It would seem that Her Majesty's personal mileage is approaching the astronomical – and in an age of space travel perhaps one day it may be truly that. Meantime, each tour is, if not a book in itself, a long chapter in a life of service.

The year 1979, for instance, produced an unprecedented sweep, with great success, through the oil-rich states of the Arabian Gulf.

The Queen's hosts, whose generosity sent their visitor home with almost embarrassing loads of jewels, were the robed sheikhs and emirs of desert lands, Saudi Arabia, Kuwait, Bahrain, Qatar, Oman, and the United Arab Emirates. Ordinarily, women are second-class persons in such lands, and wives do not appear on public view. The Queen's much-photographed appearances were something exceptional; and in Saudi Arabia – where, as everywhere, she was a smiling and miraculously cucumber-cool figure in the hot sun – she arrived swathed from neck to toe in long floaty garments in deference to Islamic laws on women's dress.

But the outstanding visit of the same year was the seventeen-day State Tour which took Her Majesty to south-east Africa: Tanzania, Malawi, Botswana and Zambia. With the Queen and Prince Philip this time was their tall, nineteen-year-old son Prince Andrew, who had just left Gordonstoun School and who on this summer-holiday journey shortly before starting his naval career was experiencing a major royal tour for the first time.

Before the tour took place, serious doubts about the wisdom of it were expressed in some official quarters and editorial columns, and the cause for concern was the Queen's safety in the closing stages of the journey when she was to attend the Commonwealth Conference in Zambia's capital, Lusaka, near which were base camps of guerrilla warfare against Rhodesia and areas of Rhodesian retaliation. The Queen's advisers had to weigh the honest apprehensions of those who felt it would be both improper and hazardous to allow Her Majesty to go at all into areas of Africa which were in political turmoil and actual fighting over the future of a Rhodesia which was then painfully being transmuted into Zimbabwe. The visit might have been a disaster but in fact proved to be, even to disapproving and dispassionate eyes, a triumph. Whilst the Queen was there, all was peace and happiness. As always, she herself had entertained no thoughts about any risks

ahead, and it would have been very hard indeed to dissuade her from going where she had promised to go, however fraught with danger the path might have seemed.

In the event, she sailed through the programme, serene and splendidly secure, above politics and yet clearly a *wished for* Head of the Commonwealth. She was rapturously received by millions of Africans, her presence had a calming and unifying influence on warring factions at that time, and she flew away from Lusaka with grouped politicians all smiles and the crowds chanting 'Bye bye, Queenie. Come again.' It was an African apotheosis.

Many other glowing royal journeys have studded the years of the reign. And independently, Queen Elizabeth The Queen Mother, the Duke of Edinburgh, Prince Charles, Princess Anne, Princess Margaret and others of the Royal Family have travelled the world on both official and informal visits. The Family are agreeable and effective royal ambassadors.

During the early summer of 1979, the Queen Mother paid yet another visit to Canada, where she is specially popular. This time the scenes were Halifax, Nova Scotia – the 'Royal Province of New Scotland', as she called it – and Ontario's capital, the great commercial city of Toronto. As they always have done, the Canadian public and the press spread an unstinted welcome for this royal lady and missed nothing of her spirited progress. Some of her quick-fire replies to hosts' questions made headlines. Would the election of a woman Prime Minister (Mrs Thatcher) have 'a significant effect on the women of Britain?' she was asked. 'More on the men', she laughed. Queen Elizabeth's own effect on big crowds of people was very significant when, in Halifax and in the pride of her own Scottish ancestry, she attended the International Gathering of the Clans, the first to be held outside Scotland.

An unprecedented event for the Queen Mother took place on the first day of August that year when she was installed as the first woman Lord Warden and Admiral of the Cinque Ports, an ancient office which used to be the post of guardian of the 'invasion coast' and defence fleets of south-east England, and is now an honorary position bestowed for outstanding service to Britain. Throughout the full day of ceremonial in Dover, Her Majesty, who invariably is a strikingly radiant figure, sparkled extraordinarily. 'It's been one of the happiest days of my life', she added. Looking at her on that day, it was difficult to credit that she was within three days of her seventy-ninth birthday.

The Queen Mother does not herself dwell on the count of her anniversaries, gratefully though the world and her own family remark them.

The Royal Family have always been assiduous in recognising the longevity and achievements of others, especially the captains and counsellors of history ... which brings to our story once again, and finally, Winston Churchill (whose passing was recalled to many minds not long ago at the time of the death and funeral of Lord Mountbatten). Sir Winston's memory was signally marked in 1965. He was buried like a king.

Several years before the end of that long life of the greatest Englishman of modern times, the Queen had quietly made it known that in the event of Sir Winston's death she wished him to be accorded a State Funeral, a rare honour the like of which had not been granted to a non-royal subject since the death of the Duke of Wellington in 1852. Churchill died, aged ninety, on 24 January 1965. So, planned to the last detail through the years, its carriage processions occasionally rehearsed through the empty streets of a London dawn, the long obsequial pageant unfolded on a bitterly cold 30 January (one of the innumerable television cameramen, positioned atop the dome of St Paul's, was brought down near to death by sheer freezing on that day). In spite of the weather, the streets were solid with people, and the winding route of the cortège

OPPOSITE, LEFT *Princess Alice, Countess of Athlone, nonagenarian granddaughter of Queen Victoria.*

OPPOSITE, RIGHT *A recent portrait of Princess Margaret, great-niece of Princess Alice.*

RIGHT *The Queen and Prince Philip arriving at the House of Lords for the State Opening of Parliament in November 1978.*

ABOVE *The Private Secretary is the working Sovereign's right hand. With the Queen here, informal but attentive aboard the Royal Yacht, is Sir Martin Charteris, who held the post from 1972 to 1977 – and is now Lord Charteris, Provost of Eton. (Compare the shirt-sleeved figure with the frock-coated Secretary on page 27.)*

RIGHT *The Queen replies to Addresses from both Houses of Parliament in 1957. Her Private Secretary for many years, Sir Michael Adeane then, is seated behind her.*

ABOVE *The marriage certificate from the wedding on 14 November 1973, in which the bride used as her surname 'Mountbatten-Windsor'.*

RIGHT *Princess Anne and Captain Phillips at the Chatsworth Horse Trials in 1977. The Princess's first child was born later that year.*

from Westminster Hall to the cathedral was lined the whole way by immaculate troops. Bands played music which the old statesman had loved as the procession slowly passed along, led on foot by the lone and imperious figure of Bernard Norfolk, wearing, as though it were part of the very man, the plumed hat of hereditary Earl Marshal of England.

At the service in St Paul's, where the coffin rested beneath the dome, every imaginable figure of Kingdom and Commonwealth was to be seen in the vast congregation: seventeen Prime Ministers, officers of State and captains of arms bearing many a famous name, Heads of Government and representatives of a hundred foreign lands, kings and queens and presidents – and, at the head of it all, the Queen and the entire Royal Family of Britain. It was an occasion of awe and solemnity, yet not a lamentation. Rather, it was a grandiose final chord of remembrance for a fighting leader, cardinal romantic and royalist, whose matchless life and its gifts had

inspired generations of men, shining the way through many a fog of halting mediocrity.

To the Queen, that funeral was the last salute to a giant of six reigns, whose youth, as he himself once characteristically put it, 'was passed in the august, unchallenged and tranquil glories of the Victorian era', and who had been so proud to live to become First Minister to herself, Victoria's great-great-granddaughter.

Present Indicative

Finally, a stocktaking and a look to the future.

The story of the Royal House as a dynasty christened by the Queen's grandfather is now in its seventh decade, and if George V were to come back he would hardly know where he was. He would seek in vain for Durbars and stand aghast at Walkabouts. In his Palace he would find no Ball for Society but perhaps a dance for the

Christmas Day, 1979: the Royal Family leaving St George's Chapel, Windsor.

staff – a Christmas ball for all the workers, high and low. At such an annual event he might glimpse one of the servants taking the floor with the Sovereign – a groundling with his granddaughter! – and each partner waltzing as though it was not only the happiest but the most natural thing in the world. He would discover some of his descendants planting ideas as well as trees, enjoying professional careers, marrying commoners, packing their children off to public schools, integrating in many ways with the world outside castle compounds.

There would be reassuringly familiar things: the sentries and the salutes in London, the fishing and stalking at Balmoral, the country-gentleman shooting parties and top-hatted race-going, with the Garter procession just before Royal Ascot, then Cowes Week and a maritime Court aboard a Royal Yacht. Princely polo would not be strange, though a Prince Consort's thrustful four-in-hand driving might cause a swift intake of breath. The uniformed pageants would not be missing either, the annual ceremonies spelling out history and tradition: the State Openings, Trooping the Colour, the Royal Maundy and Remembrance Sunday. But within the frame of such events, great changes have swept across both the aspect of the Monarchy and the attitude of the people to it. Salutary changes. Informed public scrutiny has shrivelled away the old sycophancy; and the personal lives of the rising generation of the Royal House, the young people of the family, are perceptibly 'ordinary' and unrestricted by comparison with the cabined upbringing of princes sixty years ago.

It would be foolish, however, to pretend that the Royal Family has ceased to be a *special* family, with no shine and no magic about it. The business of the Queen and her relatives is not to go about the world pretending that they are Mr and Mrs Ordinary Citizen. Nobody in his senses would wish such a thing. A First Family without distinction, a Head of State without stardom, would make a nonsense of symbolic constitutional monarchy.

The British Royal Family is the antithesis of a nonsense. It is a solid part of national life, and a majority of people, as evidenced by opinion polls, look on it as something wise and worth having. Hard times, bouts of envy, bursts of taxpaying love-hate criticism, satirical cartoons, the spasmodic invective of republican fanatics, the indifference of some of the country's what's-in-it-for-me young men and women – none of these things has tainted the general commitment to Her Majesty and her House. The personal and the representational standing of the Sovereign today is as high as anything her grandfather experienced, higher indeed, and arguably on a firmer plane than any dynasty has known. Interest in the Queen seems to be inexhaustible.

And today that interest is coupled with the attention paid to her eldest son, the Heir to the Throne. Prince Charles is the second most important member of the Royal Family – and perhaps the most promising Prince of Wales since the Black Prince. At least he has become, and understandably, the most publicised Royal Highness of our time. To vignette him is to survey the present and surmise the future of the Royal House.

Prince Charles Philip Arthur George, King-to-be, born in 1948, has had the most liberal upbringing ever given to an Heir. Unlike his mother, who was educated privately and never went to school, he was away at boarding schools from the age of eight. He followed his father and preceded his brothers to Gordonstoun in Scotland, and whilst still a pupil there spent six months on the other side of the world, two immensely enjoyed and remarkably transforming terms at Timbertop, the country outpost of Geelong Grammar School, Victoria, 'the Eton of Australia'. Between 1967 and 1970 he was at Trinity College, Cambridge – the first member of the Royal Family ever to be a full-time, full-course undergraduate – and emerged not only with a respectable Honours degree but with a reputation as a good mixer, a good musician, and a more than good mimic on the amateur stage of the college revues. His three years' residence at Cambridge was broken only by a college term spent in Aberystwyth, employing a gift for languages which showed later at his Caernarvon Investiture as he mastered the intricacies of speaking Welsh. His success there was a tribute to the language laboratory at the University College of Wales but also to the habit of plain hard work which he had acquired.

After university, Prince Charles joined the Royal Air Force, won his 'wings', and then, following family tradition, went into the

Royal Navy, served his full five years and finished as commander of a ship, HMS *Bronington*, a coastal mine-hunter. He also undertook commando training, piloted helicopters, made parachute jumps and gained experience as a deep-sea diver – all these things voluntarily, accepting challenge, testing himself. On leaves during his naval service he found time to ski, sail, surf, fish, play polo, give television interviews, attend conferences, make speeches, and carry out a variety of official royal duties, a good number of them in Wales. Like his father, Charles is a doer, not a spectator; he is congenitally incapable of idleness.

He has had his special heroes: he adored and was greatly influenced by Earl Mountbatten – and the admiration became mutual. The assassination in Sligo was to the younger man an uncommon deprival, a personal loss most deeply felt. His Royal Highness gave public expression to that feeling, and to the Royal Family's anger, when he delivered a rare and poignant address in St Paul's Cathedral just before the Christmas of 1979. The occasion was a memorial service for his murdered great-uncle and the others who died with him. The Prince of Wales spoke of the 'mindless cruelty' of the killers and of the 'vulnerability of civilised democracy and freedom to the kind of subhuman extremism that blows people up when it feels like it'.

In 1979 the Prince, already an experienced world traveller and royal ambassador, plunged into what has been described as his social and industrial education, a further part of determined preparation for his future role. This was a course of finding out at first hand something about the business and administrative life of Britain. It has taken him, with no formality, into City board rooms, Government Departments, commercial managers' offices, on to the shop floor of factories and into union headquarters, to the depths of Parliamentary labyrinths and the height of the Cabinet room at Number Ten Downing Street. The pilgrim's progress continues. No house or office gets a more inquisitive visitor.

Buckingham Palace has been the Prince's nursery, haven and working headquarters. For the last few years he has also officially had a country residence, Chevening House, near Sevenoaks in west Kent, a Georgian mansion on a Tudor foundation in an estate of 3,500 acres, a building which has been much restored and redecorated since it was bequeathed to the nation by Earl Stanhope in 1967 for use by a leading Minister of the Crown or a member of the Royal Family. Prince Charles accepted nomination as this house's resident in 1974, but relinquished it in 1980, choosing instead Highgrove, a Georgian house near Tetbury in Gloucestershire which is now owned by his Duchy of Cornwall.

The Prince is indeed a family-minded man in that he knows from his growing-up experience the happiness of family life when it is united and loving. The Palace itself cannot ever be for him merely his birthplace and the workshop of monarchy. In his memories it must surely be, even though its official function as State mansion with flunkeys at the Grand Entrance has to be accepted, the cosy home with bicycles and macintoshes strewn around the hall and, in the porch of the garden entrance, handy towels to wipe small corgi feet.

Prince Charles is part of a close-knit family and his nature has been shaped by parental example, by the training his mother and father planned, and, in more recent years, the experience of seeing the Queen and Prince Philip at work and working with them.

He was a late developer, hesitant as a child, shy as an adolescent – until that Australian experience in 1966. After Timbertop, he went back to Gordonstoun a changed boy, confident and uninhibited and relaxed – a leader. Cambridge and the Services brought out his good humour and honesty, sensibility and self-drive, the urbane wit and infectious grin. He has become a man to admire, assiduous and unpretentious, easy to get on with – though bursts of ancestral short temper are not entirely unknown. He is susceptible, and highly articulate, adventurous and ready to experiment, yet unashamedly conservative over such things as loyalty and good manners and the enduring value of the Commonwealth. He can be a comic, but not a cynic. He has faith in modern youth. He is, withal, a man of his generation and one who will move with the times.

Disarming self-deprecation allows him to defeat the critics who say that, like Prince Philip his father, he is prone to an occasional 'sounding-off' on subjects to which, as he will admit, he has had only brief introduction. But at any rate, his excursions into the minefields of industrial relations are not always on the same side of the battle. There was one day when, far from union-bashing, he 'bashed the bosses', blazing into newspaper headlines by telling the Parliamentary Scientific Committee that 'much of British management doesn't seem to understand the importance of the human factor ... Unions are people, and people are not impossible to deal with.' Shop stewards liked that. But statesmen like him too – and not simply because he is Next in Line. His appeal is partly because he seems agreeably devoid of social prejudices, and to be genuinely without bias on race and colour and creed.

Like Queen Elizabeth The Queen Mother, the grandmother he adores and with whom he has always had a special *rapport*, the Prince of Wales has, in short, an unforced charm in public as well as in private. He is in no way dependent on the trappings of royalty, and indeed regalia seems extra-theatrical on a young man so breezily innocent of pretence. The world knows his ways pretty well by now: the mannerisms, the voice and the easy informality which he gets from his father, and the tolerance, with a combination of dignity and friendliness, which is his mother's. He is essentially an out-of-doors type, as his parents are. He far surpasses them, though, in appreciation of music and books. At times he may be impatient with indoor work, the desk hours he has to put in and the committees he has to chair. But he has a driving sense of duty in whatever he does.

Watching him on an overseas tour, an American commentator said: 'The guy works so hard you'd think he was running for office. Hell, there's no need! He's got it made for him by birthright.'

One of the reasons why he is known to the world is that he is a natural television performer, as well as a great believer in TV's power to inform. Unlike the Queen, he is completely at home in front of the cameras. Like her, he has been brought by television into everybody's home. The world today knows him well.

Prince Charles has witnessed not only the alteration in the public's attitude to royalty – from the unquestioning awe of 1952 to the healthier calm assessment of the present day – but also the change that has taken place in the Palace's *presentation* of The Family to the public. An inescapable change, as the Queen, Prince Philip and Prince Charles in particular know.

The progress of the present reign has run parallel with the popularisation of television, and it has been realised that Royalty must match itself to the TV Age, must not only be there, at work, but be *seen* to be there. Modern monarchy is hallowed by camera and microphone, newspaper and magazine; and men experienced in 'the media' have come into the Palace's press office (most efficiently run as part of the Private Secretary's department), replacing courtiers of the old days who, in the eyes of Fleet Street, were primly amateur and primarily protective, conveying the impression – often understandable enough – that popular journalism was necessarily suspect and inherently vulgar. Not that the royal Press Secretaries of today are engaged in smart-Aleck selling of their employers' private lives. The royal image has been changed, not cheapened. Daylight has been let into the Palace. More facilities have been given to enable people to know the Queen and her relatives as human beings as well as public figures.

The breakthrough – and very daring it seemed at the time – was the television documentary film, *Royal Family*, which showed not only the ceremonial Sovereign but a Queen in slacks and on holiday horseback, a laughing super-mum with four likeable children and an enjoyably off-duty husband cracking his jokes at breakfast tables and Balmoral barbecues. We saw a family at ease.

The Queen's Christmas broadcasts have become progressively more relaxed, too, in the years since Her Majesty gave the seasonal Message 'in vision' before the television cameras for the first time. That was in 1957 (before that she had talked on radio only) and it marked the twenty-fifth anniversary of her grandfather's pioneer broadcast 'on the wireless' on 25 December 1932.

Such projection has undoubtedly created fresh interest in the lives of the people every editorial desk calls 'the Royals'. And international popularity was gained by such television programmes as *Royal Heritage*, the story of Britain's royal builders and art collectors, and by the not quite so factual but most attractively presented TV series on King Edward VII. Productions such as these may well go down in history as images on film of Elizabeth II as lasting and impressive as the images on canvas with which Holbein immortalised Henry VIII.

There is of course danger in what the advertising world calls over-exposure. Royalty cannot be marketed like bars of chocolate – though sometimes jaundiced news editors of Fleet Street picture papers appear to weigh the Queen and her family with an excess of coolness and dispassionate calculation, regarding them as circulation-pulling commodities which on certain days are reckoned to compete with expensive footballers and excruciating pop singers for inclusion in their columns.

Naturally enough, there are times when the Royal Family may well wish to *avoid* publicity. The Prince of Wales, for instance, is far from enchanted by the gossip columnists' obsession with his girlfriends and the Who-Will-He-Marry? game.

Another anathema is the newspaper story which suggests that it should not be too many years before he 'takes over' as King. Reports and articles in this vein must try the patience of His Royal Highness, for in fact, fervently admiring Her Majesty as a mother and a queen, he would never wish her to abdicate and hopes that she will go on from strength to strength for years. He wants to be around, *as a busy Heir*, for a long time yet. He is proud that the prestige of the Queen has risen steadily in her years on the Throne – a phenomenon the more significant in that these years have seen her country steadily *declining* as a power in the *political* world.

To look ahead – as we do when we look at the Prince of Wales – the identification of His Royal Highness with Britain as a nation will inevitably become firmer as he takes on more and more royal duties. And his outlook will not be narrow, for it never has been. He is enthusiastically a multi-racial Commonwealth man, but a European too. It is reasonable to believe that he does not see his country's 'entry into the Continent' as any abandonment of old associations round the world – any more than he would equate Common Market with Common Monarch! Were he in some future year to lay an EEC foundation stone, it would certainly not be a UK gravestone.

The future is with the Queen and her son and heir. Anyone taking stock of them must sense their problems but take quiet satisfaction from the realism with which they face anxieties that lie ahead in a society of feuding ideologies. In the troubled world of the eighties, the monarchy can remain a bulwark against extremism of Left or Right, a centre of stability transcending shabby rivalries, something round which good men may rally.

However powerless politically a democratic sovereign may normally seem to be *as an individual*, she or he nevertheless can be invaluable in drawing loyalty, national identity and purpose to a respected and representative human being scrupulously holding supreme office. It is no meaningless abstraction that justice, law, and the defence of the Realm are 'in the Queen's name'. Had Germany's Wehrmacht been able to swear allegiance to a king fifty years ago there might never have been a Hitler.

Finally, a relevant reflection from a day of *recent* history. At the sad but splendidly ceremonial funeral of Lord Mountbatten in London on that lovely autumn morning in 1979, those of us who were broadcasting commentaries on the occasion were proud and moved that the dead hero's own voice joined ours as his coffin passed before us. It was from a tape-recording, deliberately released and broadcast only then, from a moment when, not long before his tragic death, he was asked what he felt about the Sovereign he had known since she was a small child. This is what he said: 'I think she does a wonderful job in making constitutional monarchy work so well. So long as we have people of the calibre of our Queen – and her Heir – I don't think you can improve on it. My loyalty is therefore absolute and complete.'

As to the occasionally criticised *hereditary* principle of British monarchy, it is not either outmoded or unnatural. It cannot be, so long as we all belong to families and think of son or daughter succeeding the parents who have trained them and brought them up to know their inheritance. That is the case for monarchical continuity through family, the case for professional Sovereigns. It is the argument against sectional Presidents who are nominees of the moment, amateurs blown in and out of office by the winds of political change.

Many a storm has raged and retreated round the Royal Family through the ages, and today's members, from Her Majesty downwards, are exposed to tempests as never before. Sheer experience – not mere starry-eyed admiration – suggests that Elizabeth II and her family will weather the winds. This proven Queen is one of the few pieces of good fortune modern times have produced for Britain – a force to be reckoned with, a flag to follow. In the years to come, we may have cause to give thanks anew for the rock that is the House of Windsor.

RIGHT *Highgrove House, new country home of the Heir to the Throne. Bought by the Duchy of Cornwall in 1980, the Georgian mansion was previously owned by Mr Harold Macmillan's son and is situated in the Cotswolds only a few miles from Princess Anne's home, Gatcombe Park.*

Acknowledgements

Colour Photographs
Reproduced by Gracious Permission of Her Majesty The Queen 19 top, 19 bottom, 20, 29, 30, 31 top, 31 bottom, 66 bottom, 67, 86.

Broadlands (Romsey) Limited 66 bottom; Camera Press, London – Baron 88, Peter Grugeon frontispiece, 179 top, 179 bottom; Central Press, London 168; Tim Graham, London 200; Hamlyn Group Picture Library/Country Life Books 65 top left, 65 top right, 86–87, 180; Jarrold, Norwich 68 top, 68 bottom, 85 top, 85 bottom; National Portrait Gallery, London 32; John Scott, Bracknell 145 top, 145 bottom left, 145 bottom right, 146 top, 146 bottom, 155, 156 top, 156 bottom, 157, 158, 167 top, 167 bottom, 177 top, 177 bottom, 178, 198–199; Syndication International, London 197.

Black and White Photographs
Reproduced by Gracious Permission of Her Majesty The Queen, 8, 13, 27 top, 27 bottom, 36 top, 38 right, 40 top right, 40 bottom, 43, 45, 47, 57, 60, 63 top, 64, 69, 70 top left, 70 top right, 71 top, 74, 75 top, 75 bottom, 97, 107 top, 108 top, 111 top, 113 top, 114 top, 120, 121 top, 121 bottom, 122, 123, 125 top, 133 bottom, 138, 139.

Aerofilms, Boreham Wood 15, 119; Bassano and Vandyk Studios, London 26, 61; BBC, London 101; BBC Hulton Picture Library, London 9, 96, 100, 102, 104, 113 bottom, 116; British Museum, London 12 top; Broadlands (Romsey) Limited 136; Camera Press, London 151, 170, 188 top, 194 top, 203, Baron 131, 184 top left, Cecil Beaton 169, Patrick Lichfield 187, Norman Parkinson 181, 184 top right, 189, 192 right, Snowdon 154, 161; Country Life Magazine, London 184 bottom, 186 top; Department of the Environment, London 28, 33 top; Mary Evans Picture Library, London 12 bottom; Fox Photos, London 95 top, 99 top, 133 top, 134, 141, 144, 162, 196; Hamlyn Group Picture Library 10, 11, 22, 23, 25, 34, 35 top, 36 bottom, 36–37, 38 left, 39 right, 40 top left, 41, 42, 44, 46, 48, 49, 51, 52 top, 52 bottom, 53, 54 top, 54 bottom, 56 left, 56 right, 58 top, 58 bottom, 59 top, 59 bottom, 62, 63 bottom, 70 bottom, 71 bottom, 76, 77, 78, 81, 89, 93 right, 98, 99 bottom left, 99 bottom right, 103, 108 bottom, 109 bottom, 124, 126, 128, 129, 148 bottom, 152, 153; Illustrated London News 35 bottom, 73, 82 bottom; Imperial War Museum, London 55 top, 55 bottom, 105, 111 bottom; Incorporated Television Company Limited, London 201; Jarrold, Norwich 50, 188 bottom left; Keystone Press Agency, London 80, 94, 95 bottom, 104, 109 top, 130 top, 132, 137, 171 top, 171 bottom, 190, 192 left, 194 bottom, 195 bottom; Serge Lemoine, London 90 top left, 90 top right, 90 bottom left, 90 bottom right; Mike Lloyd, Guildford 191; London Express News and Features 185, 195 top; Mansell Collection, London 17, 24, 33 bottom, 39 left, 84, 127; Ministry of Defence, London 159, 163, 172 top, 173; National Army Museum, London 11; National Buildings Record, London 16 bottom; National Portrait Gallery, London 18; Popperfoto, London 21, 72, 79, 82 top, 83 top, 83 bottom, 91, 92 top, 92 bottom, 106, 164, 186 bottom; Press Association, London 143, 148 top, 150 bottom, 166, 172 bottom, 175 top, 175 bottom, 188 bottom right, 193; Reading Evening News – Steve Hartley 202; Sport and General Press Agency, London 117, 160 bottom, 172 top right, 174 top, 174 bottom, 176, 182; Studio Lisa, London 107 bottom, 130 bottom; Syndication International, London 93 left, 125 bottom, 183; The Times, London 135, 142, 149, 150 top, 160 top; United Press International, London 165; Victoria and Albert Museum, London 14, 16 top.

Index